TWO EGGS
THREE YOLKS
LEARNING TO HEAR AND FOLLOW GOD

Jan + al Cherbonneau

2-23-19

1-256-781-0070

acherbonneau@charter.net

by

Jan and Allen Cherbonneau

All Scripture quotations, unless otherwise indicated, are taken from
the Holy Bible, New International Version®. NIV®. Copyright©1973,
1978, 1984, 1985 by International Bible Society.

First published by Dog Ear Publishing
4010 W. 86th Street, Ste H
Indianapolis, IN 46268
www.dogearpublishing.net

ISBN: 978-159858-410-3

This book is printed on acid-free paper.

Printed in the United States of America

DEDICATION

From Jan: I would like to dedicate this book to Allen, my precious husband and partner; to my dear parents, James and Inez Barket, who raised me in the knowledge and love of the Lord, and to Martin Duchow, the beloved Lutheran pastor of my childhood, all three of whom now dwell in inexpressible light; and to all those English and history teachers who made me write, write, write.

From Allen: I dedicate this book, first of all, to my wife Jan, who has worked diligently at this project for many years. I am also indebted to C.S. Lewis, whose writings brought me to faith. Finally, I wish to thank all those friends and teachers who have nurtured, mentored, encouraged, and in many other ways brought this stubborn man into the great adventure of the Christian faith.

From both of us: To Phil and Vivian Omasta and our Cursillo reunion group; to Allen P. Ross, John Rodgers, and all of the faculty and staff at Trinity (Episcopal) School for Ministry; to our friend Sarah Earley, for the concept and initial editing of this book; to all who prayed while we prayed and worked; to Cindy Jones, for her friendship, prayer and encouragement; to our three extraordinary children, Alicia, Oksana and Max, and most of all, to God— Father, Son and Holy Spirit. To Him alone be the glory!

For the word of God is living and active.

Hebrews 4:12

TABLE OF CONTENTS

Part Three: An Extended Life Example

Foreword

Though my name is listed on the book as co-author, I would like to take this opportunity to provide some clarification in that regard, as well as to explain a bit further my own role in the hearing process. While the text of the book is entirely Jan's work, the experiences that are recounted are part of a prayer life that we have lived out together. My part of the book is found in the vast majority of the visions and words from the Lord, all of which have been retrieved from the journals which I have been keeping since 1989. Therefore, I will explain, as best I can, the process by which I am seeking to "hear God."

First, hearing the Lord's voice is surely a gift, but I believe that it is a gift that the Holy Spirit desires to grant to anyone who is willing to adopt the simple disciplines necessary. I do not believe that I am special or unique with regards to hearing, but I have been willing to try, and I trust that the Holy Spirit honors our efforts. The most central disciplines involved are consistent listening prayer, especially with a regular small group, and the willingness to write while praying, recording any impression or Scripture passage or image which comes to mind. Once these habits have been in place for a period of time, one will certainly begin to hear, though hearing also involves discovering and removing blocks and gaining enough confidence to write.

Second, many of the words used as illustrations in this book are in the first person, as though the Lord were speaking. However, I do not wish anyone to think that this is dictation. Rather, I start to write when, as a result of prayer, I sense that the Lord is urging me to record something. I would describe this experience as a push in my spirit. I begin to write, often not clearly discerning where it is all going. What typically follows is a series of ideas or thoughts which are quite different from anything I had been thinking or feeling concerning the subject at hand, and these form in terms which are strikingly concise and clear. Although the thoughts seem to come from outside of me, the words are my own. The process of trying to capture these thoughts in my own writing is one which I find extremely challenging, and sometimes I write at breakneck speed as I try to record a rapid flow of thoughts. Though I am utterly in control of the writing, the thinking that leads to the writing seems to originate from outside myself and to possess a unique sort of authority.

That, of course, leads to a third point: how can I, (or anyone else), be sure that it is the Lord who is speaking? The answer, it seems to me, is two-fold. First and foremost, everything I think I am hearing must be in accord with Scripture, though it may sometimes address issues which Scripture does not itself specifically address. Second, if the Lord is in what I am hearing, there will be a certain pithiness and ring of truth to the thoughts I receive, and the viewpoint will almost always be very different from my own. Often, I will be led to changes in my thinking and behavior which are very difficult for me, for the words are almost always not what my sinful nature would want to hear.

Finally, let me say that I am under no delusion that the words which I record have the weight and authority of Scripture. They do not. Nonetheless, I have found, as I hope the reader will, that engaging this process of learning to hear will not only enrich understanding of Scripture, but also provide invaluable direction for both the small and the large decisions of life. After all, the goal is to be in intimate relationship with the Lord of the universe, not only because He loves us, but in order that we may serve Him more fully.

The Reverend Allen R. Cherbonneau
Mentone, Alabama
September 17, 2007

Introduction

I wrestled for some time with what to say in an introduction to this work, my mind repeatedly scanning through what I thought were the various possibilities. However, nothing I considered seemed to strike me just right. Finally, one afternoon, in an effort to clear my head, I went for a walk, silently praying as I did so for inspiration.

Upon returning, I decided to make myself a cup of tea. As I moved about the kitchen collecting cup, teabag, milk and spoon, I found myself slowly aware that an old, familiar show tune had begun dancing through my head. The music became louder and stronger until, startled, I suddenly heard myself singing the lilting refrain from the song "Getting to Know You."

Sensing that there might be some higher purpose behind my humming, I let my mind follow the train of thought where it would, and as I did so, several things began to occur to me.

First, I felt that I was being nudged to make certain that I knew from which musical the song came, so I dutifully checked on the internet. I was again surprised when it turned out to be <u>The King and I</u>, and I smiled at the Lord's sense of humor. Second, I also realized with amazement that He had cleverly employed the very occasion of my writer's block to provide a well-timed illustration of exactly what this book is about: hearing God!

Most astonishing to me, however, was that I began to discern that the Lord had actually used the song to give me the very theme of my introduction. What He was leading me to say, I believe, is that this book is, at the deepest level, a love story, for hearing God is ultimately about being in relationship with the One who is not only the Lord of the Universe, but the Lover of our souls.

The great and terrible lie which Satan insinuated to our parents in the Garden was that God was not who He had said He was, and that He did not have their best interests at heart. They were told that they could circumvent His moral authority and attain to a new and "superior" knowledge by eating the forbidden fruit. Adam and Eve all too easily fell into the trap, and they lost their most precious possession—uninhibited fellowship with their Creator. But right there in the Garden, as the man and the woman now hid from the God who loved them, He began His passionate pursuit. He promised that, in the fullness of time, He Himself would send the Remedy for the broken relationship. And when that Promised One, His own Son, had come and gone again, God, in turn, sent the Comforter, the One who would be with us and in us—all those who believe—guiding, conforming, and teaching, until the Lord's return.

From the beginning, it has all been about relationship. From Genesis to Revelation, the metaphors which God uses to describe His intense desire for relationship with His people are those of consecrated courtship and marriage. Ever since the Fall, it has been the unceasing work of God to woo us back by showing us, over and over again, who He really is, after all. He does so through his written Word, as well as through the ministrations of the Holy Spirit in the daily life of believers. Like Adam and Eve, we still run and hide, but God continues to use every means to call out, "Look! It's Me!" It is the voice of the Lover calling to the Beloved.

As the reader will discover in the pages of this book, God speaks in a myriad of ways and for many reasons, but the overriding purpose of it all flows out of His love for us and His desire to show Himself to us, so that we will fall in love with Him again and again. His communications to us are at once eminently practical and sublimely transcendent, but they are all about a deliriously wonderful combination of romance and adventure. Satan would still trick us into believing that both the allure and the meaning in life lie somewhere else, but God wants us to know that hearing Him is about the incomparable adventure and joy of being on the path to being wedded forever to the Author of Life. For those who would listen, the eternal God is ever whispering His plan and purpose into their very being. The message is about majesty and mystery, glory and gusto, pain and perseverance, the sublime and the ordinary. The voice of God leads, comforts, guides, encourages, corrects, and warns. It sharpens and it prunes. It is profound, and it is playful.

As I worked on this section of the introduction, I was blessed with a second experience of the Lord's assistance, for I was suddenly reminded of an unusual word that we had gotten during our prayer time some months previously. While seeking guidance as to the direction of our lives, Allen reported with some bemusement that he had found himself recalling the 1980s movie <u>Romancing the Stone</u>! It is a funny, fast-paced, tension-filled, roller-coaster ride of a movie, but the thread that runs beneath it and binds it all together is a zesty, yet tender, romance—a love story with a surprise ending. Though we were perplexed at the time by the allusion to the film, I now grasped the broad-stroked analogy, for, if we choose to hear and follow God, we can be certain that the story of our lives will likewise be one filled with the romance of relationship with our Creator, the exhilarating thrill of high adventure, and not a few surprises! And we can be continually assured of a good ending, despite the ever-present battles with the forces of evil, for God's plans are always good.

For some, the thoughts in this book may be utterly new. For others, they may be of assistance on the path already joined. In either case, I am well convinced that learning to hear God and hear Him better are the most crucial endeavors in which one will ever engage. They are of eternal consequence, and they will bring unimaginable blessing.

I should add one final note. Allen and I, like all mortals who have gone before us, are fallen and fallible, and though, by God's grace, we are redeemed and anxious to be faithful, this book, no doubt, contains some errors or omissions in interpretation or insight. In His need to keep us humble, it would be unlike the Lord not to insure that this were so. May God's wisdom, discernment, joy, and peace be upon those who read herein.

PART ONE:

OUR
PERSONAL
JOURNEY

Chapter One:
A Bit of Background

In order to help the reader to understand how we ourselves began and grew in the process of learning to hear the Lord, it seems fitting that I start with a little of our own background history.

Let me say at the outset that I am abundantly aware that our personal history and experience are, in and of themselves, of little interest or consequence to anyone else. But it is in my nature to teach by telling stories, and so, in that light, I have decided that this book shall not be merely a manual but, also and perhaps even more so, instruction by example. I think the reader will approve, for the child in each of us still loves a good story. As my daughter Oksana once remarked when learning of a publisher's reactions to the book's narrative content, "But didn't Jesus teach by telling stories?" Exactly so. Besides, Allen and I cannot separate ourselves from our histories anyway, and all written here is in the context of them. Moreover, I rejoice in the fact that we are really quite ordinary people, for it means that anyone can learn to hear the Lord and follow! All it takes is a bit of faith to start and, yes, some plain old-fashioned willingness to be disciplined. Each person's journey will be unique but governed by some basic guiding principles. So, in relating how God has moved us along the path of life, of hearing, and of obedience, our goal is simply to teach, not only by describing, but also by illustrating how the process works.

Since our gifts and ministry are so inextricably intertwined, I suppose that the logical place to start our story is the point at which our lives were joined. Married in Massachusetts in 1973, my husband Allen and I had already begun to realize that the undirected nature of our liberal arts education, while intellectually stimulating, had rendered us ill-suited for employment. Parables of our generation, we had marched, with high hopes and diplomas in hand, from job interview to job interview, only to be told that we were under-, over-, or improperly qualified. Thus began a long, dreary and oppressive succession of low-paying and stultifying jobs which further destroyed our already-flagging self-images. At times our disillusionment bordered on despair.

Finally, in utter frustration, we hit upon the idea of self-employment, embarking on a long career in multi-level marketing. Here we soon learned two things about ourselves. First, we discovered that we had a genuine love for and ability to teach, lead, and inspire our large network of distributors. Second, we found that our business endeavors nonetheless did not reach to the core of our deepest longings, although we managed to convince ourselves for years that they did. It wasn't that we couldn't muster up the skills, but rather, we later realized, that this was simply not what the Lord had most gifted us to be doing. Consequently, propelled by sheer determination, we had moderate success for a time, but it was abundantly evident that our most valiant efforts ultimately produced only the most dismal results. To the observer, our lives during that time would have appeared more like an arduous trek uphill through deep mud than they would have an adventurous journey of faith. We were hard-working but stubborn, persistent but misguided, and our own willfulness had made us spiritually blind to our plight. As Pogo so aptly said, "We have met the enemy, and he is us!"

Our response to this state of affairs was to blame ourselves, and work all the harder. Eventually, Allen turned for additional income to employment in the automobile business. He did well for a time, but the pattern eventually repeated, and he again opted for self-employment, this time as a used car dealer.

By then we should have gotten the message: we were miserably out of the Lord's will. However, several more years dragged drearily on as we fought to make a living with abilities and inclinations not our own. But one cannot live in such tension forever, for ultimately we must be what the Lord has made us and called us to be, or we will suffer, emotionally and spiritually, perhaps even physically. Nonetheless, it was to God's glory that He employed even our persistent foolishness, for He used this time as a training ground, sharpening the skills which He could later transfer to service for the building of His kingdom.

Oddly enough, Allen and I had met each other at a non-denominational seminary in the fall of 1970. This fact serves to prove not only that the Lord has a sense of humor, but also that His straight lines are sometimes full circles, for twenty-two years later we would find ourselves in seminary again. Meanwhile, I had been attracted to that first seminary by the dream of studying Biblical archeology, a love instilled by a college professor and nurtured by three summers of digs in Israel, while Allen, for his part, had enrolled to study the relationship between science and ethics.

Ironically, however, though raised in church, I as a Lutheran, and Allen as a Roman Catholic, neither of us really knew the Lord; much less did we have any clue as to how to discern His will for our lives. The question, in fact, had never seriously occurred to us. Worse yet, the traditional church had left us both unprepared to deal with years of academically instilled intellectual liberalism. Neither of us was attending church when we met, nor did our first seminary experience lead us to any recommitment to faith, Christian community, or worship. We were awash in a liberal decade and had not yet returned to the Mooring. It would be seven years into our marriage before we so much as darkened the door of a church.

Now, the Holy Spirit may give us a long tether, but it is a tether, nonetheless. I, for one, had often been at the end of mine, but the bonds of faith had been tied in childhood, and there was, for each of us, a gentle, incessant tugging which began to grow stronger. Allen found refuge in denial and cynicism, but I was increasingly uneasy, and I came to a point when I could no longer abide the tension and ignore the call. Finally, one Easter Sunday morning in 1979, I arose and went by myself to a local Lutheran church. Sensing the dilemma he was suddenly in, and not to be outdone, Allen suggested the following week that we try the local Episcopal church. There was no lofty reasoning here, merely curiosity, for the rector was a fellow Rotarian, and quite a ham. "What could he possibly be like as a priest?" Allen wondered.

Our initial intent was to spend the next few weeks "church-shopping," but we were warmly welcomed by one parishioner at the coffee hour following our first Episcopal service, and so we ended our brief quest there. Besides, the liturgy and sacraments were a source of familiar comfort to us both, and thus, some months later, Allen was received, and I confirmed, by the bishop.

The next few years testified to an incredible quickening of the Spirit in our lives. Like parched sponges, we soaked up weekly worship then added Bible studies, various forms of fellowship, and service. We also immersed ourselves in books. In fact, Allen still credits C. S. Lewis's <u>Mere Christianity</u> with leading him into a genuine commitment to the Lordship of Christ. My own reading began with a friend's collection of books by Agnes Sanford and Catherine Marshall, all of which deeply affected me. From both of these godly women, I developed an enduring interest in the healing ministry, as well as a determination to someday write for the Lord. I, like Allen, went on to do massive amounts of other Christian reading, often managing several books a week.

Thus, it was a time of great growth in the Lord, and in June of 1988, at the urging of two other couples in our parish, we were led to attend a Cursillo weekend. Cursillo, for those who are unfamiliar, is a movement within the Church which focuses simultaneously on Christian community and on taking one's Christian life and witness out into the world. It centers on an initial weekend encounter, followed by a weekly small group reunion as a means of encouragement and accountability. For us, Cursillo was a profound experience which deepened our faith, gave us fresh insight into Christian community, and propelled us further into our life in the Spirit.

Soon after our Cursillo weekend, we joined these two sponsoring couples in their weekly reunion group, meeting every Sunday evening for sharing and prayer. In hindsight, I would have to say that our Cursillo weekend was the pivotal event in our early spiritual journey and the one from which everything else later flowed. Not by chance, this was also a time when Allen began to discern a possible call to full-time ministry, and it was in the nurturing context of this weekly gathering where we prayed and sought the Lord that we ultimately made the decision to attend Trinity Episcopal Seminary in Ambridge, Pennsylvania.

In the meantime, in June of 1985, Allen had begun, with some determination, a prayer journal. However, these early efforts to record his daily hopes and struggles had soon faltered and fizzled, and it was nearly four years before he started again, at the persistent nudging of his spiritual adviser, Father Bill Murdoch.

It was some eight months after joining reunion group that Allen's natural bent for writing, (he had been an English major in college), combined with the prompting of his spiritual adviser and, of course, the Holy Spirit, led him to resolutely resume his prayer journal. The journal was both an outlet for self-expression and a means of communicating with the Lord. Each day's entry was an offering-up of his experiences, hopes, frustrations, and fears, and a prayer for the Lord's wisdom and guidance.

The first entry in this new adventure in obedience was dated March 7, 1989, and it read in part as follows:

> "Lord, I sit here in bed trying to understand what it is You want of me. In some sense I know. I need to take the time to be with You— to find You in the quietness— to learn to listen. As I talked to Bill Murdoch today, I clearly understood my sense of speeding through life, compelled to do things, to make something happen. This whole process of my being called, Lord— How do I know? I try to listen— I see some signs. Are they my imagination? I am trying not to force my way forward, but to walk in Your Light. My conversation with the Bishop left me at first feeling unsure, but then it seemed to focus my resolve to not let 'practical' considerations be the deciding factors. Bill Murdoch is clearly correct in seeing my over-hurriedness. I rushed into the interview with the Bishop. I need to pray and listen to You, Jesus. I am trying to obey, yet I am plagued by the question of whose will this is— my own (some fantasy), or truly Yours. ..Help me to discern."

As I look back, I can now see that the questions and issues raised here with regard to hearing the Lord were to become the central and enduring ones in our lives and ministries.

This new effort at journal-writing continued faithfully on a daily basis for almost two weeks—not a long period of time, to be sure, but a new record for Allen! Now, for the first time, several key elements were combined. We were strongly committed to the discipline and accountability of a small-group fellowship, we were diligently seeking the Lord's will for our lives, Allen was showing a commitment to keeping a written record of his prayer life, and, encouraged by the example of the hearing of the others in our prayer group, we had begun, cautiously but earnestly, to desire the gift of hearing for ourselves.

Apparently, this was what the Lord had been waiting for....

Chapter Two:
How Our Hearing Process Began

Our reunion group on the 19th of March, 1989, began in the usual fashion, but what happened in our closing prayer-time was to change our lives forever. As we sat in silence, Allen was suddenly stunned to hear the Lord speaking directly to him, though the brief messages were most enigmatic. Repeated several times were the words, "This is the week," and then, insistently, "The sea. The sea." With amazement and trepidation, Allen reported this experience to the group. "The week for *what?*" we asked ourselves. And what was meant by "the sea?" Since this was Allen's first experience with prophetic communication from the Lord, he wondered if the words he was hearing were merely the interior ramblings of his own mind. We were at a complete loss as to the meaning of these puzzling words and could only ponder them and pray for their interpretation.

Our first answer came just five days later, with the tragic news of the Exxon Valdez oil spill. It clearly seemed to us that the Lord's urgent words on that Sunday night had been a veiled warning and an exhortation to pray, at least in a general way, against this calamity which the Lord knew would befall the sea before the week was out. Indeed, there had seemed to be a profound pathos in the Lord's lament for His creation. This, incidentally, was to be the first of many times during these early years of hearing when the Lord gave us forewarning of natural disasters and historical events, though we, of course, couldn't fully recognize them until after the fact. We believe it was His way of teaching us to watch, to trust, and to pray, for over and over again the things He showed us would come to pass.

But secondly, as we would come to see in retrospect, this word had marked the week when Allen's prophetic gifting was initiated. It was a simple and an obtuse beginning, but, even so, we were scarcely capable of comprehending the magnitude of our experience. We felt equally honored and frightened.

As we would gradually come to learn, the Lord's cryptic speech often contains multiple meanings and overlapping themes. This was our first experience in seeing two strands of one message intertwined, for the *sea* in Scripture is often used figuratively of the earth's *peoples*, for whom the Lord's heart also ached. As is the case with all spiritual gifts, the Lord had bestowed Allen's prophetic gifting in order to advance the Gospel, and it seems that this had been the week when the Lord had chosen to begin this new ministry in Allen. The timing of this first message could hardly have been a coincidence.

Confirmation of this wider, evangelical strand of meaning came several days later. Recalling with some disquiet his initial prophetic experience, and the words about the sea, Allen had mused in prayer, "Lord, I'm not a sailor." The reply was immediate: "Paul was not a sailor, either." It was true. St. Paul, the rabbi and tent-maker, once called by the Lord, had spent much of the rest of his life crisscrossing the Mediterranean by ship in order to bring the Gospel to the Gentiles. In fact, he had endured three shipwrecks, one of which left him adrift for a night and a day in the open sea. Here, then, was yet another disquieting aspect of the message to us: obedience will always take us out of our comfort zone! As time went on, we would come to recognize that this holy discomfort was to become our common state of being.

Meanwhile, powerful currents of change were swirling in our own lives during this time, threatening to drag us beneath our own black waves of discouragement and despair. We continued to grab at various business opportunities, ever hoping for success, but always settling for survival. In one year's time, Allen switched business locations twice in the elusive search for the right situation. As he wrote one night, "I have worn myself out like a moth beating on a summer window."

Personal and financial stress was accompanied by spiritual distress. We, and a few others, including our reunion group, were propelled out of our beloved church fellowship by a change in rectors which precipitated a stormy clash over the authority of Scripture. We found a new church home and were richly blessed, but not without suffering all the attending pains of dislocation and parting.

As if all of this weren't enough, we found ourselves in the midst of constant family crises. My father had lingering health problems which eventually erupted into a full-blown attack of gallstones and pancreatitis. He nearly died and was months in recovery. I so exhausted myself from worry and from driving back and forth from Massachusetts to Connecticut to check on him that I became terribly sick with an oral herpes infection—a form of shingles. The pain was so excruciating that I was put on codeine for ten days. Severe constipation resulted, and I finally resorted to a strong laxative. It worked in such a way that it too rapidly pulled the electrolytes from my system, producing violent cramping, racing pulse, and plummeting blood pressure—a crisis all the more frightening as it occurred while we were vacationing in a remote location in the Virgin Islands. Health crisis followed upon health crisis, as I also endured several other equally bizarre attacks upon my physical well-being; all of them, I believe, the result of being exhausted from the pressures of taking on burdens not my own.

Meanwhile, my elderly mother, already suffering from a lifelong personality disorder, also began to manifest symptoms of senile dementia. The combination produced frequent, violent, and unpredictable rages which we were helpless to deal with. Eventually, she broke her hip, fell, and landed in a nursing home, where she was to remain for nearly seven years until her death. My father, hardly well himself, suffered a heart attack and stroke from the enormous stress of it all. He recovered but went on to live by himself in a house too big and too full of difficult memories. Even our beloved cats suffered. One died suddenly from feline leukemia, and the other was found to have a dormant form of the disease.

The pain extended to our wider circle of relationships as well. Looking back at our wedding photos, we were sadly reminded that several close couples had already divorced, and one of our best friends was dying of cancer. Many of the other close relationships formed in our late college and early marriage years were becoming lost as well, most for a host of sad and complex reasons.

I relate these things because it often seemed that our times of greatest spiritual growth occurred during times of great trouble and conflict. In terms of our calling, the more we grew in the Lord, the more we sensed that the life we had created for ourselves was headed in the wrong direction, but somehow we couldn't break free. With each passing month and year, we became increasingly anxious, frustrated, and confused. Yet, through all of this turmoil and pain, our spiritual lives flourished and grew, for as we worshiped, continued with reunion group, and prayed and listened, the Lord faithfully continued to speak, to guide, to correct, and to conform us to His image. We had no idea where it would all lead; all we knew was that God had begun to speak, and we to listen and respond.

Allen meanwhile continued to work doggedly on, frantically striving to make his efforts bear fruit, while my life at home was a daily litany of emotional agony over who I was and what I was supposed to be doing with myself.

One afternoon, I found myself lying on the bed in a fit of despondency. Face down, head in hands, I stared forlornly out the window, not knowing whether to cry or to scream. Laughing was not under consideration. I was having yet another crisis of identity, of vocation. Whether from exhaustion, confusion, or sheer frustration, I had given up on the process of exploration and had spent the past several months wallowing in a melancholy mire of my own making. On the verge of tears, I now wailed, "How, O Lord, do I find what I am called to be and to do? Please help me." The response was clear and immediate: "You pedal, I'll steer." Astonished, I sat up and looked around, so real was the impression that not only was it the Lord who had spoken to me, but that He was there in the room. My misery quickly turned to mirth as I began to smile, then laugh out loud at the comical image of the Lord and I on a bicycle. Of course! In a pithy and graphic way, the mental picture created by the words showed me that I needed to get on the "bike" and get moving in *some* direction; only *then* could He direct me. After all, I suddenly saw, it makes no sense to try to turn the handles on a stationary bike. And yet how often had I insisted that the Lord do exactly that? And how often, I mused, had I caused myself unnecessary suffering and hardship, all because I did not know and follow His ways? It was the start of the awareness that the answers to my agonizing dilemmas lay, not in complex and cleverly devised solutions of my own making, but rather in the realization of who the Lord is, and how He guides and deals with us, coupled with obedience. I was learning once again how desperately I needed to hear the voice of the Lord, whose wisdom and compassion had instantly cut through all my despair and confusion. Hearing, I had now experienced in a very personal way, was where God's mind meets man's need.

On many other occasions, we found that we were beginning to hear the Lord speaking to us through the ordinary experiences of life. One particular day while working at the car dealership, Allen received two separate yet similar teachings from birds! He wrote,

"I think of the sparrow I saved in the dealership showroom today, flying frantically into the glass, and not knowing that it was like flying into an invisible wall. It was stunned, and I managed to catch it, bring it outside, and give it time to recover. I think I am like that sparrow. I fly into a box of my own choice and the way looks clear, but there are many walls I cannot see, and I cannot escape by myself. But if I stay quiet and let the Lord pick me up and show me His way to freedom, I can know the real joy of flight in complete trust. I couldn't also help but think about the lutina cockatiel we saw at a friend's house. It had badly deformed feet and probably could not survive in nature, but because it trusts the proper people, who love it, the life the bird lives is good for itself and for them. It is a lesson of trust that God is teaching me, but I am a stubborn student."

We also began to discover that there were times when the Lord gave us practical wisdom through dreams. Here is what Allen wrote on 6-5-89, when he was still working at the car dealership:

"I remembered one of last night's dreams this morning, and it seemed to have a clear message for me. I was purchasing a pastry like a strudel in a bake shop owned by the owners of our local Christian bookstore(!). I was being asked to share it, but at first was only willing to share a small portion. Then it seemed that a voice spoke to me, saying, 'I want you to give 50%.' That became clear to me today as I wrote a deal that I could have kept for myself but decided to split because it was the right thing to do. The principle matters far more than the money."

This, we later recognized, was one of our earliest experiences with hearing a personal message, grasping its implications, accepting its instruction, and attempting to follow. As time went on, there would be many other such instances of this process in our lives. We also began to see that the more experience we gained in hearing, the greater the responsibility to respond, and the greater the import of the messages. This principle, we knew, was in keeping with the Scriptural admonition which says, "From everyone who has been given much, much will be demanded; and from the one who has been entrusted with much, much more will be asked."(Luke 12:48b)

Meanwhile, the gift of prophecy continued to blossom and grow in the fertile soil of our Sunday night reunion group, and it wasn't long before I, though to a lesser degree than Allen, also began to regularly experience the Lord speaking to me. In fact, I can still fairly vividly recall the first vision that I received.

It was on an early morning in September of 1988, Rosh Hashanah, to be exact, and I was just awakening when my attention was riveted by an intense vision of what I immediately knew in my spirit to be the New Jerusalem. In this case, it was not like a photograph since it came, as visions do, filtered through my own mind. Nonetheless, it was quite like the image described by John in the twenty-first chapter of Revelation. What I saw was a beautiful city consisting of a compact, square cluster of buildings, all seeming to be made of solid gold or silver. Arching across the top of one of these was a large silver rainbow. I was puzzled that none of these buildings had windows, until I later recalled that none would have been needed, for in this city, as John said, "…the glory of God gives it light, and the Lamb is its lamp."(v. 23)

This city seemed to be surrounded by a wall, and it sat in the midst of an enormous expanse of emerald green land, stretching in every direction as far as the eye could see. Flowing out from the middle of the city into this green expanse was a river, brilliantly azure-blue. The vision was so startling and so lovely that I earnestly desired to hold onto it so that I could continue to gaze at it, but within seconds it was gone again. Then I heard a voice say the number "11." For years, its meaning eluded me. Then, some time ago, a friend gave me a copy of a list, produced by Streams Ministries International, of symbolic numbers in Scripture and their meanings.

Appropriately enough, according to this list, the number 11 signifies "Transition (Prophet)," and "the bridge from one era to another."[i]

On a personal level, we were indeed experiencing a transition to the role of prophet. On June 25th, 1989, our reunion group met as usual, but as we prayed, Allen received a most astounding and sobering Scripture. The verse, Ezekiel 3:17, read as follows: "Son of man, I have made you a watchman for the house of Israel; so hear the word I speak and give them warning from me." Coming three months after the gift's inception, this seemed a clear confirmation of Allen's prophetic gifting, and a further commissioning. There would be many such confirmations to follow.

We knew that, as spiritual watchman, Ezekiel was commanded to warn of God's coming judgment on the nation of Israel for their idolatry. Furthermore, if Ezekiel failed to give the warning, he would bear the responsibility for the sins of the people, whereas, if he did warn, he was delivered from blame. However, we agonized over how to apply these words to a New Testament understanding of the gift of prophecy, and how, and to whom, to give the warnings we were receiving. Ironically, the church, dulled from centuries of slumber in these matters, was of little help, and we longed to find someone with whom we could discuss what we were experiencing. However, the Lord was gracious, and the messages continued, despite our reluctance and considerable confusion.

Dreams, of course, continued to play a sizable role in our experience of hearing. All through our lives, we recognized, there had been dreams with spiritual portent, but now that we were praying, asking the Lord for insights about our dreams, and consistently recording all of the Lord's communications to us, these dreams seemed to increase in frequency and significance. Here, for example, are a pair of dreams with similar themes that Allen and I had within days of each other:

"Last week Jan and I had bizarre dreams. I had one of myself driving a large dump truck in traffic, at twilight, in a light rain. I had to stop, and got out, leaving the truck running, but it somehow got into gear, almost crushing me as I tried to hold it back. I got back in and avoided hitting the truck in front of me. Then I parked somewhere and went to meet someone to talk about something to do with *broadcasting.* Jan also had a very detailed dream. We were in a jewelry store, and after looking at the regular display, we went into the basement, and she asked to see a ring which she knew was there. It had two large emeralds, rounded and polished, on either side of a large cut diamond mounted in the center. She knew that the emeralds were she and I, and that the diamond was Jesus. Then the jeweler showed her some envelopes containing cut and uncut stones of all sorts. One of the envelopes had writing on it. Next there was a shallow velvet box with a few shiny new dimes in it, which kept falling onto the floor, and once into her shoe, needing to be picked up. She said the box of dimes was an irritation. I think that the box with dimes represents the things of this world which we pursue, even though they aren't worth much, while we are in a jewelry store full of treasures which we don't take advantage of. We also don't wear the ring, which would publicly show that we are joined to Jesus. We keep it hidden, though we know it's there."

Both dreams, I think, spoke to us of our futile and exasperating lives after the flesh—chasing after small change while surrounded by gems—and they enjoined us to turn from petty yet burdensome cares, material attachments, and other distractions which kept us from hearing the Lord's call—the dump truck, the annoying dimes in my shoe. And as I write this, I now see that the envelopes of cut and uncut stones perhaps represented those whom the Lord would have us reach with the Gospel, some as yet unbelievers, and some, those upon whom we would have further impact, helping them to perfect their faith. Or, again, they might have signified various aspects of our gifts and ministries, some recognized and in use and others waiting to be discovered and developed.

For nearly two years, we continued in this fashion, praying and listening, but often feeling that we were living in parallel and contradictory worlds, for the more we grew in the spiritual dimension, the more incongruous our everyday lives became. The tension between the two increased until it seemed we could bear it no longer. But all the while, the Lord was guiding our footsteps through our spiritual eyes and ears, teaching, nudging, correcting, and training. He was also about to bless us both with another spiritual gift. Interestingly, it involved a short journey.

Chapter Three:
An Evening in Ocala

This short but momentous chapter in our adventure began in early February of 1990, during a trip to Florida to visit Allen's parents. We had been making these trips about twice a year, but our prayer times, as we were preparing for this particular trip, had hinted that something about this visit bore special significance.

One evening, while we were out enjoying the balmy Ocala air, we happened to drive past a shopping mall, where we noticed with delight a recently opened Christian bookstore. We became so engrossed in a lengthy conversation with the owner, a former L. A. policeman, that we scarcely had time to so much as glance at the books, but as the owner accompanied us to the door at closing time, he did a most curious and remarkable thing. In an off-handed and casual manner, he paused at a shelf of books, reached up almost without looking, and with one finger slipped out a paperback from amongst its companions. "Here," he said, "maybe you'd enjoy reading this." It was Dennis and Rita Bennett's <u>The Holy Spirit and You,</u> a manual on the gifts of the Spirit. We accepted his recommendation, quickly made the purchase, and left, the door locking behind us.

The rest of the vacation left no time for reading, and so the book was tucked inside my suitcase. One night, a week or two after returning home, Allen went to praise team practice at church, leaving me by myself. I curled up in bed with my newly bought book, and began to read. Several chapters into the book, I arrived at the section on speaking in tongues, in which was laid out a description of how to receive the gift. "Well," I thought, "there's no one around to hear me make a complete fool of myself, so I might as well give it a try." I read the instructions, prayed the prayer, and did indeed begin to speak in my new prayer language. I described my experience to Allen, and, a short time later, he followed suit. I have since talked to a number of others who came to speak in tongues in exactly this way.

Here, then, was another vital piece of our spiritual armor. The experience was one key turning point in our spiritual lives, for we were now able to pray in a new way, spirit to Spirit, free of subconscious hindrances, and this gift became another significant means by which the Lord guided our steps. When feeling blocked in prayer or unsure of how to pray, we regularly found that praying in tongues brought release, resolution, and a sense of peace. Now that another piece had been added to our puzzle, the visions and words began to become more urgent, more personal, and more directive.

Chapter Four:
Indianapolis via Schenectady

Thus it was that on the night of April 29, 1990, while in prayer, Allen received the vision of the inside of a large domed stadium. The image meant nothing to us at the time, but like all the others, it was dutifully written down. When I later thought to check the dictionary, I noted that *stadium,* in addition to describing an arena for large gatherings, can also mean "a stage of growth or development." We were clearly in an intense process of growth and change. However, as mentioned earlier, the Lord is the great master of the multiple use of imagery, and so it would happen that we would soon find ourselves in a *literal* stadium, as well.

In the meantime, our rector was encouraging a small group at our church to attend a Power Ministry Conference, led by Bishop David and Mary Pytches, in Schenectady, New York. On May 3rd, 1990, we set off. While the conference was primarily on healing, Bishop Pytches, to our great surprise, decided to devote the closing hour of the last day to a discussion of the role of prophecy in the local church. Suddenly we understood more fully why we had come. We were elated to find someone who could identify with and address some of the issues and concerns we were facing with regard to hearing God. Bishop Pytches had scarcely finished speaking when we raced forward, hearts pounding, to talk with him. He answered our questions, gave us his encouragement, and exhorted us to continue in the process of learning to exercise the prophetic gifts which the Lord had given us.

The pace now began to accelerate. Barely two weeks later, while in our prayer group one evening, the Lord gave us this sobering and pointed reproach: "You are not doing my will." Immediately, Allen saw a suitcase, unzipped a small ways, with a string of pearls hanging out. "Aha," I thought. Bill Murdoch had repeatedly urged Allen to go on a retreat in order to facilitate the spiritual process of sorting out his life directions, but Allen had been resistant, due to his hectic schedule. He was ever laboring under the mistaken notion that taking that much time off would hamper his work. I assumed that the vision referred to such a retreat (and it may have, in part), thinking that if Allen did go, he would receive much sought-after pearls of wisdom. "Lord," I asked, "for how long should he go?" I felt I understood Him to say, "Four nights." However, all prayers for further clarification met with silence.

On June 11, 1990, a member of our reunion group came over to our home to pray with us. Still frustrated with the matter of the enigmatic suitcase, we brought the subject before the Lord again. The Lord does not mind if we are persistent when seeking His will; on the contrary, it is the kind of pestering He delights in. He also knows that I cannot stand to have my piqued curiosity unsatisfied, and thus I am convinced that, at critical junctures, He has used this sort of device to insure my full attention! I find myself especially driven to discover the contents of anything that is box-, or package-like! I think it goes back to the Christmases and birthdays of my childhood, and it was something that my father had always teased me about.

So, where was Allen going? Or was it both of us? And when? What treat was in store? What wisdom awaited us? As we pleaded for guidance, the Lord gave Allen this Scripture: May the Lord answer you when you are in distress; may the name of the God of Jacob protect you. May he send you help from the sanctuary and grant you support from Zion.(Psalm 20:1-2) However, to our astonishment, not to mention further confusion, the Lord then proceeded to show Allen a picture of a large yellow zinnia, in the center of which was a light! We were utterly baffled. So often, like the disciples, our requests for clarification have been met with more dark speech, so that we do not grasp the meaning, except in retrospect, and then only in part. How Scriptural, for: we do indeed see through a glass, darkly. This enticing but aggravating zinnia image was followed by that of an odd sky, full of stars, but with movement and shape in the darkness. I felt I understood this second image somewhat better, as it seemed to suggest God's design and purpose for our lives, obscure to us but at work all the same.

A few days later, Allen met once more with his spiritual adviser. While in prayer together, Allen received this Scripture: "In the church at Antioch were prophets and teachers: .... While they were worshiping the Lord and fasting, the Holy Spirit said, 'Set apart for me Barnabas and Saul for the work to which I have called them.' So after they had fasted and prayed, they placed their hands on them and sent them off."(Acts 13:1-3) It was certainly starting to sound like we were getting closer and closer to going somewhere to do something, but continued prayers for enlightenment brought only these words: "It is enough to obey."

One night the Lord showed Allen the image of a bull, standing on land which was cracked and parched in many places. Could it be that our own bull-headed stubbornness was the cause of the drought in our lives? What did obedience look like in this case, and in what ways were we being disobedient? Primarily, I believe, we were lacking in trust, and unwilling to give up control. So obsessed were we with our own situation that we were ignoring the most basic commands to fully live out the Gospel. Consequently, the Lord gave Allen these images: "I see a coastline, a south-facing shore, with a large group of arrows pointing away from the coast, like lines of force. I see a large white candle, short, but very big around." The Lord seemed to be saying, "Don't hug the shore, where it's comfortable and secure. Venture out into the sea! Be a light!" The accompanying Scripture was this: "We continually remember before our God and Father your *work* produced by faith, your *labor* prompted by love, and your *endurance* inspired by hope in our Lord Jesus Christ."(1 Thessalonians 1:3) Given the above images, this verse was undoubtedly more an exhortation to us than a commendation! As confirmation of this, the coast image was repeated a week later. This time, Allen saw a dark shoreline, with a shape like a bay, and water which was an algae-green color. How clearly this conveyed the spiritual stagnation of our security-driven lives.

During our prayer-time later that week, the Lord hinted at some of His goals for us. Allen wrote of these visions: "I saw first the image of a small boat on a trailer, and then I saw a somewhat chubby woman (I am *not*, Lord!) leaping up happily. Then I saw a steel rake, the tines of which seemed to have fallen off." From Jesus' calling of the first disciples to be "fishers of men," nautical and fishing symbols have been used by the Church, and we regularly found that the Lord employed them with us, as well. The small boat on the trailer seemed to us to suggest our transportation as believers to another body of water from which to fish, i.e. to do ministry, evangelize. I could not imagine at the time, of course, that we would be called to leave home, yet the leaping woman hinted at the joy which would follow such obedience. And what of the rake? One means by which the Lord motivated us to make the transition was that He simply made it virtually impossible for us to make a living, to rake in any money, as it were. After all, it is indeed most futile to attempt to use a rake which has lost its tines!

It was now late June of 1990. A number of friends from area churches were being sponsored by the diocese to attend the "Carry the Light International Evangelism Conference" in Indianapolis, Indiana, to be held in August. Due to a perceived shortage of time and finances, we had not considered going. The Lord had other plans.

I went to the mailbox one morning to find a packet from Episcopal Renewal Ministries which also happened to contain a brochure on the conference. Opening it, I noticed with some surprise that there was to be a seminar there on prophecy. Still, I had no inclination to go. It was too far away and too expensive, I reasoned, and so I promptly pushed the matter aside. But an hour or so later, the persistently puzzling zinnia image popped back into my head, and I decided to see if the dictionary could give me any further illumination. After all, a zinnia is a zinnia. ...isn't it? Here is what I read:

zinnia   **1.** any of the plants constituting the composite genus Zinnia (Crassina), natives of Mexico and the southwestern U.S. **2.** one variety of zinnia, Z. elegans, *the floral emblem of Indiana.*[ii]

I was speechless. When Allen called from work an hour or so later, I breathlessly related my experience. Needless to say, by that evening we had cast aside all false concerns about time and money and had called the diocese to make arrangements. To our dismay, the allotted number of participants had been filled, and so we disappointedly placed our names on a waiting list. Time was running out, but, lo and behold, a short time later one couple became unable to go, and we suddenly found ourselves with their plane tickets and hotel reservations. How often in our journey have we seen the Lord work in such a fashion! And how often would the train have pulled out of the station without us, were it not for the invisible hand of the Lord!

Consequently, it should have been no surprise when on July 23rd, as we prayed yet again about direction, the Lord offered, "That's why you're going to Indianapolis." Six days later, after praying further about these words, Allen wrote the following in his journal: "I see a mechanical blueprint—a design on a large sheet of paper. I cannot see the details. Then I see what appears to be a satellite device, box-like, with long antennas on three sides." The Lord seemed to be showing us that He had a blueprint for our lives, a master plan. Was the three-pronged satellite a symbol of the Triune God Himself, communicating His will to us from heaven?

On August 15th, 1990, we left for the Evangelism Conference which, incidentally, was to last for five days and *four nights.* But while the conference sessions themselves were outstanding, I would later come to realize that the Lord had sent us for a more precise purpose. During a break one day, in the course of perusing the displays in the huge exhibitors' hall, we happened to place our names on a mailing list to receive Trinity Episcopal School for Ministry's *Mission and Ministry* magazine. Up until this time, we were only vaguely aware of Trinity's existence, but it was through the reading of this publication that we now began to develop an interest in the seminary. We were also delighted to discover a booth run by CMJ/Shoresh, an evangelical and teaching ministry dedicated both to witnessing to the Jewish people, and to instructing the Church on Her Jewish roots. Like Paul, these things had always been close to my heart, and so we placed our names on their mailing list as well. Oddly enough, both Trinity and CMJ were based in Ambridge, Pennsylvania, one block from each other.

Even more amazing was the next "coincidence." While crossing the street along with literally thousands of others one afternoon on the way to a workshop, we struck up a conversation with the woman walking next to us, and closed the brief chat by writing her name and address at the back of our prayer journal. She was Theresa Mulligan, soon to be Mrs. Bruce Newell. Bruce was one of Trinity's deans. Theresa was also a former director of CMJ. The Lord was skillfully weaving His will into the tapestry of our lives.

"Well, Lord," I later mused, "if you can send us to Florida to buy a book, I guess you can send us to Indianapolis to get a couple of magazine subscriptions!" I was almost afraid to ask where we were going next! Thankfully, I did not know then that my next "excursion," exactly one year later, would be to the doctor's office.

Chapter Five:
The Momentum Builds

In the meantime, we continued to function on the same two increasingly dissonant planes: our spiritual lives rose and soared, while our work and family lives spiraled downwards towards chaos.

Though difficult before, the situation with my parents was rapidly becoming unbearable. My mother had now been in a nursing home since November of 1989, and her round-the-clock care should have alleviated much of the strain on us. However, even with constant medication, she remained physically and verbally abusive, self-obsessed, and controlling. For example, she, for months on end, was compulsively fixated on the order in which her clothes hung in her closet. On entering her room, she would immediately confront us with an illegible list and relentlessly attack our every attempt to place the dresses in the "correct" sequence. If we refused to engage in this absurd exercise, she became highly agitated; if we made an effort, which, of course, had no hope of succeeding, she did the same. During other periods, the compulsion involved the way in which her shoes were placed under her tray table or the evenness with which her two window shades were pulled down. A lifetime of inability to be pleased with anyone or anything had been excruciatingly refined. Senile dementia, as one might expect, played a growing role in this sad scenario.

I felt compelled to continue my frequent visits, yet the very thought of them filled me with anger and anxiety. Needless to say, even the shortest contact with my mother was intolerably stressful and oppressive; consequently, many visits lasted but minutes. Yet I was emotionally unable to put more space between them, so driven was I by groundless guilt, and a fear of hurting my father. He, on the other hand, became more and more vague, passive, and unable to cope, his emotional retreat leaving me with an ever-heightening sense of frustration and abandonment.

The tremendous burden of my family situation was further intensified by the fact that we increasingly sensed that we were being led to consider leaving home to go to Trinity. Whenever Allen and I discussed the possibility, however, we would invariably come back to the same nagging question: "How could we leave my parents, just when they were becoming the most dependent upon us?"

The Lord knew that the dilemma weighed heavily on our hearts, and one evening during prayer, He confronted us with a puzzling vision. "I saw," Allen reported, "an image of a crooked furrow winding through a field." Unraveling the meaning of the image required tracing a strand of thought, but we were aided by a sermon we had heard some time before. Furrows, the speaker had explained, can be plowed straight only if one's eyes are kept constantly fixed on a point directly ahead in the distance. If one repeatedly turns his head and looks backward as he walks, he will quickly and inevitably begin to plow a zigzag line.

Immediately, the story from Luke, Chapter 9 came to mind. As Jesus was walking from Samaria to Jerusalem, He encountered three men who each expressed an interest in following Him. They all had issues, however, which hindered their full commitment. The first man needed to be told that Jesus' itinerant ministry left no room for considerations of comfort and security. The second asked that he be allowed to remain at home until after his father had died. Now, to our human way of thinking, that sounds like a reasonable and compassionate request. After all, aren't we supposed to honor our father and our mother by taking care of them? "Let the dead bury their own dead, but you go and proclaim the kingdom of God," Jesus told him.(Luke 9:60) The third man, we find, desired that he first have a chance to go back home and say good-bye to his family. To him, Jesus bluntly replied, *"No one who puts his hand to the plow and looks back is fit for service in the kingdom of God."*(italics mine) (Luke 9:62) Now we began to discern the meaning of the vision: the work of the kingdom came first, even if it meant leaving one's security, one's ties, even one's elderly parents. In the case of the third man, the call was so pressing as to preclude even so much as a good-bye to his loved ones. It was a hard word, but one that circumstances would soon compel us to act upon.

Vocationally, our lives were in no less turmoil. Ever slow to learn, we doggedly dragged on with our various car and multi-level marketing ventures, still hoping to somehow grasp the elusive golden ring of success. We were physically and emotionally exhausted, to which the daily journal entries well testified; even now, the mere rereading of them invariably inspires in me the same fatigue.

One of the most striking images we received from the Lord during this time spoke volumes about our vocational situation. As Allen was going to sleep one night, he suddenly saw a fork, a teapot, and a white bunny. The illusion was unmistakable, and admittedly humorous; the message convicting, and embarrassingly accurate. Here was the white rabbit from Lewis Carroll's <u>Alice in Wonderland,</u> running helter-skelter from one appointment to another, all the while clutching his over-sized watch and repeating "I'm late, I'm late, for a very important date," which of course wasn't very important at all.

All in all, the consequence of the enormous strains which we labored under was that our minds and bodies were worn to a frazzle. Only our spirits found refreshment in our daily private and weekly small group prayer sessions, for it was here in the quiet that the Lord spoke to us, imparting His wisdom, His will, and often also His wit. As the above examples illustrate, the words we were now getting increasingly began to carry more personal import and involve greater risk: risk not only in terms of the courage required to take a step in faith, but also risk in terms of the blessing lost if we chose not to obey. It was clear that we were being drawn irrevocably closer, not only to a crisis of decision, but also to a watershed—a major dividing line in our lives. Thus went the year following our return from Indianapolis. It would prove to be a time during which the Lord was actively and aggressively teaching and preparing us for what lay ahead.

In January of 1992, a routine visit to my gynecologist revealed three massive pelvic growths which, I was later to discover, had miraculously protected me from the ovarian cancer which lurked inside. Through diligent prayer, we were able to understand that the root causes of my illness were to be found in the overwhelming and under-addressed issues of our lives, and that only radical change would bring physical and emotional healing. The Lord had taken His own calculated risk in allowing it, based on His knowledge of our willingness and ability to pray, hear, and discern the reasons for which He had allowed the illness, and then to respond accordingly. My cancer, surgery, and the inner healing which began then would prove to be profoundly life-changing events that catapulted us forward—first to Trinity, and then beyond.

It is time to cut our own story short at this point, for it is not possible within the purpose or scope of *this* book to recount the details of that extended healing experience, though I shall attempt to do so in my companion book, <u>Hearing and Healing</u>. Nonetheless, it *is* essential for the reader to understand that it took the combined crises of health, family, and vocation—conjoined, most importantly, with an understanding, based on our hearing, of the purposes behind those crises—to shake us free and get us moving further onto the path the Lord had for our lives. One of our Old Testament professors was fond of saying that when God wishes to get our attention, He often does so in one of two ways: health or finances. In our case, we had obviously been hit with both barrels, which surely testified to the urgency of the change required. Just four months after my surgery, we had packed up, moved, and were sitting in our first classes at Trinity. In retrospect, we recognized that much of our training in hearing the Lord up to that point had been for the purpose of leading us to this critical juncture.

It is fair to say that by this time, we had acquired some significant practice with and experience in hearing, and we had come to realize that it was the very stuff of life. In awe, we regularly wondered how we had ever functioned, indeed ever really lived, without the application of the Lord's direct guidance and wisdom to both the small and large challenges we faced. Nevertheless, though we had learned much, we knew that we had vastly more still to learn. Scarcely, too, could we have then imagined the even bigger adventures that were yet ahead of us!

That is enough of our own story for now. Having given the reader some idea of how we came to be where we are, both in our lives and in our hearing, I will turn to a discussion of the actual reasons for and ways in which hearing comes and functions.

PART TWO

THE MECHANICS

Chapter One:
Why God Speaks

Psalm twenty-three gives us some profound insights into the reasons why the Lord speaks to us, and it begins by telling us that He is our Shepherd. As we continue to move through the psalm, we see that He provides, refreshes, leads, guides, restores, protects, comforts, corrects, blesses, and communes with us.

We also know from many Biblical texts that Christ, who called Himself the Good Shepherd (John 10:14), also holds the office of Prophet. (see, e.g., Luke 24:19) It therefore follows that His prophetic communications to us are intended to shepherd us. In other words, they will impart not only the Scriptural truth about God, and God's general will for mankind but also His specific will and guidance for each of us as individuals. If we are listening, He will be the Shepherd of our souls. In fact, no less than five times in His Good Shepherd discourse in John Chapter 10, Jesus defines being in relationship with Him as discerning His voice. And the point of our hearing is this: "I have come that they may have life, and have it to the full."(v. 10b)

Learning to hear God, then, is not about being entertained (though the process *is* fascinating!), nor is it merely a way to get help when, and in the way in which, we think we need it. As He once reminded us, God is not a genie in a bottle, there only to grant wishes when we cannot attain them by our own efforts. Rather, our two-way communion with Him is no less than our very life and breath. Since it is a continual source of amazement and cause for praise that we have such a God who is willing to reveal Himself, to converse with us and to share His very nature with us, let us now look in greater depth at some of His purposes in doing so.

1) God speaks to reveal himself

First and foremost, the God of the Bible is a God who is *self-revelatory*. He is intensely desirous that we know who He is and how He thinks and acts. In the Book through which He has chosen to speak to humanity, He describes Himself as real, absolute, sovereign, and personal, fervently seeking to communicate with His creation, to speak His will into that creation, and to bring all who will to Himself through His Son Jesus, the Word made flesh. God continues to speak to show Himself to us, and to draw us into relationship and fellowship with Him, so that we may do His will and enjoy the benefits of participating in the work of the Kingdom.

2) God speaks to declare what is and to foretell what is to come

Second, as we know, the Lord's prophetic communication to us can be said to take two general forms: *forth-telling and foretelling*. *Forth-telling* is declarative, proclaiming the will and word of God, while *foretelling* is predictive, providing supernatural knowledge of future events. In truth, this distinction is often somewhat forced and the functions difficult to separate. For example, when the Lord foretold to Abraham and Sarah that they would have a son, He was also declaring, in and through that promise to them, His purposes in salvation history for the nation of Israel and for Abraham's spiritual descendants, the Church.

Neither *foretelling* nor *forth-telling* as gifts and works of the Holy Spirit ceased with the writing of the Holy Scriptures. *Forth-telling* encompasses the ongoing work of preaching, teaching, writing, witnessing, prophesying, and in other ways speaking forth God's message. This book, then, could be seen as an example of *forth-telling*. In contrast, the ongoing purpose of prophetic *foretelling* is to reveal future events in the life of an individual, the church, the nation, or the world. Let me cite some examples of the Lord's use of *foretelling* from our own experience.

While we were staying at Christ Church Hospice in Jerusalem in January of 1993, Allen wrote this during one of our morning prayer times: "I saw the face of a boy with kind of sandy, stiff hair, around twelve or thirteen years old...." Naturally, the vision baffled us, and no amount of speculation could have brought us any closer to its meaning. Four and a half years later, however, we welcomed our first exchange student, Hanno, from Germany. Some time afterwards, in going back through the journals, I came across the record of this image, and realized that it described Hanno quite accurately. His wiry hair is one of his defining physical characteristics, and, when I checked his passport, I noted that, even there, his hair color had been described as "sandy." Even the age that Allen had discerned was accurate, for Hanno would have been a little over twelve at the time of the vision.

Likewise, in January of 1998, almost exactly five years later, and again while we were at Christ Church Hospice in Jerusalem, Allen saw a vision of a young woman with whitish skin and wavy black hair parted in the middle. Immediately after our return from that second trip, we made the decision to take another exchange student and began the selection process. Months later, after we had chosen Revital from Holland and received our first photos of her, we were struck by the similarity between the vision and her appearance. I have no idea why the Lord chose the timing of a trip to Israel and our stay at Christ Church to send each of these visions. However, as with most of Biblical prophecy, the meaning of these images was recognized only in retrospect.

Again, one evening in July of 1989, while praying with our reunion group, another member of the group felt led to ask the Lord if there was going to be a large earthquake in the United States. Allen immediately saw the red outline of a distant city skyline, followed by the image of a short, squared watchtower. Next, he seemed to be seeing portions of that city: first, a section of concrete highway; then a bridge; then an area of low buildings in flames. We were, needless to say, stunned by the reports of the San Francisco earthquake three months later. The television news repeated over and over again the images of the ruptured bridge, collapsed highway, and low, burning buildings, all bearing witness to the accuracy of the vision.

Nearly a year later, Allen and I had just finished our prayer time one evening and turned off the light, when I suddenly heard him exclaim, "I just saw the strangest thing!" He sat up, switched the light back on, and described this vision: "I saw the picture of a map, with a river flowing south to north, emptying into a body of water. There was a crack of large proportions opening in the earth along the left side of the river." "Another earthquake," I thought. Five days later, while driving in the car, we turned on the radio just in time to hear the news of a massive earthquake in Iran. Studying the atlas, we saw that the geography of the quake was just as Allen had described it.

These two earthquake images raised some difficult questions. Why were we being shown these things, and what was to be our response? For years afterwards I felt some guilt regarding these experiences, for I realized that we were perhaps being exhorted to pray against these terrible events, or at least to pray that lives be spared and damage minimal. However, we also recognized that the Lord was using these early experiences to teach us to trust, both in Him and in His gift, since this process of seeing events, and seeing them fulfilled, was repeated many times in the early years of our prophetic call. Further, we reasoned that we were being taught that, if these things which He showed us came to pass, then we could surely count on the other things of which He spoke, as well. It was all part of our apprenticeship. In fact, one night, the Lord showed Allen an image of a line of open freight cars, each containing a rolled up scroll. We sensed that the scrolls contained the messages and images that we were being given, and we chuckled at the pun: the Lord had us "in training."

Nonetheless, as I was working on this paragraph, I felt that I needed a further word from the Lord regarding the matter, for the dilemma was a basic one. How could these early images we were shown be both training in hearing and something we should pray against, since, if our prayers were effective and the event was pre-vented, we would never know if we had heard and understood cor-rectly? Why was God speaking in this way? Here is what Allen thought he heard the Lord say about these messages:

"They were training, since at the stage you were at you could not have really even known about what to pray. There are, however, some things that prayers will do, once you suspect you should be praying. The prayers will not stop this sort of event, but prayers will provide extra support and encouragement in the spiritual realm for My peo-ple to hear and act upon the warnings I give during these times. Your prayers, then, can greatly affect individual lives, and they have done that in the past, in many ways which you will never know. Indeed, prayer is always effectual, though it often accomplishes very differ-ent things than what you are praying about."

3) God speaks to comfort, exhort, correct, rebuke, encourage and warn

In each of these areas the application may be personal, or it may be wider in scope. Following are some examples:

Several years ago, while our Dutch exchange student Revital was staying with us, we received a call in the middle of the night that her mother had died in her sleep. Revi, overwhelmed with grief, left immediately for home, while we continued to pray for her and for a word of comfort for her. One day, the Lord showed Allen an image of a woman walking peacefully through a sunlit field of intensely yellow flowers. The sense of peace and the color of the flowers seemed to be the predominant emphases in the vision. When Revi returned from her mother's funeral, we shared the image with her. She was astonished, and tears welled up in her eyes. Yellow, she informed us, had been her mother's favorite color, so much so that her mom had worn a yellow dress, and her dad a yellow suit, at their wedding! The vision spoke directly to Revi's heart at a time when she so desperately needed *comfort* and reassurance.

The Lord also uses words and images to *exhort,* meaning to strongly urge us to His desired action. Many years ago, the Lord showed us a vision of a fishing net hung over a peg on a wall. Obviously, the net was not in use. We recognized this message immediately as an exhortation, for Jesus' clear instruction to His disciples was that they be fishers of men. We were likewise to take down our net and go fishing— to share the Gospel. We may not all have the spiritual *calling* of evangelist, but none of us is exempt from the Great Commission. However, since nets in Biblical times were hung, dried and repaired in anticipation of the next day's work, the image could have further signaled a time of Sabbath rest and preparation for the new ministry which lay ahead of us. Yet again, we find connections to the fourth chapter of Hebrews, in which our own Sabbath rest becomes ultimately tied to the finished work of Christ on the cross, a rest which we, in turn, labor to invite others to enter into by faith, and so on. This rest, then, becomes the focus and goal of our work, just as it is our work to believe.

Finally, the image seemed to hint as well at Jesus' words in John 9:4: "As long as it is day, we must do the work of him who sent me. Night is coming, when no one can work." This, it struck us, was both a reminder of the brevity of life, and an intimation of the close of the age; hence, the exhortation may have contained an element not only of personal, but of eschatological urgency.

There are also times when we need *correction* and *rebuke*, and often it is in our attitude towards others. I particularly remember an evening in our prayer group some years ago, when, to our shame, we had been rather harshly discussing someone who had a tendency to be a difficult person. Later, at the end of our prayer time, Allen saw the cover of a book imprinted with the words "Will To Love." The agape love of which Scripture speaks is not about feelings but about a settled determination of the will. This correction was also a reminder that the Lord knows our hearts and hears every word we say. We began to be more deeply aware that our conversation always needs to be pleasing to Him.

There is further a category of visions which I would call beatific, and these seem to be primarily for the purpose of *encouragement*, for they focus on the sovereign majesty of God, the Lordship of Christ, the ministrations of the Holy Spirit, and the glory of the creation and of the heavens. They produce a response of great joy, peace, praise, and awe, and may come at times when we need a glimpse of tran- scendence. I suspect that these visions, by their very nature, are especially difficult to grasp second-hand, since they are usually accompanied, upon seeing, by a response of intense emotion. Nonetheless, I will relate two such visions just as Allen described them. In the first, he wrote:

"I saw a series of what seemed like very beautiful paintings from the time of Jesus. There were people in prayer, or gathered together in groups. In one of the paintings there was a white dove woven into the fabric of the picture and moving it along, as the Holy Spirit moves us all."

In this case, there was a profound sense of our connection with the communion of saints, who have gone before, and a deep realiza- tion that we are bound together by our life in the Spirit.

On another occasion, Allen reported seeing the following astounding image. Though obviously difficult for him to articulate, it nonetheless gives some hint of the glorious scenes awaiting us in Heaven:

"I had a profound vision which showed me a brief glimpse of some heavenly scene of light and power—I'm not exactly sure of what— but underneath the glorious light there was a layer of translucent, pale gold, shimmering and moving in a way that I cannot fully describe, except that there was a certainty in my spirit that I was seeing a sea of angels under the throne of grace, like a cloth of indescribable beauty and power, pulsing with life and praise. Though pale in comparison to the light above them, the angels were clearly connected to the light, and they formed a floor of translucent gold which seemed ready, in a moment, to act on a word from the light. All of this description is completely inadequate, but the glimpse was so brief and the light above so intense that I'm not sure I can do any better."

Continuing on, I will relate an example which illustrates how the Lord may give a *warning* of danger. During our reunion group one night, one of the other women announced that she was about to fly out to Colorado to visit her children. At the end of our prayer time, we prayed for a good visit with her family, and for safe travel. After Allen and I had gone home and gotten into bed, Allen received a startling vision of an airplane with the side door falling off. We were puzzled, and initially hesitant to even connect this vision directly with our friend's trip. However, though it was already quite late, we decided that we needed to call her and tell her of the alarming image, just in case. On the phone, we all prayed again, asking that there be no such incident. When our friend returned from Colorado, she told us that her plane had just begun to roll into position for the taxi down the runway when it suddenly stopped. Several flight attendants came down the aisle, halting in front of the emergency exit door, and a mechanic was called on board. He examined the door for several minutes, opening it and closing it and making some adjustments, until he appeared satisfied that everything was in order. It was only then that the plane was allowed to take off. For those who view prayer as boring, ineffectual, or too "spiritual," I would instead suggest that it is the most eminently practical of all endeavors! Who knows what disaster may have been averted simply because we prayed? In the above illustration, we can further see how the elements of foretelling, warning, and a word of knowledge actually *combined* to offer protection.

On a sadder note, however, some time ago there was a tragic plane crash over a body of water, and the subsequent news photos showed several Bibles floating on the surface. A friend of mine was stricken by this, and asked, "Lord, why did You allow so many of Your people to die in this crash?" With sorrow, He replied, "None of them thought to ask Me if it was safe to take the flight." Similarly, some months ago, there was a tragic plane crash involving some believers, and I was very troubled. I asked the Lord if the deaths could have been avoided. Allen thought he heard,

"Of course, many things could be avoided, especially particular accidents like this. There are also larger scale tragedies which require hearing and taking action in advance. Do you not think that I was telling My church in Germany to stand against the evil when Hitler rose to power? I told them, but they were too deaf and complacent and sinful to hear. Some heard, of course, but they were not enough to alter the course of events. I always warn, and I always guide My people, but My people usually do not listen. Sometimes, it is because they do not believe I speak, or because they don't believe I'm concerned with small events like plane trips, but most of the time they simply do not wish to have the predictable course of their lives disturbed. Of course, I am a Disturber. It is easy to let patterns form which stop up the ears and blind the eyes, and I always seek to save My people. I seek to save all of My creation."

4) God speaks to provide help of various kinds

Fourth, the Lord works in the life and heart of each believer to bring His *help* in specific and concrete ways. Often the word given is for the believer himself, but it may sometimes also be given for a larger group— even, as we know from Scripture, for a nation. Here are some of the ways in which that functions:

a. *To provide physical, mental, emotional, and spiritual healing*

Unfortunately, the nature of our Western way of thinking has led us to want to compartmentalize and disassociate these aspects of our being. In truth, however, the Biblical concept of healing is rooted in the Hebrew words *shalom* and *rapha*, both of which convey a profound understanding of integrated completeness, soundness, and wholeness. In light of this, when speaking of healing, we must insist that God always desires to heal the *whole* person.

Consequently, it must be emphasized that a simplistic understanding of healing which says that all prayers for physical healing should be answered immediately, and in the manner in which we desire, far misses the mark, and can only result in frustration, disappointment, and even anger at God. While God does on occasion choose to heal instantly as a witness to the Gospel, healing is generally a more complex event, and its processes are unique to each situation. Some illnesses and ailments are simply the result of the Fall and the sin in the world, but many others have their roots in our own sinful attitudes and behaviors. Though we may not like to acknowledge or wrestle with this fact, God is more than willing to deny or delay healing in order to do the larger spiritual and emotional work which He deems necessary. The process of complete healing involves sovereignty on God's part, and humility and hard spiritual work on ours. I believe that this is part of what Paul meant when he said, "…continue to work out your salvation with fear and trembling…." (Phil. 2:12) Every illness, therefore, should cause us to seek the Lord as to its root cause.

Volumes have been written on the subject of healing, and a general treatment of the topic is not my purpose here. Rather, it is my specific desire to awaken in the reader the realization that healing, in the context of wholeness, is intimately and inextricably bound to hearing, and that this is yet one more reason why learning to hear the Lord is so crucial.

b. *To offer consolation*

I have already spoken of God's general desire to comfort, but His role of consoling in grief deserves special mention here as an aspect of helping. When my father was dying, I expressed concern over his suffering, and I also asked the Lord if he would get to see my mother at his death. Allen thought he heard this:

"Of course, nothing could be more certain. There is much that you do not understand about all of this, for Scripture reveals truth, but it does not give all of the details, for you would not believe them. I have made plans, and by comparison, your best imaginings are as nothing. You have the essential idea from Scripture, though you cannot comprehend the vastness of what I do. I take special care of the weak and struggling, so you need not worry about your father."

Three days after his death, we also received this word in the context of another response to prayer:

"For Jan, I want you to know that your father is with Me. He was faithful in his walk with me, though he did not become all which I had planned. He is enjoying the magnificence of praise right now. You may hold to the certainty that you will see him again when I return to rule. That is a great truth which should sustain you in your grief. You know I love you."

I was deeply grateful to the Lord for the enormous comfort and consolation which I received from these words, for they helped me in very deep ways to move through the grieving process.

c. *To impart wisdom*
The reader has, by now, seen ample evidence that all of these categories of hearing, more often than not, have some overlap. Here, for example, is a word given for me which combined comfort and God's wisdom.

Some years ago, I realized that I had always struggled to internalize the meaning of the word *grace*. Although I intellectually acknowledged that I was the recipient of it, grace remained largely a theological term to me, and I had great trouble grasping its truth at the core of my being. Finally, I decided to ask God to give me a definition I could understand at a different level. "That's easy," Allen thought he heard the Lord reply, "You just do the best you can, and I make up the difference." Not only did I now suddenly understand far better, but I received much comfort from that new understanding. And how like the Lord it was to cut through libraries full of theological dissertation with a simple sentence. Now, lest anyone think that this word contradicts the Biblical doctrine of salvation by grace and not by human effort, let me say two things. First of all, the "difference" of which the Lord speaks is always a humanly insurmountable gap, bridged only by Jesus' finished work on the Cross and by the work of the Holy Spirit. Secondly, Scripture does indeed, in many ways and in many contexts, exhort us to wrestle with, strive for, contend against, and do battle with. Faith and obedience are by no means passive states.

I had a similar experience of benefiting from God's wisdom just recently as I sought an understanding of what it means to be salt and light, based on Jesus' exhortation in Matthew 5:13-16:

"It is impossible to win souls without being salt and light, despite all the best intentions. Salt is the savor—the zing—the very immediate power the Gospel should have. Light is the understanding that comes from seeing My work in the world and My work in salvation history, and knowing the journey that the Church has been through, with all of the lessons from that. All of this, certainly, comes from the understanding that the power and work of the Holy Spirit is utterly necessary."

d. To impart knowledge

The Lord gives words of knowledge in order to aid us in particular situations, even those on the most simple and practical levels. Many believers, for example, have had the experience of asking the Lord to help them to locate lost objects. Some years ago, we stopped by the home of our pastor one evening, only to find the family in a bit of a dither. It seems that one of their young daughters had lost a cross which was very dear to her. She had spent considerable time scouring the entire house, and especially her room, but the cross had not turned up. We offered to pray with the family, and Allen thought he got a sense from the Lord that the cross was in the daughter's room, in one of the drawers of her dresser. She tearfully protested that she had looked through the dresser several times, but she dutifully went back up the stairs to look one more time. In a few moments, she came tripping back down, smiling and holding the cross. It had, in fact, been found in her dresser drawer, where it had somehow fallen behind some clothes.

I must, however, add here that on occasions when I have lost things, I have often found the Lord speaking to me on a far deeper level about the situation. Once, after a pair of new shoes had been missing for months on end and repeatedly searched and prayed for,

He asked me a probing question: "Do you care that much about those who are spiritually lost?" Just as illnesses are occasions for self-examination, so also a lost object can become a reminder to reorder our priorities! I will deal with words of wisdom and words of knowledge again in the chapter on *how* God speaks.

5) God speaks to conform us to Christ's image and set us on our path of life

God also speaks in order to conform us to Christ's image, as well as to set us on the specific path which He has for each of us. In fact, an examination of Scripture shows us that these two things are inseparable in God's thinking. In John 17:17, for example, the apostle quotes this word from Jesus' prayer for his disciples: "Sanctify them by the truth; your word is truth." To Jesus, it becomes clear, sanctification and revelation are the complementary and necessary parts of one whole. Recently, in referring to that same prayer, the Lord had this to say to us: "'If you love me, you will obey what I command,'(John 14:15) means more than just the *commandments*—it means obedience in the daily journey along the path I have planned for each believer." Not by accident, the following verse, John 14:16-17a, goes on to say, "And I will ask the Father, and he will give you another Counselor to be with you forever—the Spirit of truth."

If we connect the dots here, the conclusion must necessarily be that obedience to the Lord *includes* obedience to His ongoing, specific instructions to each believer, given through the guidance of the Holy Spirit. And though we often stumble and fall along the way, God's word, both written and given through the daily ministrations of the Holy Spirit, guides, corrects, and leads.

In prayer not long ago concerning the challenge of living with the uncertainty involved in this hearing process, the Lord laid out not only the blessings to His followers of hearing and following on the daily path, but also the consequences of not doing so:

"For those who make their own choices, it does not mean that they are not saved, but it does mean that they will miss great blessing, and they will know forever what might have been if they had but been willing to hear. They will, of course, know My joy, which will wipe away tears, but how much better it is to listen and obey and receive what I have planned. My way is always the best choice, for many reasons. Your job as always is simply to obey to the best of your ability. I love you and will not forsake you."

6) God speaks to equip believers for ministry, advance the Gospel, and work out His eternal Kingdom purposes

A few months ago, as we prayed about how to do the training of others which we felt we were being led to do, we received this word regarding the relationship between hearing and equipping people for ministry:

"They are to be trained to use their gifts to engage in the battle in the ways in which each of them is called. The first training is in the central discipline of listening to Me, and that is the key to the other training. Listening to Me involves knowing My Scriptures and hearing My Holy Spirit. I speak through each of those, but I give My specific instructions for each life's adventure through the Holy Spirit. You don't have to establish some sort of comprehensive training curriculum, for you could not successfully do that anyhow to cover everything that will be needed, but you will find that what you need at a particular time will be available to you and the people I will give as fellow journeyers."

Paul himself was intimately acquainted with the direct guidance of the Holy Spirit as he sought to share the Gospel. Look for the signs of the Holy Spirit's direction in this passage from Acts, Chapter 16:

"Paul and his companions traveled throughout the region of Phrygia and Galatia, having been kept by the Holy Spirit from preaching the word in the province of Asia. When they came to the border of Mysia, they tried to enter Bithynia, but the Spirit of Jesus would not allow them to. So they passed by Mysia and went down to Troas. During the night Paul had a vision of a man of Macedonia standing and begging him, 'Come over to Macedonia and help us.' After Paul had seen the vision, we got ready at once to leave for Macedonia, concluding that God had called us to preach the gospel to them."(vs.6-10)

First, we see that Paul was sensitive to the leading of the Holy Spirit. Second, he was responsive to God's timing. He was learning that because something was generally right to do did not mean that it was to be done at that time, or even necessarily by him. He was "tuned in." Third, we note that once aware of God's divine blockages, he did not press his own agenda, but obeyed. And finally, crucial to the effectiveness of the Holy Spirit's guidance was not only Paul's willingness to obey, but to obey without delay.

7) God speaks to illuminate world and national issues

Several years ago, during our reunion group one night, I felt led to ask the Lord if there was to be a great disaster in the United States. Allen thought he heard the Lord reply, "It has already happened. It is only the results which you haven't seen." The vision he received the following night amplified the reason behind this sorry state of affairs. Allen wrote, "I saw a series of images. First, I saw a woman's face, looking up, with lightning going to the face and back. Then I saw another woman's face. This time, it was not looking up. Then, I saw the image of the United States, seen from above. Lastly, I saw an ugly woman's face, looking down."

This vision, I believe, graphically depicts the spiritual history of our country. We at first looked up to God for our physical, moral, and spiritual sustenance, and we received His light and strength. Then we came to look outward, glorying in our position and power among the nations. Finally, having forsaken God, we are looking down to the dark powers beneath us, and we have become ugly. "What will happen to this nation if we continue on in this way?" I asked. Allen saw an image of people wearing white sheets, even over their heads.

Here is a dream of mine, recorded on 12-7-00:

"Allen and I were seated with a group of people, and our group seemed to get word that the Russians had been planning a major attack on the United States, via ship. They had many, many ships headed for ports along the coast all over the country, and they were filled with perhaps a million men who were planning to invade, and to attack and kill as many people as possible. We were all concerned, and became rapidly more so as the reality of this news began to sink in. However, among this group there seemed to be little sense of what to do. There was no group effort to respond, either with prayer or a course of action. Rather, people, including us, seemed to decide to begin to break up and pack to go home. I remember heading back to our room to try to find and gather up my things, feeling somewhat confused and frustrated, as well as anxious. At that point I woke up."

When we sought the meaning of this dream, here is what Allen thought he heard the Lord say:

"The dream that I gave Jan is symbolic of the forces of evil over-running this nation of America. The 'Russians' are not literally coming, but there is, in fact, an invasion of demons, and they are emboldened by the foolishness and ease of so many of My people. These demons have already spread out across the land, and they are reinforcing those who already have strongholds. I am, of course, still infinitely stronger, but My people must call upon My power. The fact that most of My people do not even know what to do shows how desperate the situation has become. I have many warriors, but I have many whose main interest is their own comfort, and who confuse love with 'niceness.' There is no time for that, as the enemy is not deterred for even a moment by 'nice' people. It is only those who wield the weapons of truth and real love, dependent upon the power of My Holy Spirit and resting upon the revelation in Scripture, who can triumph over the enemy. I will ultimately triumph, but there is also a battle here and now, and I expect My soldiers to stand in My power. Do not be afraid, for I am with you, and I have given all that is necessary to win this battle. Do not be deceived or intimidated by the enemy. Truth is powerful, for I am the embodiment of truth, and I am behind and in front of every true soldier of the Cross."

On a larger scale, the following is a sobering word that we received concerning the spiritual state of much of Western Christianity:

"There is a need to testify to life in the Spirit, for most of those who call themselves by My name in the affluent West are using Me as a sort of white frosting over the devil's food cake of their everyday lives. You are all going to struggle with sin, but I am seeking the hearts of those who think they are O.K. with a dose of Sunday 'sanctification.' It is not enough to say the words of allegiance to My commands when I am asking for everything, and most won't even consider giving that. Of course, I give everything in return, but it takes trust to make that step. It is hard, but without it there is no real life. Indeed, I am calling My *church* to become *My* church."

God also has a role for each faithful, hearing believer to play in the fulfillment of His great Kingdom purposes. Recently, He described it this way:

"I am seeking those who would understand who I AM, and how I work, and how I speak, for it is through those that I can work. There are some, though fewer than are needed— those who know that I am calling to adventure, not comfort, at each stage. This does not mean that I do not give blessings; of course, I do— but it means that I expect every talent, every gift, every bit of intelligence, all that you are— to be used in serving Me along the way. It is by this commitment that the Church will be restored. Though I desire that all come, there are some— many in the churches of the West— who will come only on their own terms— and no one ever gets to go on this journey on their own terms. There is only one way to be on this King's highway, and that is to do it My way— to hear, to follow, and to obey. It is certainly a difficult and sometimes painful act of trust, but it is the only way to be My servant: one who is woven into My great tapestry of history."

I will close this chapter on God's purposes in speaking by reminding the reader that there are two things we must avoid as we seek to hear the Lord. The first concerns the desire to use the process of hearing for our own spiritual entertainment and self-gratification. In our own case, I must confess that for a time in the early stages of our hearing, we found the experience of receiving veiled foreknowledge of a future event so fascinating that we typically got caught up in the process of trying to figure it all out, while sadly neglecting to pray for or against those things which we were being shown. We had ignored our responsibility, and had often failed to be obedient. The

Lord was patient, but, after some time, He finally gave a somber rebuke: *"This is not a game."* Having been thus reprimanded, we thereafter made a far more conscious effort to pray and not just speculate. While the Lord has delighted in giving us words and images which are always fascinating, and often entertaining, they are not for our entertainment. They must bear fruit through our response. This cannot be overemphasized.

The second thing we must eschew is the temptation to use hearing from God for our own self-promotion. Recently, we attended a gathering where a stern warning was given concerning those who have been acquiring wealth and fame from their prophetic ministries. We must always bear in mind these words from Revelation 19:10: "For the testimony of Jesus is the spirit of prophecy." To God alone be the glory.

Chapter Two:
The Basics of Listening

In the beginning chapters of this book, my goal was to relate how it was that two ordinary people came to be able to hear the Lord with enough clarity and certainty to begin to make small and large decisions and to take the steps that forever changed their lives. From my hysterectomy and miraculous deliverance from cancer to leaving our home in Massachusetts four months later to go to Trinity Episcopal School for Ministry in Pennsylvania to ordination and a rector's position in Alabama, life with four wonderful exchange students and numerous trips to their homes in Germany and Holland, the adoption of three Russian children and the possibility of a fourth and perhaps more, and, most recently, the emergence of a new ministry vision, as yet not fully discerned, we have lived the adventure of hearing and following the Lord. And we know that the adventure has only just begun.

In light of the fact, then, that this book is largely set in the context of our own experience, this would be a good place to clarify two things. First, as I have already said, I am fully cognizant of the fact that the world cares little about how Allen and I got to seminary and beyond. But I do believe that many people care passionately about how they can learn to hear God for *themselves*, and about how they can begin to act in faith on that hearing. So, from the beginning, to inspire them to do this has really been my central purpose in writing. When all is said and done, can there be anything in this world more essential or exciting to an individual than learning to be in communion with his Creator and hearing and following His voice?

Second, I should add that some of what I have offered here and throughout this book is *prescriptive,* having universal application, while some is merely *descriptive* of our own journey, reflecting specific instructions to us at particular points in time. For example, it should go without saying that not everyone is called to seminary, to ordination, or to adoption. These *descriptives* are largely the things which propel the narrative of our own story, and, as the Lord once reminded us when praying for direction for someone else's life, *"I tell no one any story but his own."* However, even in the case of our personal guidance, I do believe that behind each word, vision and dream lays a rich storehouse of *general* wisdom dealing with the nature of God, Biblical theology, prophecy, truth, Scriptural exposition, and the life-long process of sanctification, from which the attentive reader may also glean many appropriate and valuable lessons.

Having said these things, I will now undertake the task of explaining the basics of hearing by spelling out in greater detail just how our *own* hearing process began and was facilitated. I will start by reminding the reader that our own adventure of hearing and following the Lord, though hidden in the mind of God from all eternity past and manifested throughout our earlier lives in many ways, really took on flesh and bone in the supportive context of our Cursillo reunion group, which we joined in June of 1988. This, of course, is not to say that one has to attend a Cursillo weekend to learn to hear the Lord. This is a descriptive. The crucial point was that we became involved in a small group fellowship where we saw listening and hearing being modeled (a prescriptive). In this group of six, three couples (all initially from the same church), there were three key elements present which fostered both the development of our spiritual gifts and our ability to hear the Lord's voice:

The *size* of the group was small enough to provide intimacy, but not large enough to be intimidating. I will again take this opportunity to endorse small home fellowships, for our own experience and that of many others along with the testimony of Scripture, confirms that they are designed to be the birthing place for spiritual gifts and the training ground for effective ministry.

Because our group met every Sunday night, week in and week out, for four years, there was a clear sense of commitment to the meeting and to one other, providing the strong and necessary elements of consistency, dependability, mutual trust, and accountability. It was a *discipline* which we took seriously.

Like infants learning to walk, we emulated what we saw demonstrated by the others in the group, in terms of learning to pray and listen. *Modeling* was crucial.

These are the *specifics* of what we did in that early setting. After our reunion meeting, we entered into a time of prayer. (I should pause here and note that prayer time, particularly an extensive one, is not a given part of the Cursillo reunion group format, and it is likely that many groups do not engage in any or, at least, any *extended*, prayer time together. This just happens to be something that *we* chose to do). We often found it helpful at this point to lower the lights, as it served to minimize distractions and quiet us down, but this is another descriptive. There were also times when we discerned that we needed to begin by praying for spiritual protection. On one occasion, having done this, Allen immediately saw an angel with a flaming sword standing over us.

We often began with a time of praise and thanksgiving, and I must say that we seemed to pray more effectively when we took this extra time, although of course the Lord graciously heard and responded to us even when we didn't start this way. Typically, we spent from five or ten minutes to a half hour or so engaged in praising God with songs, psalms, and individual thanksgivings. Over time, we came to the understanding, as modeled in the Lord's Prayer and elsewhere in Scripture, that prayer should always begin with praise. "Our Father in heaven, *hallowed be Your name.*" And again, "Enter his gates with thanksgiving and his courts with praise; give thanks to him and praise his name. (Psalm 100:4)

In other words, Scripture shows us that entrance into God's holy presence rightly begins with praise—not, by the way, because the Lord needs it, but because we do! Praising takes the focus off of us, and places it where it belongs. True praise is probably one of the most neglected activities of the Church, for we tend to jump into intercession, driven by the perceived urgency of our own agendas.

Next, we simply began to pray, each as led, in no particular order, for friends, family, neighbors, local church, wider church, nation, and world. As noted earlier, we often felt led to use the gift of our private prayer languages, particularly when feeling distressed or blocked in prayer. After each petition, we sat quietly, waiting to see if the Lord would respond in any way. These moments of silence generally lasted from one to a few minutes, but there were also times when we sat in utter silence for up to a half an hour or more. The waiting, we found, was a crucial element.

Early in the process, we began to discover that the Lord would not infrequently use our prayer time to speak to us concerning things for which we had not been praying at the time. It was as though He were using the opportunity of our quiet listening to speak to an issue He deemed important. Sometimes, He would even interrupt suddenly with an answer to or comment upon something we had prayed about in an earlier session! It was almost as though He were saying, "You may have your agenda, but this is what *I* want to talk about right now!" I also believe that the Lord sometimes uses this particular device when we are so emotionally tied to the question we are raising that we doubt our own objectivity in hearing. Consequently, to insure that we know it is He speaking, He delays the answer and interjects it when we are focused on something else. Since I cannot call to mind an earlier example of this phenomenon, let me cite a more recent illustration.

Some time ago, I received a phone call from my cousin in Seattle, inviting Allen and I and our three adopted Russian kids to come out to visit. Her mom, my mother's sister and the last remaining sibling from that large family, had turned ninety-five, as had my uncle, and it had been several years since I had last seen them. Up to this time, no one in my family in Seattle had met our children, and I felt it especially important that my elderly aunt and uncle have that opportunity. Allen and I talked about the possibility of making the trip, pondering, as we did so, the considerable and intimidating factors of distance, expense, and timing. We also prayed about it on several occasions, and, although such a trip would certainly have seemed to be in His general will, the Lord did not seem to give us a specific word about going. One morning, near the end of our prayer time concerning completely unrelated matters, Allen received this Scripture from Genesis:

"Now Israel's eyes were failing because of old age, and he could hardly see. So Joseph brought his sons close to him, and his father kissed them and embraced them. Israel said to Joseph, *"I never expected to see your face again, and now God has allowed me to see your children too."*(Genesis 48:10-11—italics mine)

Although the verses did not come in direct answer to prayer about the trip, it certainly seemed that their connection to the issue was far too obvious to be coincidental or unrelated, particularly since my aunt is now legally blind. I therefore took the words as a strong encouragement from the Lord to go.

Timing then became the central concern. Several weeks later, in response to our asking the Lord when we should make the trip, Allen received this Scripture from Mark 14:1: "Now the Passover and the Feast of Unleavened Bread were only two days away...." Curious, I checked the calendar, and finding that Passover was on April fifth that year, I concluded that perhaps we were being encouraged to leave on the third. I then emailed my cousin, a high school counselor, regarding our tentative plans, but I was a bit surprised when she replied that her vacation week came at the end and not the beginning of April. Oh well, I reasoned, perhaps the Lord was simply giving us a general time frame. However, I was amused to get a second email from my cousin a few days later, stating that she had been in error and that her vacation was in fact scheduled to begin on the third! As we began searching for plane tickets, we further found that the fares on that date were the best in the surrounding two-week period.

The chance to spend time with my family, especially my aunt, was a profound blessing in ways too numerous to recount. Further, we discovered upon arrival that we were just in time for the opening day of the spectacular Skagit Valley Tulip Festival. To top it all off, the Easter Sunday that we were there was on record as having the best weather for that day in the past 50 years! The Lord had clearly provided for a beautiful reunion, but His hand had also been evident in so many other delightful details.

Similarly, on numerous occasions we were astonished to realize that the Lord had responded to a prayer just prior to its being verbalized! Our daughter Oksana once asked us, "Does God know what I'm thinking, even before I say it?" The answer, attested to by our personal experience and confirmed by Scripture, is a resounding "Yes!" In the Anglican tradition, we affirm this reality each week as we begin the liturgy: "Almighty God, to you all hearts are open, all desires known, and from you no secrets are hid...."[iii]

Having given the reader a little window into what our small group prayer sessions looked like, I will now turn to what I firmly believe was in point of practicality the most crucial factor in this entire beginning process of hearing for Allen and me. After several months of reunion group participation, of watching and hearing the others with whom we met, Allen renewed in earnest the discipline of keeping his prayer journal. Evidently, this was precisely what was necessary because, as I described earlier, it was very shortly afterwards that Allen himself began to hear words and see visions during the prayer time. Everything was dutifully recorded. I estimate that since we began this process in 1989, at least 90% of what we have received from the Lord has been written down. In addition, upon seeing a vision, Allen has often attempted to sketch as well as describe what he has seen. Consequently, his prayer journals are *full* of intriguing little drawings!

I do not exaggerate when I say that our very lives began to move and change when Allen began this disciplined process of hearing *and recording.* For many reasons, it was clear that the Lord wanted us to have a written record of our journey and of our dialog with Him. Without those, we would have no permanent archives of our own history, no lasting testimony to God's activity, no record of His speaking, no written documentation of His answers to prayer, and no way to tie together the threads of a message given over a period of time. Without the journals, the possibility of writing this book would have been nonexistent. Likewise, had the prophets and apostles not been obedient to God's instructions to write what they heard and saw and testified to, we would have no Bible.

The journal-keeping led to the beginning of Allen's prophetic gifting. At first, he recorded what he received after he got home from reunion group, but, as the prophetic gift developed and the messages increased in quantity, we soon found that he had to bring his notebook to the group and write as we prayed, for the visions and words became too numerous to be retained until we got home. In the subsequent years, Allen has filled nearly thirty notebooks, and I several more of my own. They provide a remarkable record of our spiritual journey and the Lord's guidance, as well as an astounding testimony to answered prayer. We have often commented that, if the house ever burned down, after first making sure that the kids were safe and the animals were out, we would next save the journals. In addition to being a record of our personal history over the last eighteen years, they represent thousands of hours of our shared prayer life.

Incidentally, our writing book of choice has always been colored, spiral-bound, 91/2" by 6" journals. After the first few, we learned that we needed to buy the ones with hard plastic covers, as otherwise they begin to disintegrate with constant use. Lately, with their advent, we have found that we also prefer those with fabric-covered rings, as the covering provides even greater protection. With these spiral-bound notebooks, there are no loose sheets of paper floating about, and they can be easily carried, packed, or kept by the bed. Of course, the reader is free to write on whatever he chooses, and, in a pinch, anything—a napkin, a grocery receipt, an envelope back—will do until the messages can be more formally recorded. The important thing is to get it written down. Over the years, people have often asked us about the process of hearing, and what we have consistently said is foremost is this: "Begin the discipline of writing as you pray." To our dismay, these same people will come back to us weeks, months, or even years later to complain that they are still not hearing from the Lord, yet when we ask if they have begun the practice of quiet time with pen and paper in hand, they say no.

Let me add one further bit of helpful information. As I first began the daunting task, some years ago, of going through the journal material in order to write about it, I became acutely aware that I needed some system for quickly finding and easily sorting through the different topics and themes about which we had prayed. Spurred by a suggestion from Pat Miller, the educational consultant at Trinity, I adopted a method of using colored felt-tip markers to underline the text. The colors I assigned were as follows: purple for praise, as well as for all prayers relating to our personal situation; brown for intercession for others; green for prayer concerning the Church, local or otherwise; red for national issues; blue for world issues; black for eschatology (end times); and yellow for all direct words from the Lord. (Please note that when I say "direct," I mean so circumspectly.

This is not dictation!) I had originally also assigned orange for what I called general theology—insights into Scripture, the nature of God and of man. However, I quickly realized that it was all theology! With dreams, I underlined the word "dream" in turquoise, and then drew a little puffy cloud shape over it in the same color. When a journal is filled, I affix a self-adhesive label to the front cover, noting on it the starting and ending date of the entries and its journal number in sequence. Finally, I store it in a plastic bin under my desk for easy access.

While it certainly has taken some extra time to reread and mark our journal texts, this system has been absolutely invaluable in helping to go back through the journals. There is simply no way that I could manage the material without it, and, interestingly enough, I have also found that I can glance at stretches of text and get an overview of our concerns. To my chagrin and shame, I have generally been all too painfully aware that much in our journals is underlined in purple for "personal concerns!"

In addition to developing a system by which to manage the journal entries, I soon realized that I needed to do some serious work in another area, as well. It didn't take Allen and me long to discover that the Lord was employing a rich and vast range of archetypal Bible and Christian imagery in the dreams, visions and words which He was giving us. Some of this was immediately familiar to us and reasonably obvious; much, however, was considerably more difficult and enigmatic. In those beginning years of hearing, I made many trips to the library to research these symbols, and I gained much insight. I also realized that it would be helpful to have a resource of our own to use at home, and I opted for <u>The New Unger's Bible Dictionary</u>. In addition to being a wonderful, general Bible lexicon, it has proven to be very helpful in dealing with the figurative meaning of images, though it is of course by no means the only good book on the subject. Many Bible dictionaries devote at least some space to the figurative meanings behind Biblical imagery, and the reader will want to find the one that most appeals to him or her.

We also learned that the Lord has designed it so that hearing comes and is facilitated when we ourselves consciously create the favorable conditions. Interestingly, these all involve a willingness to commit to certain disciplines. I would divide these into three areas:

Outward conditions

Discipline #1: The willingness to commit to a regular *quiet time*. Most people find that either early morning or late evening work best, but the reader will need to find a consistent time in his or her own schedule.

Discipline #2: Within this quiet time, the willingness to commit to *reading and pondering the Scriptures.* Many people from liturgical traditions often find it most helpful to use the schedule of the daily office. Others may choose a book of daily meditations, while still others simply prefer to let the Lord guide them to a Scripture passage.

Discipline #3: The willingness to do these two things with pen and paper at hand, ready to *write* down one's thoughts and reactions to Scripture, the day's experiences, the previous night's dreams, and whatever it is that we think we may be hearing from the Lord as we seek Him. As I repeatedly emphasize, it was Allen's commitment to journal-keeping that started this whole process in us. The key in all of these things is consistency.

Why is writing so necessary? To begin with, our prayer journals are the record of our personal history and our spiritual journey. Like the Israelites, it is easy to forget where we've been, and why we've been there. I have been amazed and grateful to be able to go back through the journals to trace the record of our own life and growth. When Joshua, Caleb, the priests with the ark, and the whole nation of Israel crossed over the Jordan into the Land of Canaan, they were commanded to erect standing stones to commemorate the place where the Lord had parted the waters. Our prayer journals could well be seen as our own standing stones, bearing permanent testimony to what God has done in our lives. Second, I am also convinced that writing brings healing, clarity, and resolution. There is something uniquely helpful about putting things on paper. Last, we need to write because I believe that the

Lord requires it. To Moses and the prophets, to the apostles and to Paul, the Lord's command was, "Write."

Inward conditions

First and foremost, we must make a full assent to the Lordship of Christ. If we are to seek the Lord's wisdom and will in openness and honesty, we must have an abiding determination to put aside our own perceived needs, desires, preconceptions, and opinions. Further, there must be a clear commitment to what we believe that we are being called to, regardless of the potential consequences. If we allow our own wills and desires to take precedence, we will simply hear the reverberating echo of our own voice. Many of us have known people who were convinced that the Lord was prescribing a certain course of action, when it was obvious that what they were "hearing" was precisely what they wanted to hear. In our experience, the Lord's ways are usually significantly different from our own, which is one reason why obedience is a test of faith. Listening faithfully requires humility, trust, submission, and a repentant spirit, accompanied by praise.

Second, I must also address the profoundly important matter of what is variously called the baptism of the Holy Spirit or the in-filling of the Holy Spirit. The record of the New Testament shows that this in-filling did not follow a rigid pattern or time sequence with relation to either conversion or water baptism, and so I cannot prescribe one. Neither do I see it as my place here to debate issues of terminology or theology concerning this subject but, rather, to exhort the reader to avail him or herself of the Spirit's power for ministry. What is of utmost necessity is that the believer has a sincere desire and willingness to use his or her gifts in the Lord's service. Further, as with both accepting Christ and receiving water baptism, Allen and I feel that this commitment should be made in the context of the Christian community, with other believers laying hands on, praying for, and agreeing to support the person in his or her life in the Spirit.

An excellent resource in this regard is Dennis and Rita Bennett's <u>The Holy Spirit and You</u>. When I asked the Lord to assist me in discussing this in-filling of the Holy Spirit, Allen thought he heard the following:

"It is not the action which causes the gifts to be given, but it is the willingness to be obedient. When a person is willing to commit further to obedience and earnestly desires to hear Me, then I make that possible. There is no 'magic' to the specific act, except as a visible symbol of that willingness to obey, but that visible confession of willingness is very important. The process of receiving gifts is not a one-time event but, as you are willing to obey and follow into places and situations which require more, I give more. I am not stingy with My gifts, but I do not give them as toys. The gifts are intended to be used to prepare and enable My people to do My work. In a sense, gifts are like muscles. If they are being used, they get stronger, and if they are not, they atrophy. The idea is, obviously, that the gifts are given to further the Gospel in some way and to win people to the truth about Me. The world is awash with lies of every sort, and those who choose to call themselves the Church are often the perpetrators of the most harmful lies, because they deny My people the things they need in order to fight, and Satan rejoices at this. I would have each of My people claim the full complement of gifts which I have planned for them in order to bring the truth of the Gospel into the battle for the souls of mankind, but some are too deceived to claim their gifts, and some are too comfortable to claim their gifts. As you have found, the gifts are great blessings, but they move each believer, step by step, into a life of trusting in Me—life on the edge—and there are many who cannot bear that thought, even though they don't fully know what it would be like. I empower for that to which I call, and I do My miracles among those who are willing to trust. After all, they are the only ones who appreciate miracles for what they are, though I do use miracles to bring people to Me who are ready to hear. You see this issue of 'gifts' is both simple and complex. The only real necessity in receiving is a heart that is willing to obey, and, as that heart stays on the path, My gifts will flow to accomplish My purposes. However, the gifts are under My control, and no amount of manipulation will cause them to be given where I have not purposed."

The role of community and accountability

I have already spoken amply about the function of the Christian community, and especially small groups, in nurturing and supporting the hearing and gifting process. I will only add here that I have known of too many unfortunate instances where believers in self-chosen isolation have misheard or misinterpreted what they thought they were hearing, misleading others in the world and in the Body in the process. In some instances, this has had tragic consequences. The Church was designed so that we need each other's prayer, spiritual insight, and correction. Literally everything I have thus far described from our own experience was birthed, nurtured, or facilitated in the context of Christian community. As Paul instructed, "The spirits of prophets are subject to the control of prophets."(1 Corinthians 14:32)

Chapter 3:
How Our Listening Grew and Developed

We indeed learned an enormous amount about the basics of hearing in those early years of our experience, but, over time, we also discovered that there were some interesting changes and progressions occurring in the means by which the Lord spoke to us. Below are some of the ways in which we found that to be happening.

First, I will address some of the changes we experienced with regard to the *methods* which the Lord employed in speaking to us. Initially, as I have shown, the Lord's communications to us were in the form of senses or impressions, short references to Scripture verses, single visions, single words or very short phrases, and, of course, dreams. I guess one could say that He started feeding us by giving us small bites. However, as Allen gained confidence and practice in hearing, the length of the words he felt he was getting expanded to a sentence or two, then a paragraph or two while the visions grew in complexity and quantity and the dreams and Scripture citations continued in abundance. In those first years of our hearing experience, Allen was literally peppered with hundreds upon hundreds of visions, words, and Scripture references. So voluminous was the Lord's outpouring of prophetic material that I would have to say that by far my most difficult task in writing this book has been to select material from amongst the plethora of words(short and long), dreams, images, and other prophetic expressions with which the Lord graced and continues to grace us. In truth, I have often wondered why the Lord has sent us so much, especially since we cannot understand most of it, but I suppose that I might as well ask why plants produce so many seeds that never come to fruit or flower. God is simply a God of abundance in whatever form.

As time went on, we began to observe that we were receiving increasingly longer spoken messages—many several pages in length. We attributed this to a combination of the practice we had acquired in hearing and the confidence we had gained that at least much of what we were hearing was truly from the Lord. As the spoken words got longer, we noticed that, for a time, the number of visions diminished, though they did continue with a fair amount of regularity.

The nature of the visions themselves did not seem to change significantly with one notable and fascinating exception. In July of 1999, Allen had surgery for a detached retina. A gas bubble had been injected into his eye to hold the repair in place, and, consequently, he had to live for several days with his head down, eyes directly facing the ground. This awkward position was not only highly uncomfortable but soon rather boring for him. On several occasions during this time, however, he received lengthy and elaborate visions, one continuing for about twenty minutes. While the meaning of most of these has almost totally eluded us, I can't help but wonder if the Lord in His compassion wasn't, besides imparting much spiritual content, simply providing some heavenly entertainment for His immobilized patient. Bear in mind here that I use the word "entertainment" cautiously, for the Lord does nothing lightly. To date, this experience of receiving such long and complex visions has not recurred.

I do not wish to imply, by the way, that this shift in *methods* of hearing over the years connotes any superiority in one form of the Lord's communication over another, and other people's patterns of hearing may be different. The only change which I might attribute to our own growth is, as I mentioned above, that of Allen's ability to receive longer verbal messages with time and practice. Beyond that, we have found that the Lord simply uses whatever we are most spiritually receptive to at any given time, be it dreams, words, visions, or other means, and His methods of speaking are, as the saying goes, "subject to change without notice."

I will make note of another way in which our gifts developed and matured, especially in regard to *community*. As I have mentioned, when we first began hearing from the Lord, Allen saw visions and heard words primarily in our reunion group setting. After continuing for several months in this fashion, the two of us began meeting separately during the week with one of the members of the group for additional prayer, and shortly thereafter Allen's prophetic gift soon became evident amongst just the three of us. After some time, the same thing happened when just Allen and I prayed together, and of course, somewhere in the process, he increasingly began to hear when he was alone. I am not exactly sure why this progression occurred, but it does seem to underscore the training of the small group experience.

While at Trinity, we had an intriguing addition to our experience of hearing which also seemed somehow related to the theme of community, though we never really understood exactly how or why. We went through a fairly long period of time when the Lord seemed to be giving Allen words in other languages. Amazingly enough, we discovered that, during this time, precisely this same phenomenon was happening to two or three other fellow seminarians, who were as baffled as we were! In hindsight, I wonder if we had simply missed the obvious: perhaps we should have gathered with these others for prayer, but the idea didn't seem to occur to any of us at the time! Some of these foreign words we recognized because we were studying them in Greek and Hebrew. But there were also words in other languages unknown to us, though at times we at least recognized the language. Some of them, I suppose, could also have been "tongues of angels."(1 Corinthians 13:1) I scoured the dictionaries and prayed for insight, and, on very rare occasions, we would figure out a word, but the vast majority of these were lost to us, except that we dutifully wrote them all down to the best of our ability. When we complained to the Lord that we didn't understand, He only said, "I know." He neither explained nor justified Himself. However, He did add that there would be a time when we would understand. It may be in the age to come! At any rate, this experience remains a mystery to us, and perhaps the Lord was only seeking to underscore His sovereignty. Eventually, these foreign words largely stopped and have, to this point, only rarely reoccurred.

It is important to add that there is one interesting, not to mention frustrating, way in which our hearing has *not* seemed to change over the years. Neither our immediate nor our subsequent comprehension *rates* seem to have increased perceptibly, suggesting that that particular aspect of the hearing process cannot be improved with practice or experience. God has apparently designed it that way. Each time I read through our old journals, I am rewarded with a few new insights, but I am amply convinced that there is richness and a depth to what we have been given that is deliberately and vastly beyond our ability to decipher and comprehend. It keeps us humble. God never intends for Himself to be fully figured out, for in the relationship between finite man and the infinite Creator, there must always be room for mystery. It recently occurred to me that heaven will likely include many "road to Emmaus" (see Luke 24: 13-32) experiences in which the Lord opens to us what He has shown and spoken to us on earth, both personally and through His written Word. I can imagine the Lord and I walking or sitting together as He illuminates the journals, shedding His light on what was for so long dark speech, for "…then I shall know fully…."(I Corinthians 13:12)

While the Lord, then, regularly blesses us with practical guidance which is immediately understandable and applicable to a specific need, most of what we hear we do not initially grasp. Understanding with regard to deeper issues, we have found, generally comes in retrospect and, even then, is only partial. Often there are onion-like layers which get peeled over a period of many years. This seems to be especially true with the more visual and, therefore, more highly symbolic forms of communication— dreams and visions. If this experience of hearing was otherwise, we would not have to exercise faith. But, as it is, we are in good company, for the record of Scripture shows that the prophets themselves often fared no better. Their task was only to be obedient in recording. Like Mary, they no doubt spent their lives "pondering in their hearts" what they had been shown and told, wondering about and waiting for the outworking which, in many instances, has not yet come in its fullness.

I will relate here one remarkable incidence of our coming to an unfolding understanding of a word over a period of time. As I mentioned earlier, the latter part of our time in Massachusetts was marked by extreme angst on my part, as I desperately struggled to understand what I was supposed to be doing with my life. Having suffered from childhood emotional abuse, the situation was further complicated by the deep inner healing issues with which I was wrestling. One night, as we prayed about the situation, the Lord showed Allen a tri-fold vision. First, he saw a playing card— the ace of clubs; next, a teddy bear wearing a little jacket; and, last, a pair of kittens sitting together. I felt from these images that the Lord was urging me to regain the sense of carefree childhood playfulness which had been lost, and I remain reasonably certain that was the message to me at that time.

Several years later, we began the process of taking exchange students, and, in the fall of 1998, we welcomed our second student, Revital, from Holland. We had, also, already planned to take Katharina, the sister of Hanno, our first German student, the third and following year, followed by her brother, Heiner. Though I had not really thought about the three-part vision for a long time, for some reason, on the night before Revi's arrival it came back to me strongly, and I even went back to the journals and located it. Suddenly, my heart racing, I now saw the images as relating to our exchange students. Hanno was our first—the ace; Revi was somehow connected to the teddy bear; and the kittens were Katharina and her "litter-mate," Hanno, or perhaps her younger brother, Heiner, who eventually came to live with us for a year, as well. I was even led to muse to Allen while Revi was downstairs the following night unpacking, "Wouldn't it be funny if she brought a little teddy bear with a jacket?"

She had arrived in the evening, exhausted, and had only partially unpacked, but the next morning I heard her bustling about in her room and went downstairs to see if I could help. As I walked through the door, she reached over to her window shelf, exclaiming, "Would you like to see what I brought?" I recall that I actually let out a small shriek, for she handed me a little brown teddy bear wearing a blue denim jacket! Even more amazing was this: Revi explained that she was not really a "teddy-bear sort of person." Furthermore, this bear had not originally come with a jacket. However, her friends back home had decided to give her a going-away gift of money, and her mother had made the jacket, complete with little slits cut into it, through which the bills were cleverly woven. Hence, the bear and the jacket had been very specifically connected with her coming to us. We were in awe. If the three-part vision has yet more layers of meaning, only time will reveal them.

I am convinced that it is as much fun for the Lord to watch us delight in discovering these hidden treasures as it is for us to find them, and I'm sure that is partly why He does it. However, to catch these things, one needs to be attuned, to keep one's spiritual ear to the ground. All of us surely miss things much of the time, for the "still small voice" is subtle.

People have often remarked to Allen and I about the way in which our individual gifts have come to compliment one another and function together, so let me also say a few words concerning that. The pattern we operate with was, I believe, set from the very outset, being inherent in our personalities, our gifts, and the ways in which we relate to one another. The prime prophetic gifting was and remains clearly Allen's, and I would go so far as to say that his gift falls into the category of that described in Ephesians 4, verse 11: "It was he who gave some to be apostles, some to be prophets,….." However, I also regularly receive prophetic visions, words, and dreams. Amazingly, in fact, on a number of occasions during prayer, Allen and I have received nearly simultaneous words or senses, and there have also been a few remarkable instances when we have had dreams of almost identical prophetic content and imagery on the same night, providing a strong confirmation of a given message.

Nonetheless, from the beginning, the complimentary role that the Lord has seemed to assign me has been that of helpmate—reviewing, sorting through, pondering, writing about and, in general, tracking the things that the Lord has given us. Indeed, in many ways, the present culmination of those efforts has been the writing of this book. Allen, for his part, has always been more reluctant to go back through the journals, mainly because he is fearful that will influence his hearing, and it is only fairly recently that he has resolved somewhat in his mind that this does not have to be the case.

As with any two human beings living and working so closely together, there are ways in which we function almost as one person in our hearing, as though we were two parts of one whole. On the other hand, there are clearly areas in which we mature in our gifts at different rates and, therefore, must correct, complement, balance, and encourage each other. Let me cite an example. Odd as it may seem, despite my strong awareness of the necessity to be writing while praying, I spent years relying on Allen to do most of the writing during our prayer time, all the while being frustrated by the fact that I wasn't hearing more myself! Clearly, there were some emotional and spiritual factors involved here that I needed to work through, but, when I complained to the Lord about my sparseness of hearing, He reminded me that I needed to be consistently praying with my own notebook and pen in hand. Here is what Allen heard Him say:

"You must learn to write while you're praying, for I give words to be recorded and remembered. If My people are not able to remember what I say in detail, it will not be of much use to them. You do write when you are journaling, but I would give you more. Most of My people have their hearing and, thus, their understanding crippled by never being willing to make the effort to write down what I am saying—or what they even suspect I am saying. I speak more and more completely to those who record—it is that simple."

Finally obedient to this instruction, in the past few years I have begun to receive visions and words with increasing frequency.

Lastly, with regard to growing in hearing, I must address an issue with which we have continually struggled in our attempts to be obedient to what we think we are receiving, particularly when it comes to the larger life decisions. Intrinsic to the process of listening and following, it seems, are two opposing impulses. On the one hand, we always hesitate to act, fearful that we may be moving precipitously and prematurely, driven by our own assumptions and anxieties. On the other hand, we fully recognize the need to test a word by stepping forward in faith from the light on the path into the darkness, knowing that the next light will come on only as we step and not before.

To make things even more complicated, there is also the counterpoint of our personalities. I tend to be the one who is more receptive to and less fearful of change, while Allen is more resistant. Naturally, these leanings in our own natures have some impact on how we hear and on how we respond to what we are hearing. Consequently, regularly faced with dilemmas of timing and directions, so much of our prayer over the years has been, "Lord, are we getting ahead of You, or are we lagging behind out of fear of doing something which might not be Your plan? How hard do we push on the doors, or do we even push at all?"

This particular question persistently nagged at me as I worked on this chapter, almost as though the Lord wanted me to pay special attention to it, not only for our own benefit, but also for the sake of others wrestling with the same question. Finally, feeling that I could not address the matter adequately without the Lord's further input, Allen and I prayed about it, and this is what He seemed to say:

"There is no real tension, for I work in such a way that when you feel a need in the Spirit to push on a door, that is of Me. Waiting is also of Me, for I do arrange things over time, and they do not come together immediately. The 'pushing of doors' does not violate the principle, as long as you submit to Me in prayer, for I do use that to show the way—or not the way, more often. It is when you break down the door in your rush to do something that it can become a problem. I very well know the nature of humanity, and I recognize that the circumstances of your lives do make you wish to batter down some doors and 'make something happen.' I will assure you that something *will* happen in My time and in My way, if you are merely obedient to what you understand. You could not 'make something happen' in the way that you need to anyhow, and I have planned it that way. I desire that you place your dependence on Me."

I wished that we had asked the question long ago, for hearing the Lord's answer helped us enormously, as I hope it will others, enabling us to move on to a new wisdom in hearing. This word was also a confirmation to us, for over the years, the Lord's consistent answer to our questions concerning timing and initiative has seemed to be that, if we continually seek Him, He will correct any missteps. Nevertheless, when all is said and done, I confess that this process remains a decidedly scary one. "It is quite normal," the Lord once reminded us, "to be anxious when you are seeking to operate from faith. Do not think that Abraham was perfectly serene as he sought to obey, for he was in turmoil much of the time."(We know that, on at least one occasion, he and his wife Sarah did batter down a door!) (See Genesis 16:1-3)

This word, on the surface, seems as though it should have caused great disillusionment with regard to Abraham's walk of faith. On the contrary, it left us feeling enormously relieved, encouraged, and comforted. Now, instead of viewing Abraham as a dauntless and inimitable superhero, we saw him as one who, while trusting God's overarching promises, faltered along the way and yet, ultimately, held to the path of obedience despite what must have been enormous fear and frustration. Here was someone with whom we could readily identify. Like Abraham, too, it has often been only in hindsight that we have received full assurance that we have stayed on the path. If it were not so, trust would not be required. Over the years, learning to live with and even to have joy in the midst of this anxiety has been one of the greatest areas in which our spiritual muscles have been exercised and our skills in hearing strengthened. "Now faith is being sure of what we hope for and certain of what we do not see."(Hebrews 11:1)

I trust that this chapter has given the reader some further insight into how hearing may undergo growth and change, based on our own experience. I will now turn my attention to the topic of the many ways in which the Lord speaks to His people.

Chapter 4:
How God Speaks

As I began to work on this chapter, I sought the Lord about it, expressing my anxious concern about selecting just the right examples to illuminate the various ways in which God speaks. Since the Lord had earlier advised me not to first take the time to reread through all of the journals (a formidable task), I asked Him to help me to remember those things from our own experience that would be most interesting and helpful. I thought it would be fun to include the Lord's response to that request here, as a lively and pertinent illustration of His ever-present guidance. Here is what Allen thought he heard:

"This is not a matter of finding the perfect illustration, for you cannot know how any particular story or incident will affect readers. You must make sure that the focus is on hearing Me, and how that has changed your lives, for I desire to do the same work in every heart which comes to Me. I will remind you of particular images and incidents as you proceed, but you also know that there are certain things I have shown or said or done which are especially vivid in your memory, and you will find that those will help others as much as they've helped you. I am surely speaking to anyone who comes to Me desiring to hear. However, there are many who do not believe that I would speak to them, so they are not listening for the 'still small voice,' or the image that comes unbidden, or the circumstance which seems so odd, or the words of another person delivering My message even when they themselves do not know they are a messenger. It is very helpful for My people to understand that I speak in the silence of waiting, and I often seek just to find out if there is obedience in the small things. Will they take the trouble to write? I am certainly there to help My people, but I do not exist to grant wishes. I lead people along the path to exciting, phenomenal adventures which bring great fulfillment, but that path is not anything which might be expected, and it often seems like something you do not want at first. Sadly, many of My people are not willing to walk the path of great, great blessing because it does not seem to be what they want, and their main concern is some strange idea of personal fulfillment found in doing things their way. I insist on obedience because it is the only way to break the cycle of self and move My people onto the path where they can truly see that I have incredible plans and that their gifts will be used in great ways by the Giver of all gifts— Me."

I will now detail some of the various ways in which hearing the Lord may come, citing illustrations from our own experience and that of some others. I have divided these expressions of God's communication to us into nine basic categories. In each of these, I have necessarily tried to limit the illustrations, and I hope that the reader may be stimulated to supply some of his or her own. I also ask the reader to bear in mind that this list of ways in which God speaks is neither exhaustive nor definitive. It is simply my list, and I remind the reader once again that hearing is more art than science. This means, among other things, that there is overlap and flow between these categories, and someone else may choose to organize these things a bit differently. I have tried to group the various ways of hearing according to the ways in which they come to us.

I. Words, Spoken and Written

A. The General Reading and Study of God's Word

Psalm 119, verse 105 tells us, "Your word is a lamp to my feet and a light for my path." Before and above all else, it is through His written Word that God reveals Himself, sets forth salvation history, conveys His general will for mankind, and teaches His people. We cannot expect to know and follow Him if we are not willing, first and foremost, to find Him in the pages of Scripture. That is where we are called to begin, and to abide.

Moses declared on receiving the Law, "These commandments that I give you today are to be upon your hearts. Impress them on your children. Talk about them when you sit at home and when you walk along the road, when you lie down and when you get up. Tie them as symbols on your hands and bind them on your foreheads. Write them on the door frames of your houses and on your gates." (Deuteronomy. 6:6-9)

Likewise, the New Testament gives abundant evidence that, for the disciples as well as for Jesus Himself, Scripture was the touchstone. When Philip encountered the Ethiopian eunuch reading from the book of Isaiah, he was invited to climb up beside him in the chariot and elucidate the text. (Acts 8: 31) While Jesus walked with two of his disciples on the road to Emmaus, he "explained to them what was said in all the Scriptures concerning himself."(Luke 24: 27) When Peter addressed the crowd in Jerusalem at Pentecost, he challenged their assumptions about the strange behavior of the apostles, using Scripture as his reference: "No, this is what was spoken by the prophet Joel."(Acts 2: 16)

In the normal course of our reading of Scripture, the Holy Spirit will also, if we are attentive, begin to move our hearing from the realm of the general to the specific by drawing out what we most need to hear at any given moment. The same passage, at different times, will produce in us different responses. In the course of my own life, for example, as I have read the story of the Magi from Matthew, Chapter 2, I have had various reactions. As a small child who spent hours gazing up into the starry night sky, I was always fascinated by God's use of this wondrous star to guide. As an adult, I was drawn to the spiritual attentiveness of the Magi and to God's protection of His divine plan in the face of blatant evil. When we began our adoption process, however, the mother's heart inside me suddenly saw the Lord supernaturally leading to the place where the Child was.

B. Scripture Guides and Devotionals

There are hosts of helpful guides and devotionals available, and one need only to peruse the racks of any good Christian bookstore to find one that is suitable. As a general rule, guides and devotionals tend to come in one of two forms. Some may offer a daily meditation based on a cycle of Scripture readings, while others may be thematic. An example of the former would be Oswald Chambers' enduring classic, <u>My Utmost For His Highest</u>.

I must say that our favorite *thematic* devotional over the years has been Frances J. Roberts's <u>Come Away My Beloved.</u> With regard to printed material, it is, next to the Scriptures, the book which the Lord has seemed to use most regularly to speak to *us*. I recall, for example, our fervent prayer concerning whether or not we should accept a rector's position here in Alabama. During the week of our interview, we experienced brooding skies, blustery winds, and heavy spring rains. We also discovered that the town we were in was quite famous for its summer camps. As we asked the Lord if this were truly the place to which we were being called, Allen was led to read an entry from Roberts's book which began:

"Lift thine eyes to the heavens, for lo, they are filled with clouds; yea, they are heavy with water. Get thee back to the camp. Set out the buckets and make preparation: For already the wind rises, the leaves rustle in the trees..."[iv]

I had an immediate knowing in my spirit that the wording was no coincidence but, rather, a sign from the Lord—one more confirmation in a list of many which convinced us to come. On this and numerous other occasions, Roberts's book has provided wisdom and insight and helped us to discern our path. I highly recommend it, but I do not prescribe it, as the Lord obviously uses different things with different people, based on their leanings and personalities. I should also add that this wonderful book has recently been carefully updated to speak in today's language.

For those in liturgical churches, God may also speak through the use of a *daily lectionary,* a prescribed cycle of Scripture readings used in some denominations. In our case, for example, we follow the readings assigned in the <u>Book of Common Prayer</u>. It is no small amazement to me that this cycle of readings, set up so very long ago, can so consistently and directly speak to an immediate personal issue or need. Also, we have noted, the themes in the assigned passages often seem to coincide with events going on in the nation or the world. To illustrate, the following verse was from the Old Testament readings in March of 2003:

"Oh, my anguish, my anguish! I writhe in pain. Oh, the agony of my heart! My heart pounds within me, I cannot keep silent. For I have heard the sound of the trumpet; I have heard the battle cry."(Jeremiah 4:19)

The date? Thursday, March 20th, 2003, the day after the United States had declared war on Iraq!

C. *Liturgy: sign, symbol, and sacrament*

Even the briefest survey of Scripture reveals that God uses symbols to describe Himself and His work. Indeed, from beginning to end, the Scriptures abundantly attest to the fact that the Lord speaks and teaches through sign and symbol, through simile and metaphor. If all symbolism were removed from the Bible, it would not only be vastly reduced in its content, but also largely bereft of its richness of expression. Jesus Himself continually chose to describe His activity and His very Being in terms of metaphor: He called Himself the Bread of Life, the Door, the Alpha and the Omega, the bright Morning Star. The Lord recently told us:

"I use symbolism in Scripture, for reasons which should be obvious to you, after all of your time praying and listening. Symbols have a certain sort of power and comprehensiveness which the simple declarative statement may not have. I am also a God who likes surprises, and symbols allow a level of mystery, and also allow room for the exercise of faith. However, I do not always use symbols, because I also choose that some things be completely clear, in order that there be no mistake."

With regard to sacrament, volumes have been written on the deep meanings contained within the ordinances of the Old Covenant—circumcision and Sabbath rest, and of the New—baptism and Eucharist. It cannot be my purpose here to unpack all that finds its expression in the symbolism behind these commanded observances. I will only say that, for Israel and for the Church, obedience to these corresponding outward signs was designed to point to the inward graces of sanctified commu*nity* among the faithful and their commu*nion* with God. Furthermore, as with the worship at the tabernacle and the temple, Christian worship, from its inception, has been steeped in sign and symbol. Much, for example, has been written about the symbolism in the Eucharist alone. Dom Dix's classic The Shape of the Liturgy is generally accepted as the authoritative work on the subject.

For those in liturgical churches, God may speak through the ministrations of the *Daily Office,* those services appointed for the canonical hours of morning, noonday, evening, and compline. Speaking for myself, I have always felt God's deep peace and presence especially strongly in the reading of compline, the prayer for the last hour before retiring.

The Lord may also speak through the cycle of the *liturgical calendar*, for there is beauty, rhythm, and instruction in observing the seasons of the church year. So lasting was its impression that I can still recall, from the age of fifteen, a wonderful Confirmation class in which my Lutheran pastor taught on the symbolic meaning behind the colors representing the liturgical seasons of Advent, Christmas, Epiphany, Lent, and Easter, and Pentecost.

Some years ago, during our prayer time about another subject entirely, Allen suddenly thought he heard the Lord say, "Return to my symbols." It struck us, at the time, that this was a call to the wider Church to rediscover the richness of, and to re-institute the use of, the historic symbols of the faith. The reason, we discerned, was that these rich symbols are not only ancient, enduring, unifying, and universally understood, but also less susceptible to manipulation and doctrinal distortion than words alone. It's hard to argue with or explain away the meaning of the Cross yet, sadly, I have been in several modern church buildings where I have been astonished to find that, in their perplexing move to do away with all symbols, they have eliminated even this—Christianity's most central and defining token.

In the past several months, as we have found ourselves directed to a process of visiting a wide variety of churches, this word regarding symbols has come back to us most strongly and repeatedly. One night, in fact, the Lord seemed to punctuate this message with an unusual dream in which I found myself standing in front of what seemed to be a lectern. An unseen hand was sprinkling me with holy water, and I was filled with a light-hearted joy in response. Attached to each side of this lectern was a long stemmed tulip-style flower made of brass. Suddenly the stems began to gently sway, and I realized that the buds at the top were actually bells. This was followed by a knowing that the smell of incense was about to fill the room. The clear impression from the dream was that much of this rich sensory experience was missing from today's Western worship.

In response to this dream and to the word regarding symbols, we felt compelled to seek the Lord further, and this is what He seemed to say:

"The Church has gone on many different paths, but I originally gave the symbols as a strong stamp upon the fickle human mind. It is easy for a church to be led aside by the words of an attractive and well-spoken leader, but the symbolic representation of the faith is not so easily distorted. Indeed, the feasts of Israel were unchanging symbols of My actions in the past or the anticipation of My actions in the future. Even with those, the people of Israel often forgot. The symbols alone are not enough, but they help provide a standard pole and a focus which work with Scripture and the leadership of good men (and women) to bring My people to active, living faith. There is much to be said for the enthusiasm and excitement of modern music, so I am not telling the Church to forget the present and live in the past. I am saying that there must be a powerful appeal from various directions to call the heart to follow and understand. A church with only good preaching, or only good music, or only well-done liturgy is in danger, for the full range of the human mind is not engaged. I want My people to understand that I expect everything—their whole heart, mind, and body—and I give everything in return. My word to you about symbols is simply a part of the broader message about hearing Me. I am calling in every way possible, and I am calling with a great urgency, that all who might respond will get the opportunity. I intend that worship give the fullest possible picture of the excitement, adventure, and shalom of following."

The message behind these words may be difficult for some, but it is inescapable. In abandoning the historical, liturgical worship of the Church and its profundity of symbolism, we have lost much. I am led to suggest that "Return to My symbols" is a command which the Church can only ignore to its own spiritual impoverishment and worse, for in our Reformation zeal, we have sometimes thrown the baby out with the bath-water.

Allow me to give just one example of what that impoverishment looks like in practical application. In many non-liturgical churches, the service often begins with a brief time of greeting those standing around us. We are invited to introduce ourselves, to "meet someone new," to "greet your neighbor." However, in abandoning the historic liturgy, we are seeing through our own glass darkly, for what has actually been lost is the Passing of the Peace—an act of worship which is meant to occur after the ministry of the Word, confession, and absolution, and immediately before the offering and communion.

Why at that point of the service, and for what purpose? First, there are profound theological connections to the peace offering and communal meal of Leviticus, chapters 3 and 7, and they in turn have connections to the Passover meal we call the Last Supper during which Jesus instituted the New

Covenant in His body and blood. Second, in Matthew 5:23-24, Jesus exhorted anyone whose brother had something against him to *first* leave his gift at the altar and be reconciled. The peace offering was to be a time of joy and thanksgiving in which worshipers experienced fellowship and a communal meal with God and with others in the light of God's acceptance of the worshiper's vow-, free-will-, or thank-offering. Peace, blessing, fellowship, and shared meals are intimately connected in Scripture. Stripped of its meaning and wrenched from its place in the service, the Passing of the Peace as an act of worship has devolved into a sociable but largely meaningless handshake. Having grown up in liturgical churches, I will certainly attest that people can become blasé about the meanings behind our acts of worship, but we nevertheless set those aside at a cost which is more than we can afford.

Finally, if sacred imagery is to be a central facet of the worship life of the Church now, neither will the close of the age bring an end to God's use of signs and symbols. In Matthew, chapter 24, Jesus discusses the events which will accompany His return. Then, in verse 30, He describes His Second Coming this way: "At that time the sign of the Son of Man will appear in the sky, and all the nations of the earth will mourn." We do not know what that sign will be, and a list of the possibilities is not to the point. What is significant is that at that most awesome and long-awaited of moments, at the very culmination of this present age, God has again chosen to employ a sign, a symbol.

D. Preaching and Teaching from Fellow Believers

Words from the Lord may also come in the form of *sermons, formal and informal teachings, Christian speakers, radio and television programs, videos, conferences, and seminars.*

It would, of course, be impossible to list all the resources available here, but the opportunities presented to hear and be guided by good teaching and preaching are innumerable.

Suffice it to say that the Lord has designed the Body to be one major means by which we hear His voice through the spiritual gifts of other believers. The very Church itself, we note, was birthed at Pentecost when Peter preached to the gathered crowd.

In our own age, technology has added immensely to the tools at our disposal. We recently discovered, for example, Zondervan's outstanding video teaching series entitled <u>That the World May Know</u>, taught by Ray Vander Laan. In these insightful and convicting lessons, filmed at the relevant Old and New Testament sites, the Lord's will for believers in confronting their culture comes through loud and clear. Allen has been using the series for a class he is teaching to the teens at our weekly combined home school gathering, and it is causing them to think more seriously about how they can impact their world.

Likewise, not long ago, while visiting Allen's sister in Lecanto, Florida, we were drawn by its soaring architecture to attend Seven Rivers Presbyterian Church, where we were immediately attracted to the gifted preaching of senior pastor Ray Cortese. We bought some earlier sermon CDs in their bookstore, and on returning home downloaded a number of others, laying the stack on the coffee table in the living room. While praying the next morning, we suddenly noticed that there was a large and lovely rainbow arching across the length of the ceiling, at one end of which were two bands of white light. We were baffled as to its source until our son Max came in and offered to help solve the mystery. In doing so, he discovered that the beautiful colors were reflecting off of the stack of sermon CDs, and we remembered that for some time we had been lamenting our lack of access to good, application-focused preaching. The discs, we realized, were an answer to that prayer—the treasure, as it were, at the end of the rainbow. Others may relate to different teachers, but the point is that hearing also comes in the form of gifted preachers and teachers whose message has been made more widely available thorough the tools of technology.

Often the fellow believers helping us to hear the Lord are those closest to us. God meant it to be this way. After all, in the Hebraic world-view, it was mother and father who were to be the primary conduits of God's teaching. I can still remember my mother taking me to church and Sunday school for the first time, and I can recall many of those early Bible lessons. In addition, some of my strongest childhood memories are of my father watching Bishop Fulton J. Sheen on TV and later debating theology with our pastor, as well as of him watching and reacting to the early televised Billy Graham crusades. My father provided a wonderful example to me of someone who was zealous of hearing and following the word of God, both written and exposited.

E.   Bible commentaries

We can often be blessed, informed, and even guided by someone else's insights into a verse or passage from Scripture. There are many good commentaries out there, but the three that I find myself using most regularly are The Bible Knowledge Commentary, edited by John Walvoord and Roy Zuck, The Expositor's Bible Commentary, edited by Frank Gaebelein, and Matthew Henry's Commentary. Following is a recent illustration of how Henry's commentary, for example, has played a role in helping us to hear the Lord.

Although we left Ambridge over six years ago to come to Alabama, we have maintained close emotional ties with our dear friends there, and we had longed to be able to get back for a visit. Some time ago, I suddenly found myself thinking repeatedly about one friend in particular, Ann Dickinson, and I even commented to Allen about it. One morning, not long afterwards, what should appear in the mail but a card and note from Ann!

We have long since learned that in God's economy, there are no coincidences. Consequently, the card instilled in us a deeper sense that we really needed to seriously consider taking some time off and making the twelve-hour drive to Pittsburgh. As we were praying one morning, Allen thought he was being led to Acts 18: 22, a verse which mentions Paul's visit to the church in Jerusalem. I decided to see what Matthew Henry had to say about it. Here, in part, is his exposition: "The increase of our new friends should not make us forget our old ones, but it should be a pleasure to good men, to revive former acquaintance. *God's people are dispersed and scattered; yet it is good to see one another sometimes.*"(italics mine)[v]

I read the passage to Allen, and that word, along with other confirming words and circumstances, was a factor in convincing us to go. Needless to say, we had a marvelous time reconnecting with Ann and with many of our other old friends. In this instance, the Scripture verse alone would not likely have given us the insight or the impetus to make the trip, but the amplification in the commentary helped us to hear the Lord's will and perspective more clearly. It must be noted that the full confirmation that we had been in God's will by going was not given until after we had returned. In the meantime, though we *felt* we were hearing correctly, we had to go on faith that that was so.

F. Christian Literature

Christian fiction and non-fiction works have both played an enormous role in helping people to hear the Lord. Here again, it is not my purpose to provide a list of suggested books and authors, assuming that were even possible. I can only relate the joy that Allen and I have found in being reached by the Lord's voice through the pen of a good writer.

Allen has always credited C. S. Lewis's <u>Mere Christianity</u> with leading him to an acceptance of Christ as Lord and Savior, and he continues to recommend the book to others. Because he sees himself as a linear thinker, he believes that what he needed were solid, well-written, and rational arguments in defense of the faith—i.e., a vigorous apologetic. In his case, no emotional appeals would have prevailed.

For my part, as an adult I finally got around to reading Lewis's <u>Chronicles of Narnia,</u> and I found that I simply couldn't put the books down. They spoke to me mightily, as they have to millions of others, of the nature of Christ, of the sanctification process, and of the Kingdom now and to come. I often found myself amazed and chagrined at how well something in a character's dialog or experience spoke to an issue in my own life. Our kids, for their part, have been relishing Tolkien's <u>Lord of the Rings.</u>

There is also an important connection between Christian literature, hearing the Lord, and our evangelizing and discipleship of others. On a number of occasions, frustrated in our attempts to present the Gospel or to lead someone further along in their relationship with the Lord, we have sought Him as to what books might be helpful. Since the Lord knows the hearts and minds of our friends and loved ones far better than we, He is able to suggest that which is most suitable to a particular person's tastes, personality, spiritual needs and receptivity at any given point in time. As a result, we have found ourselves lending books, giving books as gifts for Christmas and birthdays, and even sending books overseas. Here again, we see that, while Scripture provides general guidance, it is in hearing through listening prayer that we receive the Holy Spirit's wisdom for practical application.

G. Group Bible Study

While individual study is very important, there is a dimension of learning and growth, not to mention corrective judgment, which is added in the context of group fellowship. Proverbs 27:17 tells us, "As iron sharpens iron, so one man sharpens another." True in our relationships in general, it is especially applicable to our joint study of the Word as we benefit from the knowledge, wisdom, and insight of others.

The only counterbalance I would interject here is that we Christians tend to like to study, study, study, since that's where we are comfortable, while often doing little about what we hear and read from the pages of Scripture. Group Bible study is probably the single most common activity in the Church, yet our lives often seem to be but dim reflectors of the lessons God speaks to us through the pages of His Book.

As James exhorts us, "Do not merely listen to the word, and so deceive yourselves. Do what it says." (James 1:22)

The following three categories of hearing by means of words address messages which come through more directly *supernatural* means. These may be found among the spiritual gifts listed in I Corinthians, chapter 12.

H. *Words of Knowledge*

Simply put, this spiritual gift provides God's help, healing, or guidance by means of supernaturally revealed information which would not otherwise be known.(For further information on this and other spiritual gifts, I recommend David Pytches' book Spiritual Gifts in the Local Church, as well as Dennis and Rita Bennett's The Holy Spirit and You). I will share some examples of how this particular spiritual gift has operated in our own lives.

Several years ago, we needed to take a trip to see my father in Connecticut, and I prayed about the safety of the flight which we had booked out of Atlanta. I had an unusual heaviness in my spirit about this flight, and we continued to seek the Lord, wondering if we should cancel and reschedule. During our prayer one morning, we received an Old Testament verse which spoke of a violent spring storm, but we did not get a sense that we should change our flight, so we proceeded with our plans, albeit somewhat apprehensively. I had a sense that there was indeed some element of danger, but that we were to go and to trust.

As we drove to Atlanta, the sky grew ominously black, signaling an impending spring storm, and we indeed flew out just as a severe thunderstorm was breaking. On landing in Hartford, also in a strong thunderstorm, we drove to Allen's parents' home, turning on the evening news just in time to learn of a violent thunderstorm in the Atlanta area which had caused a fierce bolt of lightning to strike the airport runway, gouging an impressive hole in the tarmac. The time given for the incident was within minutes after our departure!

While this experience was rather dramatic, words of knowledge are often provided for even the most mundane of life's circumstances. The following illustration happened to us recently. Cindy Jones, the treasurer of our fellowship, had made up the weekly deposit slip from the Sunday offering, placing it and the checks in an envelope to be mailed to the diocesan office when she got to work. Upon arriving, she took the elevator up to her twelfth floor office and, after checking in, got back into the elevator to return to the lobby to mail the envelope. On the way down, the elevator stopped at the eleventh floor, where some construction work was being done, and Cindy held the door open for a worker who was getting on. The envelope was in her hand as the man brushed by her, but he had apparently knocked it out of her grasp as he passed, for she suddenly realized when she arrived at the lobby that it was gone. She diligently searched the area, returning to the eleventh floor to look there as well, and she even made some attempt the following day, with the assistance of the maintenance man, to see if the envelope had slipped between the elevator and the shaft wall down onto a lower floor. The search was fruitless. Cindy then called the diocesan office, asking them to let her know should the errant envelope manage to somehow arrive there.

When we met for our usual Wednesday prayer session, Cindy told us the story, and we sought the Lord, asking Him to give us some indication of what had happened to the envelope. Now, this was certainly no crisis; after all, the checks could simply have been stopped, reissued and another deposit sent. But God is the Lord of the little things as well as the great, and so we felt free to lift this matter up to Him. As we did so, I thought I saw an image of a long white envelope, but it sported the cutest pair of small but energetically flapping white wings. Cindy reported that she had also gotten an image of a wing-shaped object. Given these images, we felt that the envelope had likely been found by someone and placed in the mail, but all we could do was wait for word from the diocesan office. Sure enough, they called a few days later to report its appearance, and we could only chuckle at the confirmation of the Lord's word to us.

Sometimes words of knowledge are given which increase our natural knowledge or understanding of the created order. Not long ago, we were having a discussion with friends regarding the Book of Genesis and the six-day creation account. We later asked the Lord for insight as to how science and the six-day account could be reconciled. Allen thought he heard,

"I have given you eyes, and I have given you minds. I have put evidence everywhere that I have carefully designed this earth. My Scripture is, of course, true, but the understanding of its truth is subtle, for the six days could not be in human reckoning. I do not intentionally mislead, and I never contradict Myself. Your minds need to be expanded to understand that the six days are true, and the evidence of proper science is true, and they do not contradict each other. I made the world. I wrote the Scripture through My human agents. I am now illuminating the wonders of what I have done."

I. Words of Wisdom

This spiritual gift is closely related to words of knowledge but differs somewhat in that it provides the Lord's insight into the *how*, or the means by which, a particular situation may be helped, healed, or in some other way positively changed, to God's glory. A word of wisdom may also reveal the *why* of, or the reason behind, a particular situation.

One of the common ways in which the Lord gives a word of wisdom is in response to a prayer for healing. One of my most memorable instances of this occurred while we were living in Ambridge. We had driven to Connecticut one week to visit with my father, who was by then living alone, and I had spent several hours vigorously vacuuming his house for him. In the process, I had evidently incurred a great deal of back strain, and all it took the next morning was a slight twist as I was getting up to send an agonizing spasm through my back. I spent the next few days lying on the couch alternating ice packs and heating pads, but all to no avail. So severe was the pain that it was difficult to stand up or walk. We were on a tight travel schedule, as we urgently needed to get back to seminary to complete another portion of Allen's ordination process, and we were getting panicky, for I knew that there was no way that I could endure the ten-hour car ride back to Ambridge. For two or three days we had been praying for healing, but now, in desperation, Allen laid hands on my back, asking the Lord if there was anything we should do. Immediately, Allen thought he heard the words "mustard plaster."

We recalled that this was an old-time remedy, so we hurried down to the pharmacy to purchase one. "We haven't carried those things for years," the pharmacist said with a mixture of apology and amusement. It seems they had gone the way of wringer washers and crank telephones. "Well," we thought, "perhaps we could make our own."

We were staying at Allen's sister's house, and we remembered that she had some books on herbs and herbal remedies, so we drove back to check for a recipe for mustard plasters. The ones we found all called for dry mustard, so out we went again, this time to the supermarket. A short time later, I found myself lying, hot-dog-like, on my face on the bed, topped by a pungent mass of mustard paste which was sandwiched between two dish cloths. After a half an hour or so, I sensed that the plaster had done its work, so I got up and removed it. To my amazement, the pain had diminished considerably. Within the next half hour, it had disappeared entirely and never returned! We made the trip back to Ambridge the next morning, and I rode in absolute comfort. In fact, for weeks afterwards, my back felt far better than it had for a long time.

Nonetheless, the Lord never desires to stop with the physical healing; He is out to heal the whole person. In the case of my sore back, the Lord also used it to work a long-needed healing between my father and me. Years of painful interrelationships in my family had resulted in an awkward emotional and physical distance, and it had been a long time since my father and I had hugged each other. However, a day or two before we received the word about the mustard plaster, I had been to visit him, and he observed me hobbling about in considerable discomfort. After a while, he came to me and offered to walk me around the house, in the hopes that the movement would do me some good. He slipped his arm around my waist, supporting me, and we walked several times in circles through the living room, dining room, and kitchen. It was a tender moment, and more than worth the pain I was experiencing. The *how* of the word of wisdom healed the physical problem, but the *why* gave me insight into the reason that the Lord may have allowed it in the first place.

As the above example illustrates, words of wisdom are very often given to assist in the process of physical or emotional healing, and our journals are filled with many other examples of receiving such words. It should go without saying that the key to healing, in instances like this, is obedience, even if what we think we are hearing seems unusual, embarrassing, or even downright silly.

Some time ago, I suddenly developed a bad earache just before going to bed. I did take a decongestant, but those alone never seemed to completely do away with the problem. As we prayed, Allen thought that he heard the Lord say that I was to put a few drops of olive oil in my ear, followed by a clove of fresh garlic! I went to bed smelling like an Italian restaurant, but, in the morning, the earache was completely gone. On another occasion, the Lord's remedy for a persistent congestion in one ear was the olive oil, followed by a raisin. I have no idea why the raisin, except that it may have held the oil in without soaking it up as cotton does, and its gentle expansion with oil overnight might have drawn out some impurities. I laughingly remarked to Allen, "I bet I'm the only woman in town tonight with a raisin in her ear!"

Obviously, one still has to practice discernment here, and it should also go without saying that these are not prescriptions for anyone else. If the reader has a health concern, he should seek the Lord himself for healing, and, of course, if necessary go to the doctor. But, more often than not, we have found that the remedies the Lord offers are based on foods, herbs, or exercise, at least in part, and we have experienced

His help in these ways perhaps hundreds of times. Of course, there are also times when He directs us to see a physician instead of, or in addition to, His remedies, and still other times when He simply heals sovereignly.

At times, it may be difficult to distinguish between a word of knowledge and a word of wisdom, for there may be an overlapping or an intertwining. Consider this example. One evening during our prayer time with our friend Cindy, she described a distressing situation she had encountered earlier in the day. It seems that a beautiful little male hummingbird had somehow flown inside her porch and become trapped. She tried her best to save it as it beat itself frantically against the walls, and she earnestly prayed for the Lord's help. However, it finally broke its neck and died in her cupped hands. Cindy felt awful about the tiny creature, and she asked us to pray with her, seeking God as to why He had not answered her fervent plea to save the bird. Here is what Allen thought he heard:

"You surely do not know all of the circumstances which accompany My wild creatures. In this case, there was a territory issue involved, and there would have been a resolution leading to the death of one or another of the fighters. This is the state of the Creation. Of course, I also provide you with numerous parables of what is happening in your life and the life of the Church. There are many who are like that hummingbird, trapped and confused and unwilling to accept help, yet also dangerous to their own kind, as harmless or helpless as they may look. All is not always as it appears, which is why I ask you to keep all in prayer."

Apparently, this bird had been engaged in a territorial fight to the death with another male hummingbird when it had somehow flown into the porch. Here, then, was a word of knowledge— a supernaturally provided piece of information which explained the circumstances under which the hummingbird had managed to get inside. This word gave Cindy an immediate sense of comfort, peace, and resolution, for she now realized that, even had she managed to get the bird back outdoors, either it or the other bird would have been killed in the ensuing struggle. However, the Lord also took the opportunity to present a word of wisdom, using the situation as a parable. How often must He have done exactly that same sort of thing with His disciples, as He taught them using the illustrations from ordinary life and nature which He continually found all about Him. Scripture gives us a sampling of His skill in this regard. Of course, this word concerning the little hummingbird also gave us further insight into the nature of the created order in this fallen, groaning age.

Once again, I must pause to emphasize that my distinctions of category are somewhat arbitrary. Hence, with regard to both words of knowledge and words of wisdom, the term "word" should be understood loosely. The message may indeed come through the medium of words in some form, but it may also come in a variety of other ways, including the imagery of dreams and visions, as was the case with Cindy's errant envelope. The focus, then, should more properly be on the intention and function of the word, rather than on the specific means of its transmission.

J. Tongues (and Interpretation of Tongues)

Tongues and its partner gift of interpretation are perhaps the most misunderstood of the spiritual gifts. I feel as though I'm wading in over my head on this one, but I will attempt to give a brief overview, and to relate the ways in which these gifts assist in hearing God.

Let me begin this discussion by saying that I believe that the gift of tongues manifests itself in three forms. In the first, the speaker is given a spontaneous ability to speak in a human language unknown to himself for the purpose of witnessing to and blessing a speaker of that language. This is the form of which we read in Acts, Chapter 2. While the widely dispersed Jews were gathered together in Jerusalem for the feast of Pentecost, they suddenly saw tongues of fire appear on the heads of the disciples and overheard these Galilean men speaking, not in Hebrew or Aramaic but in their own native languages. This form of tongues obviously needs no interpretation and speaks to the hearer about God and His work, as a sign of the kingdom.

In the second form, that to which I believe Paul addresses his counsel in I Corinthians, Chapter 14, the speaker is spontaneously led to speak in a worshiping assembly using the private prayer language, be it angelic or human, with which the Holy Spirit has gifted him or her. In this case, the Holy Spirit must also provide an interpretation—a spiritually discerned sense of its corresponding meaning—*without* which the message does not bless the assembly. Here we see the body operating together to give an edifying word from the Lord to the group.

Let me give an illustration of this second form of tongues. While attending a Wednesday morning Eucharist at Trinity, someone, in response to a prayer offered in the group, gave a message in tongues. Immediately, another student spoke up. With a note of awe in his voice, he reported that he had somehow understood the words of the message, adding further that he had even been given knowledge of the identity of the language he had heard— Cherokee. The message he delivered through interpretation was very moving and pertinent to the prayer that had been offered, blessing the gathering of worshipers. What's more, the tongue-speaker was happily surprised to learn the identity of his prayer language. I might add that it is possible for an individual to have more than one prayer language, and to use different languages for different spiritual purposes.

In the third form, which also seems to be addressed in I Corinthians 14, the gift is used privately and does not need an interpretation, though one might conceivably wish to ask the Lord for one. Again, the language employed could be angelic, it could be a human language unknown to the speaker, or the language might even change on occasion. Because the gift of tongues bypasses certain unhelpful defenses of the conscious mind, thereby opening our spirits to God's Spirit, this particular manifestation of the gift serves a number of unique and highly important purposes in the spiritual life of a believer. Among these are the imparting of wisdom, removal of barriers to inner healing, guidance for spiritual warfare and intercession, deeper insights into the mysteries of God, creative inspiration, a restoration of body, soul and spirit, and, of course, unhindered praise. Speaking for ourselves, we have found the private use of tongues to assist enormously when blocked in prayer or seeking wisdom. In addition, I can personally attest that praying in tongues while struggling with the writing of this book has resulted in new insights and greater clarity, the removal of blockages, new spurts of inspiration, and even increased energy for the task. In other words, the gift of tongues for private use is meant to be a significant component of the process of being in communion with and hearing God. This begs a question for, as Paul says, in tongues it is *we* speaking to God. How then, one might ask, does that activity come to involve our *hearing* God? The answer, I suppose, is that tongues, like prayer, initiates a conversation which invites and expects a response.

I must also caution that the gift of tongues seems especially prone to abuse, since it can be manipulated consciously or subconsciously by someone to put forth their own message or advance their own agenda. Hence, its proper public use takes wise pastoral oversight, and in First Corinthians, Chapter 14, Saint Paul gives necessary instruction for its orderly operation in worship.

I must finally add that the subject of tongues as described in I Corinthians 14 is a difficult one, producing significant differences of opinion. My goal here is not to sort through the various positions or to attempt to write my own definitive statement on the matter. I desire rather to relate, through the medium of my own understanding and experience, the role that this gift plays in hearing God.

K. Inner Voice

This kind of hearing usually comes as words which are formed from within the mind, yet are discerned in the spirit not to have originated in us. Such an experience will invariably illicit a surprised, "Where did that come from?" reaction, since the knowledge, wisdom and wording are so foreign to our own ways of thinking. A few months ago, I was having a conversation with a young friend who was longing for some adventure. He was contemplating taking a summer-long trip through northern Africa. As I prayed about this afterwards, I thought I heard the Lord say, "Adventure is not a place, it's a Person."

In another instance, at the height of our struggle to determine the best course of action for my father during the earlier stages of his Alzheimer's, I agonized over issues of when and how to step in. I was deeply concerned for his safety, but, as we prayed, Allen thought he heard the Lord say, "Safety is not the highest value." In each of these instances, the Voice we heard was not externally audible but came as a clear hearing from within, yet also as something which we clearly knew did not come from our own minds. Often these words will stun, amuse, unsettle, or disarm.

Not long ago, Allen and I were praying about our lengthy challenges with finding a way to bring this book to a larger audience. Since we are currently pursuing the possibility that our three children may still have a half-sibling in Russia, a friend had offered that perhaps the Lord Himself had caused the publishing delays in order that we might get to include that episode as the end of the adoption story. However, when we sought the Lord about it, Allen suddenly thought he heard, "What makes you think that's the end of the story?" If God sent email, I imagine that He would have punctuated that sentence with a winking smiley face.

L. Audible Voice

In my own experience, it has been in dreams that I have most often heard what I sensed to be the *audible* voice of the Lord. For example, I first became aware of the possible existence of a fourth child through a brief dream in which I saw our son Max. With him was another boy, perhaps four or so years younger but with similar facial features and chestnut brown hair. In the dream, I knew his name to be Zechariah, though I was given to understand that was not his birth name. Suddenly a voice, which I somehow knew to be the Voice of the Lord, spoke to me, saying, "You have four children." I reasoned and argued, as though I of course knew better, saying, "No, I have three children: Alicia, Oksana, and Max." Again the Voice repeated the same message: "You have four children." Again, I argued. The Voice came a third time, now with a no-nonsense sternness: "You have four children, and you have *always* had four children." End of discussion, end of dream. On awaking, I recalled from Hebrew class that Zechariah means "God remembers."

I will relate one other rather amazing experience of hearing God's voice which occurred on our trip to interview for Allen's rector position here in Alabama. The March weekend of our visit, as I have mentioned, was miserably gray, windy, and rainy, and I was quite depressed. The last thing I felt I wanted, after living in the close community of Ambridge, was to come out here to live in the woods on the top of a mountain with few neighbors in sight. The afternoon that we were leaving to drive back to Ambridge, we stopped by the church one final time, just as the sky was becoming heavy with black clouds. As we walked back to the car, I insisted to Allen that I absolutely did not want to come down here to live. Immediately, as I was reaching out to touch the door handle, there was an enormous, solitary, and terrifying clap of thunder, but somehow, in my spirit, in a way that I can't explain, I knew that it was directed at me. I had heard the Voice of the Lord. It was His will that we come here, and I was not to disobey. In Hebrew, this manifestation is called a "bat qol," meaning "daughter of a voice." I am now better able to understand the event described in John, Chapter 12. Jesus had asked the Father to glorify His name, and a voice from heaven replied, "I have glorified it, and will glorify it again."(v. 28b) John remarks that the crowd that was present and heard it said that it had thundered. It is spiritual discernment that allows us to hear the Voice in the thunder.

As stated earlier, there is often an overlap or a blurring between these categories of hearing. For example, it is sometimes difficult to know where an inner voice leaves off and an audible voice begins. Precise descriptions are often elusive.

II. Pictures

Scripture itself verifies the fact the Lord uses symbolic imagery to convey His messages: "When a prophet of the Lord is among you, I reveal myself to him in visions; I speak to him in dreams."(Numbers 12:6) That being the case, let us next examine how the Lord may speak to us through pictures, both in our waking and in our sleeping.

A. Visions

For those who have never had visions, I must confess that attempting to describe or compartmentalize them is a little like trying to lasso the wind, and I humbly submit that others may explain and classify these experiences of "seeing" somewhat differently than I have. Therefore, I will simply say that, in our own experience, we have found that visions seem to come in the following general forms:

1) Perhaps the most striking, though rarer, form of vision is that of an *externally* projected picture, as though one were actually watching an image on a screen. In even more graphic instances, the image may appear to be free-standing and nearly three-dimensional. These visions often come utterly spontaneously, though they may be stimulated by prior prayer, thought or conversation about spiritual matters. They may contain action, or they may be "stills." Though they may come at any time, they often seem to come while lying in bed before going to sleep or at the moment of awakening. They cannot in any way be controlled, though I assume that they could be prematurely ended through distraction or an act of the will. I have found, in my own case, that I always want to hold on to these images, to make them remain, so that I can

gaze at them and study them. However, I am completely unable to do so, for though these projected images are frequently very striking, they are usually fleeting, lasting but a few seconds. Further, they are often highly symbolic and enigmatic in content. These features combine to distinguish this type of vision from something that could arise from one's own imagination and, for this reason, I have always trusted their divine origin.

These externally projected visions are, of course, seen with the eyes open, and they tend to leave a strong and lasting mental impression. Often there is intense emotion, such as fear, joy, peace, or love, conveyed along with the image. Sometimes, there is also given some further sense about the meaning, which is more perceived than seen. In addition, physical sensations such as heat, cold, pain, or pressure may sometimes accompany the vision. The color in these visions may be brilliant or luminous, at times beyond description, as though not of this world. I once saw, upon awakening, a vision which included a ball of light which was so fiercely bright that it burned my eyes, forcing me to turn my head to the side. In fact, to this day, the very recollection of that image produces the same reaction. Again, this startling physical response confirmed for me that the vision was from the Lord, and not from my own imagination.

2) More commonly, a vision will be *internally* discerned, as though appearing on the screen of the mind. While still perceived as a projected picture, as distinguished from the work of the imagination, such visions may even take the form of a visually-depicted thought process. In my experience, these images tend to be less clear and colorful than the externally projected ones and can be less spontaneous. They often come as the immediate result of prayer, a prayerful conversation, or a direction of thinking; they may be seen with the eyes open or closed; and they may or may not contain action.

I will take some time here to describe two of the visions which have particularly impressed and remained with us over the years. One of our favorites was given to Allen while we were at Trinity. In it, he seemed to be seeing, as though look-ing down on it from a height above, a white dove-like bird in flight. He noted, with amazement, that he soon became aware that the back of the bird was actually an open cockpit, and he found that he could look inside. As he did so, scanning the interior, Allen suddenly realized that there were no controls and no steering mechanism—only a seat! We quickly grasped that the bird was the Holy Spirit and that we were being invited to ride in the open cockpit. The catch was that the flight—life in the Spirit—would require total trust and a complete willingness to relinquish any desire to control, for there was no way to direct or alter the flight. Reasserting "control" could only be accomplished by bailing out of the process.

The second occurred one evening years ago as I was pray-ing about my elderly parents, who were both showing symp-toms of dementia. The situation was enormously difficult and stressful, and I grieved for them. As we prayed, Allen saw the letters "I reck" written vertically in script. I went to the dictionary and found that *to reck* means "to have care, regard, or concern for."[vi] If the Lord had simply said "I care," we might have doubted that the message was really from Him, but the vision, combined with the archaic language, convinced us of its source. The image was followed by another: a vision of a windshield wiper which swept across a surface, leaving blankness, and then swept back again, expos-ing clear, joyous colors. Revelation 21:4 immediately came to mind: "He will wipe every tear from their eyes. There will be no more death or mourning or crying or pain, for the old order of things has passed away."

3) A vision may sometimes be a pictorial representation or dramatization of a Scripture verse or text. In fact, there is often likely to be at least some element of direct Scriptural reference underlying the imagery in many visions, though few of us are well enough versed in Scripture to always or, even occasionally, recognize it. To make matters even more interesting, these textually based images may sometimes be

translated into those with which we can more readily identify from our own cultural and historical vantage point. Some years ago, the Lord showed Allen a vision of a pavement roller, as well as other heavy road-building equipment, sitting in a large, flat area in a desert-like scene. As I pondered the image, I was reminded of Isaiah 40:3: "A voice of one calling: 'In the desert prepare the way for the Lord; make straight in the wilderness a highway for our God.'" The New Testament connects the voice with that of John the Baptist, whose message of repentance prepared the way for Christ's first coming. The Lord, we reasoned, had simply given us a culturally-contextualized exhortation to likewise prepare ourselves and the Church for His return.

I will relate another fascinating experience we had with the issues of imagery and cultural-contextualization, this time combined with an image I had during sleep. For some time, while we were at Trinity, the Lord seemed to be speaking to us about Texas and about cowboys. Over a period of time, Allen and I both had striking dreams and visions about cowboys, and persistent words and images relating to Texas. Oddly enough, during this same period of time, a friend back in Massachusetts also reported that she was receiving visions relating to cowboys. All of this was occurring during our job search process, and we began to be convinced that the Lord was calling us to go to Texas. However, though we did interview for one position in El Paso, it eventually became clear that we were going to Alabama instead, and we were puzzled and confused. Finally, I asked the Lord what all of the imagery relating to cowboys could possibly have meant. Allen thought he heard Him reply, "The cowboy is the North American version of the shepherd." Suddenly I gained an interesting insight. I began to realize that the cowboy represented the Lord and, perhaps also, his under-shepherds, and Texas was a symbol of the Kingdom, both now and to come. This seemed to be confirmed when I asked the Lord why we hadn't gone to Texas. "You're not ready for Texas," He replied. Now, I should add that it is certainly possible that at some point in the future we could also be called to go to Texas in the literal sense; however, this would be a good place to remind to not to jump to conclusions about interpretation!

Now, I will share my vision. I had been praying for salvation for my son Max, who was then eleven years old. One night, in my sleep, I had a single strong image of him, standing before me. He appeared to be somewhat taller, and I saw him from about the waist down, in black jeans. My attention was drawn immediately to his feet, and I saw that he was wearing a brand new pair of cowboy boots. Since I was now familiar with the meaning behind the symbol, I knew that the Lord was reassuring me that he would soon come into the Kingdom. Sure enough, a few months later and completely on his own initiative, he went forward at a youth rally and accepted Christ.

I would also add that these and other similar experiences have given me insight into the reality that many of the visions seen by Ezekiel, Daniel, and the Apostle John, among others, were culturally contextualized for *them* as well, and that, divine veiling aside, this is one reason why we may struggle so today to rightly grasp their meaning. T he same, of course, could be said for the parables of Jesus and, in fact, for much of the Bible. Furthermore, anti-Semitism and a certain long-standing arrogance on the part of the Church have separated us from comprehending the Jewish roots of our faith and from seeing Jesus in His first- century Jewish context. Hearing God, among many other things, *must* also mean placing Jesus and the Scriptures in their right religious and historical setting. This is no small matter, for uninformed and mis-guided interpretations have led to centuries of wrong and confusing doctrine. The most help we have received, in this regard, has come from good preachers and teachers whose own diligent study has enabled them to unearth and illuminate the cultural and historical settings which undergird the Scriptures. One of our favorites is Dwight Pryor of the Center for Judaic-Christian Studies in Dayton, Ohio.

4) To add another little twist, we have discovered that sometimes, as I have noted, word and picture categories can overlap. Thus, for example, after Allen had begun receiving visions, he would not infrequently *see* a chapter and verse

citation written out! On at least one occasion, he actually saw the Scripture citation as though written across the sky!

5) Just as words and visions may overlap, so may visions and dreams. Hence, as illustrated above, visions may also occur at night, sometimes in the form of, or as a portion of, dreams. Conversely, a graphic dream of intense spiritual imagery and significance might legitimately be seen as an extended "night vision." We see numerous instances of this overlap or blurring of categories in the prophetic Scriptures. On the one hand, Daniel's dream of the four great beasts in Chapter 7 is also called a vision, while in certain other instances in Scripture referring to night visions, the prophet is said to be awake rather than asleep. The prophet Zechariah, for instance, had all eight of the visions comprising his book in one night, while he was fully awake. Likewise, Paul also describes a number of visions which he received at night, while still awake. Incidentally, I'm not sure why God often chooses the night and early morning hours to speak to His people in this way, but it may simply be that the mind is in a quieter, less distracted, and more receptive state.

In general, I distinguish *sleep* visions from other prophetic dreams mainly because they typically consist of a single, intense image, or a series of brief images, and do not have much "plot," although there may be some limited action or movement. Other than the fact that they occur during sleep, however, these sleep visions are identical to other visions. Simply put, then, waking *night* visions are, I think, like all other waking visions, except for the hours at which they come.

In my case, both prophetic dreams and sleep visions have at times been accompanied by a short, internally-heard message, or sometimes by an audible voice, as stated earlier. In those situations, the message has consisted of one or a few brief but intensely meaningful sentences, sometimes couched in highly symbolic language. The voice, when I knew it to be the Lord's, was unquestioningly authoritative and clearly perceived as masculine, though it did not seem to possess gender in quite our regular human sense.

B. Dreams

I must mention once again that we found we were being led by the Lord to write down our dreams, asking Him to help us to understand those which seemed significant. Recently, the Lord had this to say to us about why He sends dreams, and why we are to record them:

"Any dream which I cause you to remember in detail is intended to have some message for you. Remember that your dreams are times when your normal filtering process is suspended, and I can tell you certain things which would not get through at other times. However, you already know that the symbolic nature of dreams makes them hard to interpret. Nevertheless, I use them regularly for communication, especially with those who don't think they hear from Me but also with those who are learning to hear more, like yourselves. If you seek the meanings, I will make the symbols clear, and you will understand, at least in part."

Having been instructed by the Lord to do so, we began to record our dreams if we could recall them at all upon waking. Obedience brought blessing for, as we began recording, we quickly found that our recollection was aided by the very recording process and that the sooner the dreams were recorded, the more we remembered.

Our general process has been as follows. First, we try to write down our dreams as quickly as possible, though we are admittedly faulty in this regard at times. Second, as we are recording them, we pray for illumination or an interpretation, and we do sometimes receive and record a further sense about them or a Scripture verse which helps us to understand. Third, we also ask each other, and, if need be, other prayer partners for any insights they might have. The majority of our dreams seem to have no lasting significance and would be totally forgotten almost immediately if not committed to paper. Nonetheless, our understanding has always been that we are to record them all. However, we have learned to sense which dreams are from the Lord, for they have a lucidity, intensity, and spiritual authority which sets them apart. Sometimes their message is for us, and sometimes it is a more general prophecy, but it may take further prayer to discern which is which.

As an example of how the Lord may speak to us through dreams, I will relate a dream that I had some time ago. This is what I recorded the morning after the dream:

"Allen and I were below deck in a large old battleship. It reminded me of the USS Alabama that we had seen in Mobile harbor. We had long-handled paint rollers, and we were painting the gunmetal gray ceiling a very intense red. I can still picture the chunky, heavy old metal look of this ship ceiling. Our son Max seemed to be present. At one point, there was something slightly humorous spoken by or to someone, but I can't remember what. It may have had something to do with my commenting to Allen about not covering one spot completely with paint. The red color was striking. Maybe we will be helping to prepare the Church for spiritual warfare."

Here, several significant elements had come together. First, I had had a dream which contained some striking and archetypal imagery. I knew that a ship was a symbol of the Church and that red symbolized the Holy Spirit. Second, I remembered the dream with great clarity upon awakening. Third, I took the time to write it down. Fourth, I already had some strong sense in my spirit, due to the nature of the imagery and the clarity, that it was from the Lord. And fifth, Allen and I submitted it in prayer that morning, asking the Lord to help us to understand its meaning. This is what Allen thought he heard: "How could something like that not have spiritual significance? The red color is obviously important, as is the battleship and the ceiling. Remember that you are in a spiritual battle along with all of My Church, but the weapons of warfare have been allowed to fall into disuse." This explained why the old ship seemed to be "in mothballs.," and the ceiling, of course, was a metaphor for the heavens, where the spiritual warfare originates.

III. Senses or Impressions

A. An Inner Knowing

Communication from the Lord comes in other ways, too. At times, a message may be given as a persistent thought, a strong knowing, an inner urging, a nagging, disquiet, or an intuition—all variations on a theme. Sometimes, these things are not even quite at the conscious level. These senses might arise during prayer, or as we are going about our daily activities.

A few years ago, for example, we took a vacation to Florida to see Allen's parents. They lived in a gated community, and we had taken our three kids down to the clubhouse to swim in the pool. After a while, the girls were ready to return to the house, and Allen drove them back, but our then twelve-year old son Max and I stayed behind. A short time later, I came out of the changing room and decided to see if Allen had returned for us yet, so I headed toward the clubhouse, passing Max as I did so. He was near the shuffleboard courts, busily bouncing a tennis ball up in the air with a racket. A fleeting nudge told me to call to him to come with me, especially since Allen was due to be back for us within minutes, but Max seemed to be enjoying himself, so I continued on into the clubhouse. I had barely been inside for a minute when a man came bursting through the door. "Is that your little boy outside?" he asked with urgency in his voice. "He has hurt himself badly." I dashed back to where I had last seen Max, only to find him sitting, head in hands, blood-stained and sobbing. It seems that, focused on the ball, he had tripped over the heavy bench by the sidewalk and, in falling over it, had tipped it over onto himself, hitting himself squarely in the face. We spent the next three hours in the emergency room. I knew, in retrospect, that the inner nudge to collect him on my way by had almost certainly been from the Lord, but, engrossed in my own thoughts, I was not listening carefully enough to change my course of action. I believe that we all receive these kinds of divine prods on a regular basis, but our fallen nature and the distractions of our lives usually keep us from hearing.

One related issue deserves attention here. A friend asked me how the nudge I received would differ from "mother's intuition," or is it the same? My immediate response was that I felt that all inner senses which have as their end godly outcomes must have their origin in the work of the Holy Spirit, whether or not the person is a believer. Nonetheless, I felt that this was a good time to seek the Lord about the general question of what we call "intuition," versus hearing. The word which we got confirmed my own understandings of the matter:

"I am speaking all the time to your circumstances, but there are times when I speak more urgently so that anyone could hear. There is, of course, heightened awareness of parents regarding their children, so the message often 'gets through' even to unbelievers. I speak more subtly about the complex issues of direction and call and the use of gifts. These are not mere responses to a crisis, but they relate to long-term willingness to hear and to obey. I am constantly warning people, though many times their sensitivity is so hardened or misdirected that they do not hear My warning. Sin is always a wall— sometimes a thin one and sometimes a great one. If the wall is thick enough, no hearing is possible. The answer to your question, then, has to do with the nature of what is being heard."

I will offer another example. As I related earlier in telling part of our story, my mother had been confined to a nursing home in 1989 after she fell and broke her hip. After seven months, my father, terribly lonely and frustrated with the care she was receiving, brought her home in an effort to care for her himself. It was an extraordinarily difficult task, and the toll on him was enormous. Allen and I tried to convince him that the job was too much for him, but to no avail. All we could do was to try to help out by making frequent visits and by calling regularly.

One morning, just a day or two after I had last spoken to my father, I had a compelling sense that I needed to call him right away, though I didn't know why. When he answered the phone, he sounded strangely weak and breathless. When I asked what was the matter, he said, "I think I'm having a heart attack. It feels just like it did when I had the last one (twenty years earlier)." Stunned, I pressed, "Did you call an ambulance?" The answer was no. He had instead called his doctor's office, but it was a Wednesday, the traditional day when doctors' offices were closed. He should have known that, but, of course, he was not thinking clearly. He had simply left a message on the office answering machine and then lain down on the couch to await a return call! If it hadn't been such a desperately-serious situation, it would have been comical. I sprung into action. "Hang up right now and call 911," I commanded. He said he would.

As a backup, I immediately called his pastor and asked him to get over to my father's house as fast as possible. Then I jumped into the car and drove the forty miles to my father's house, not knowing what to expect when I got there. I was met at the door by the pastor, who had decided to stay with my mother until I arrived. He explained that when he had arrived at the house, the ambulance was already there, and that my father had been taken to the hospital where he spent a week recovering. Had I not called when I did, the outcome of it all would undoubtedly have been very different.

B. A Burden

Also referred to as a "passion," this form of hearing may be described as a divinely implanted impulse to care deeply, to pray intently, and to act compassionately with regard to people, causes or situations. A burden could involve a long-term commitment, as in giving monthly to help support an overseas orphan, or it might manifest itself in a more immediate or urgent sense, as when one feels a strong call to drop his or her own work in order to help in a soup-kitchen in a disaster-stricken community.

Obviously, the issues of burden, calling, and ministry are closely intertwined, for the Lord usually leads us into areas of ministry and mission precisely by giving us a heart for certain people or situations. We recently watched the film <u>Beyond the Next Mountain</u>, the remarkable story of young Welshman Watkin Roberts's passionate desire to bring the Gospel to the Hmar headhunters of northeast India. Though he remained with them only a few days, the resulting conversion, ministry, and translation work of Chawnga Pudaite and his son Rochunga changed the lives and history of their tribe forever, while Rochunga's *Bibles for the World* project continues to bear fruit, not only in India but throughout the world.

This kind of burden operates in cooperation with our God-given personalities and inclinations. Sometimes, however, God may *create* a new burden in us by arranging things so that we are allowed to experience suffering in some way, since we often minister best out of our own painful histories. A married couple who were classmates of ours from Trinity had been operating a successful business for several years when unanticipated misfortune suddenly caused a total reversal of finances. Before they knew it, they and their two young children were living in their car. Today, they have a challenging and fulfilling ministry to the homeless in downtown Pittsburgh. They would be the first to admit that without receiving a burden for the homeless in this way, they may never have changed life directions.

A final example is especially close to our own hearts. Shortly after receiving our three kids from Russia, it became evident to us that the public school system was not prepared to deal with the language issues involved at the high school level. We opted to home-school the girls, but, needless to say, we felt a bit daunted by the task. To our great amazement and blessing, however, we got an unexpected phone call from a retired English teacher in town. She had heard about our situation through a mutual friend and volunteered to tutor the girls herself. Dee Dee came to our house four mornings a week for a year and a half, and, besides enjoying her presence immensely, we all owe her an enormous debt of gratitude.

IV. Circumstances

A. *Words or Confirmations from Others*

The Lord may sometimes choose to speak His will to us through another person or persons. The word may be intentionally directed toward us, and godly counsel is one of the functions of the Body, but it may even come simply as an off-hand remark to which our spiritual ears are attuned. For obvious reasons, discernment should be exercised and independent confirmation sought here. Nonetheless, we have at times found that the Lord has sent someone along at just the right time to confirm a decision or encourage us toward a particular course of action.

We entered Trinity Seminary out of obedience to the Lord, not knowing what He had in mind for us there. It was only at the beginning of our third year there that Allen began to discern a call to ordination. Shortly afterwards, first a faculty member and then a fellow student came forward and told Allen that they strongly believed he was being called to pursue ordination, though they had never said anything previously. We considered these timely words to be one confirmation from the Lord of Allen's call.

Again, we had been praying with another couple for some months regarding job possibilities and directions for them, as well as for us. To his surprise, Allen had a dream one night about having gone to live in the Carolinas, in a place somewhat south of our location here in northern Alabama, and we assumed that the dream likely pertained to us. Two days later, however, the other couple received an unsolicited invitation to interview for a position in South Carolina, not far from Charleston, and went on to accept the offer. They did not, needless to say, make their decision based on Allen's dream, nor should they have, but rather on other confirming evidence. Nonetheless, in retrospect, the dream seemed to be the Lord's way of providing an externally corroborated affirmation of His will. (I might add that it is certainly *possible* that we could move to the Charleston area, at some point, our-selves, but, to date, the Lord has not indicated that, and I'm also aware that the idea of Charleston could have a symbolic rather than literal meaning of some sort for us).

In that most amusing and fascinating example from the Old Testament, God even used a donkey to speak a rebuke to his master, the pagan prophet Balaam. (See Numbers 22:21-30) From this example we can see that the "others" from whom we might get a word don't necessarily always have to be human. I, too, recently had my own experience of hearing a word from the Lord through an animal. I had gotten a bad case of stomach flu and was exhausted and dehydrated from several bouts of vomiting. I began to sense that I was sup-posed to drink some sort of herb tea, but I couldn't discern which, so I asked Allen to help me pray about it. The words were no sooner out of my mouth when Rachel, our little tor-toise-shell Manx cat, raced into the room and squawked out a loud and emphatic meow. "Catnip tea," I reasoned. "Maybe I'm supposed to drink catnip tea." I asked Allen to confirm by looking in our herb book, and, sure enough, catnip tea was recommended as an effective means of quelling nausea. The tea, by the way, worked quite well. Here is an entertaining example not only of the benefits of practice in hearing and of staying attuned, but also of being receptive to a wide variety of means, without which I may only have only heard "meow." My immediate response to the word was understandably one of gratitude, but I was surprised by a further sense that it was worth having been sick just to be able to share the story—an interesting "take" on servant-hood.

B. Coincidences and Timing

Seminary was a time when we repeatedly saw the hand of the Lord at work in our circumstances. Our first year in Ambridge—and what we had originally assumed would be our only year there—found us living in a rented house on Church Street. In March of the following spring, we began to sense that we would be staying longer, and we had assumed, hearing nothing to the contrary, that we would be able to continue renting where we were.

Meanwhile, one Saturday morning, with Allen off at a youth ministry function at church, I was looking for some way to amuse myself. Our neighbors several houses down the street, John and Joyce Miller, were graduating and had just put a "For Sale" sign up in their front yard. With typical female curiosity, I walked over and asked Joyce if I could see the house. I found it quite charming and, when Allen got home, I asked him to go and take a look at it with me.

Now, mind you, we had no real reason to be taking any personal interest in this house. However, a few days later, we got a call from our friend Ann Ridley, who was the agent for the house we were renting. It seems that the owners, who were former seminarians, had originally intended to move back to Ambridge after retirement but had now decided instead to remain in California. The house was going on the market, and we would need to be out in a few weeks! Finding another rental was well-nigh impossible, as we had two cats. The owners had been most gracious about our animals, but they were clearly the exception among landlords.

Now, our interest in the Millers' house became genuine, not to mention urgent. We talked to them again, and Allen made a trip to the bank to discuss a mortgage. However, we were forgetting one minor detail. Even though we did have some capital, we needed it for living expenses, and the bank quickly reminded us that, without any income, we were unable to qualify for a loan. Dismayed, and now genuinely worried about where we were going to live, we went back and talked to John. He thought a bit and then offered the fact that it was his dad in Florida who actually owned the house. John said he would call him and ask if he would be willing to give us a private mortgage, but I was not hopeful. After all, John's dad had provided this house for his son as a way to help him through seminary, but what would prompt this man to give a private mortgage to total strangers? He could simply have sold the house. To our amazement, John's dad did agree to a private mortgage, and, when our house in Massachusetts sold a year later, we became the proud owners of our little house on Church Street. How astonished we were to see how the Lord had moved in that situation. He had known of our need before we had and had gone before us to provide.

In a similar way, in the spring of our last year at Trinity, my faithful old Peugeot, our only vehicle, began to falter. We had desperately hoped that it would get us through our last year of school and into Allen's first rector's position, but, in March, the engine began to develop serious problems, and there was no Peugeot mechanic to be found in our area. Allen decided to drive the car back to Massachusetts while it was still possible to do so, and he felt strongly that he was to go alone. Our own mechanic in Massachusetts had already told Allen that he would be unable to work on the car, and so Allen had been referred to another fellow who agreed to do the job. However, on arrival in Massachusetts, Allen discovered that this second mechanic's son had unexpectedly become seriously ill and was in the hospital. After three days of waiting, by which time we had thought that Allen would already be back in Ambridge with our repaired car, it became evident that this second mechanic would also be unable to work on the Peugeot. Allen and I were six hundred miles apart, (it now seemed like six thousand), and neither of us had a vehicle, nor did we have any money at all to buy even the most inexpensive of used cars. Allen didn't even have a way to get back to Ambridge!

Meanwhile, he had been borrowing his sister's spare car and was driving to Connecticut each day to check on my father and to help him with his bills, paperwork, and other household tasks. During his stay in Massachusetts, and strictly out of curiosity, Allen had wistfully contacted his old friend Dave from the car business to ask what might be available in late model used vans. Knowing a move to another state was likely imminent, a van would have been our purchase of choice, and we had begun to dream of somehow being able to have one. Dave mentioned that he did have access to a nice, one-year old, white Pontiac Transport. The price, with tax, was $14,100. There was no real reason for

Allen to have even made this call to Dave, since, as in the case of the house, we had no way to make a purchase.

However, on his eighth day (interestingly, the Biblical number for new beginnings) in Massachusetts, a most remarkable thing happened. While Allen was at my father's house that morning, an envelope came in the mail. My mother had passed away a few months before, and the envelope was from a bank where, unbeknownst to my father, she had apparently had an old savings account. Allen showed the letter to my father and offered to drive him to the bank to help him withdraw the balance and redeposit it. My father, always a generous soul, instead offered, "Do you need the money? If you do, you can have it!" The amount on deposit? $14,100! On the tenth day, having purchased and registered the vehicle, Allen arrived back in Ambridge driving our new white Pontiac Transport van, and we have it to this day.

While we, so often during our seminary years, had bemoaned our lack of money, without this vulnerability we would never have known the joy of the Lord's stunningly surprising, timely, and miraculous provisions.

Also while at Trinity, I saw the Lord's hand in the timing of a gift. On a visit back home shortly after my mother's death, my father had given me her wedding and engagement rings. Of all of the things that had been hers, these probably meant the most to me. During the Christmas holidays, we finally found the time to take them to the jeweler's to be resized, and I was very eager to get them back and wear them. However, the jeweler informed us that he was swamped with orders from many other people wanting their Christmas gifts of jewelry resized as well, and I found myself waiting days longer than I had anticipated for a call that the rings were ready. Finally, on January 2nd, which happened to be my birthday, we got an afternoon call that the rings could be picked up. On the way home in the car, as I studied them on my finger, it suddenly occurred to me that the timing of their receipt was no accident. They had been a birthday gift from the Lord.

Some time ago, we had another amazing experience, this one in the form of a "coincidence." We have been to Holland several times to visit Revi, our Dutch exchange student, and on two of those occasions we were treated to visits at the home of her elderly grandparents. We fell in love with both of them, and on our second visit, Revi's grandmother presented us with a lovely crystal bud vase. When I returned home, I filled it with dried flowers and placed it on an end table in the living room, next to the sofa where, every morning, Allen and I sit to have our prayer time. One morning, just as we were settling down, Allen glanced over at the little table and noticed that the bud vase was lying down on its side on the doily. I gently stood it upright again, commenting to Allen on how odd it was that the vase had fallen over, since in the three years we had it, that had never happened before. A few days later, we got an email from Revi informing us that her grandmother had died. When we compared dates, we realized that the vase had fallen on the day of her grandmother's death. As we prayed about the conjunction of events, Allen felt that it was indeed a sign from the Lord—an assurance that all was in His hands, and that Revi's grandmother was with Him. As further confirmation, Allen received Jesus' words from John 14:1: "Do not let your hearts be troubled. Trust in God; trust also in me." I asked if the Lord if He would give us yet a further sense regarding Revi's grandmother's presence with Him, and Allen thought he saw an image of her sitting at a yellow table on a terrace, surrounded by a glow of warm light with many flowers all around her, mostly in red and yellow and white. She was holding a beautiful flowered and white porcelain cup in a position as though she was about to drink some tea. Since this image was so much like the picture of her own garden at home, I pressed the Lord as to whether or not the image was really from Him. Immediately, Allen got a second image of a beautifully decorated pair of wooden shoes sitting on the floor—empty.

V. Angelic Visitations

Allen and I have also seen both angels and demons, in dreams, in visions, and through the spiritual eyes of discernment, in a number of different settings. However, I would like to instead share a wonderful story from a *friend's* experience.

Several years ago, our friend Denise from Massachusetts related this remarkable incident. For some time, she had been heavily involved in caring for her aging father, who lived in a senior housing complex a few miles away from her. His health was failing, and, though Denise desperately loved her father, the incessant demands on her time and energy were wearing her down. One winter's evening, having taken her dad out to do his grocery shopping, then washing, drying, and folding his laundry and finally feeding him dinner at her home, she set out to drive him back to his apartment. They left her house later than she had wished, since snow had been forecast, and Denise soon found herself driving through a miserable and dangerous mixture of sleet and freezing rain which soon turned into a full-blown snowstorm.

By the time she pulled into the apartment complex, she realized that for her father's safety, she needed to get him as close to the front door of the building as possible, and so she drove down the sidewalk between two rows of bushes. Her first goal was to get her father securely inside the building, so she helped him out of the car and into the vestibule and then returned to the car to struggle with two large bags of groceries and the laundry. Her next task was to get the car back into the parking lot. She reasoned that backing up rather than turning around would be the best option, but that proved easier said than done, and, by the time she reached the lot, the sides of her new car had become badly scratched by the rough branches. She was by now frazzled and irritable, and, as they took the elevator to the fifth floor, she and her father broke into one of their many arguments. Once on the fifth floor, Denise set the laundry bags down and, still juggling the groceries, proceeded to navigate her way down the hall by alternately kicking the two bags a few feet at a time.

She at last got her father settled into his apartment, bid him good night, and got back into the elevator. As the door closed, and she found herself alone, she leaned wearily against the wall and began to weep. The physical and emotional stress of the past months had taken their toll, and she cried out, "Lord, I just want to laugh."

It was by now about 8:30 P.M., and the building was utterly quiet, as the elderly residents had all long since gone to bed. There was nary a soul stirring. When Denise reached the ground floor and stepped outside into the cold winter air, she was surprised to see that it had stopped snowing, and that the streetlights on the fresh snow were now causing everything about her to glisten. It was a dazzlingly gorgeous winter evening.

Denise took a right onto the sidewalk and started to walk toward the parking lot, but she had scarcely gone more than a few yards when she began to hear beautiful singing from somewhere behind her. She quickly discerned that the voice belonged to a woman and that the woman seemed to be gaining on her. Somewhat nervous at being followed, yet not fearful, Denise turned, and the woman came into full view. She was striding along on cross-country skis, and she was wearing black stretch pants and a striped turtleneck sweater knit of rich and brilliant colors with shimmering golden threads woven through it. Her mittens matched her sweater. The woman's face was framed by strawberry blond hair which fell in golden ringlets, and she wore large golden bangle earrings. As she passed under each streetlight, she literally sparkled. Denise started left into the parking lot, and, when the woman began to ski past her, Denise turned once more, and their eyes met. As they did, the woman raised her ski poles and said, with vibrant enthusiasm, "Hi!" She was laughing, bubbly, exuberant, and bursting with joy and life, and Denise suddenly found herself laughing as well.

Then Denise turned again and took five or six short steps to her car. Putting the key in the lock, she glanced up a final time, wishing to speak to the woman, but there was no one there. Astonished and baffled, Denise hurried back to the sidewalk and stood looking in all directions for some sight of the woman. She had a clear view of the sidewalk, the parking lot, and the field next to the building, but she found herself to be utterly alone. In the time it had taken her to take those last few steps, there was simply no way that the woman could have skied completely out of sight. It was then that Denise remembered her spontaneous prayer, "Lord, I just want to laugh."

I myself had a fascinating encounter with angels, this time at the hospital in Birmingham where Allen was recovering from his eye surgery. While waiting for the doctor to clear Allen for discharge, I lay down to rest on the bed next to his in his room. After awhile, as I lay on my back looking up at the ceiling, I suddenly had the sense that the large, square, white ceiling tiles were being parted, and that an opening was being formed. Immediately, I became aware that there were several young angels gathered around the edge of the opening, and the focus of their attention seemed somehow to be me, for they would alternately peer down with a mixture of great interest and curiosity, and then glance knowingly at each other. I remember asking the Lord, at the time, who these adolescent angels were, and I thought I heard Him say, "step-guardians,"— a term I thought very odd and more so since I couldn't find it in the dictionary. Needless to say, I was puzzled and intrigued. It was July of 1999.

Meanwhile, in March of that year, we had begun to realize that the Lord was calling us to the adoption of three Russian children, though we did not yet know which three, as we were still in the very earliest stages of the process. Amazingly, when we later prayed about these curious young angels, Allen felt the Lord to be saying that they were the guardians of the children whom we would be adopting, sent to "check out" the prospective new mom! Moreover, Allen had the sense that the apparent age of the angels—late childhood to early adolescence—reflected the age of the children over whom they were watching. Now I understood the word "step-guardians," for they were not *my* guardians but guardians over those who would soon be related to me—guardians once-removed, as it were!

Recently, we prayed again about the matter, asking for confirmation of the vision, and of the word concerning it. We received this further insight: "It is true that angels, as you see them in visions, assume the general appearance of those whom they oversee, yet that, of course, is not what they look like. What you saw was a taste of angels being given a bit of My plan and exercising their own unique gifts in seeing their charges and also you. It is not important how that happens, since it is something which you would not understand anyhow, but it does give an interesting dimension to spiritual warfare, does it not?"

VI. Visitations of the Lord

On several occasions, Allen and I have each seen Jesus in visions. In my case, for example, I once saw Him standing before me in a vision which gave me much-needed comfort and encouragement at a time of grief.

During Christmas vacation of our first year at Trinity, we had taken a week-long trip home to see my father in Connecticut, leaving our two beloved cats in the care of a neighboring seminarian. Melissa, our beautiful black and white angora, had been discovered, as I mentioned earlier, to be a carrier of feline leukemia, but she had lived a happy seven and a half years with no signs of the disease. Melissa had always been especially endearing for, from the time she was a kitten, she had delighted in riding about the house, draped around the back of Allen's neck as he shaved, or read or ate. However, on our return from our Christmas trip, I opened the front door of our Ambridge house and walked into the living room to find her stiff little body on the sofa. She had been dead for just a few hours, the victim, finally, of the leukemia. We were devastated, and we both cried and cried. For hours, we both felt like we were under a dark cloud of oppression for Melissa's death was now added to the already immense weight of school pressures, exams, financial stress, and the terribly difficult situation with my parents.

That evening we sat down to pray, and Allen thought he heard the Lord say, in response to my grief, "But child, I love you." However, Allen also got the sense that the oppressing spirit was one of self-pity, and he heard the Lord say, "There is much to be done." I understood Him to be referring to the work of the Kingdom. It was a hard but a necessary word. Likewise difficult was another word which we received: "There is a cost to following Me." I surmised that the stress of our lengthy move three months earlier had precipitated the breakdown of the immune system which had kept Melissa's disease at bay for so long, and why the Lord did not simply protect her I have never, given the word, asked.

Later that night, just after I had gotten into bed, deeply sad, and lonely for the cat who had always slept under the covers by my feet, I was suddenly astonished to see a strong and clear image of Jesus standing in the room near the window. Most amazing, he had Melissa draped around his neck! However, despite the clarity of the image and the poignant sign from the Lord which was its focal point, I was not willing to automatically accept that Melissa was with Jesus, for my theology had never assured me that our pets went to be with the Lord. I was resolved that I would only accept the Lord's truth, despite what I wanted to believe, and I needed assurance that the vision was really from the Lord.

Early the next morning, Allen arose and went downstairs to have a bowl of cereal before dashing off to school. He was sitting at the table, by now quite preoccupied again with matters of schoolwork but also still feeling some self-pity, when, utterly unexpectedly, he heard the Lord break in: "How could anyone who knows Me think that I would not have animals in My heavenly Kingdom?" He asked, adding, "They are part of the Great Praise." I remember pondering the thought of heaven filled with the joyous sounds of barking, meowing, chirping, neighing, mooing, quacking, and thousands of other creaturely noises, all in praise of their Creator!

Several nights later, as we were lying in bed, I again prayed about how badly I felt about Melissa, for I still had not fully accepted the image and the words. Immediately, Allen thought he heard the Lord say, "I have given you reassurance."

When I expressed my guilt about not having been there to help her, the Lord replied matter-of-factly, "You could not have done anything." Then He gave us this Scripture: "He tends his flock like a shepherd: He gathers the lambs in His arms and carries them close to his heart...."(Isaiah 40:11) With a weight of doubt still remaining, I sighed, "Lord, I feel so badly because I'll never see Melissa again." He instantly replied, with a playful wink in His voice, "Don't be too sure of that." With that, I was finally at peace in the matter.

The timing of Melissa's death was surely the Lord's provision for, truly, given the nature of her disease, we could have done nothing to save her. Our presence at home with her during that last week could only been one of anguish and fatigue as we desperately tried to help her and hang on to her. By grace, only a week after her death we were scheduled to take a seminary-led trip to Israel and so were able to occupy our minds during the days prior to our travel with shopping, packing, and with anticipation.

The following week, as the saga continued, we were amazed and amused to be the recipients of another form of visitation from a very interesting little visitor. Now in Israel, we arrived one evening on the shores of the Sea of Galilee, to spend several nights at Kibbutz Ma'agan. We all piled off the tour bus and were given our rooming assignments. The resort consisted of a number of small condo-like units, and we located ours and then went back for our bags. As we approached our door, key in hand, from around the corner and down the sidewalk trotted a little short-haired black and white cat. She made a bee-line for us and reached the door of our unit before we did. When Allen opened the door, she walked in ahead of us, hung a right as if she knew exactly where she was going, went into the bedroom, and jumped up onto the bed, purring loudly. We could not budge her and finally decided to let her stay. Every night of our stay there, the process repeated, and we slept with this little cat, who clearly seemed to be "on assignment" from the Lord to bring us comfort in our loss. No one else in the tour group had any experiences with cats coming into their condos, much less wanting to sleep with them, and even the manager commented that the cats were not in the habit of entering the buildings. We took a picture of her curled up on the bed-spread, just to prove that she had really been there. When we recently told our friend Cindy the story, she jokingly imag-ined that the cat, upon first gaining entry into the condo, had put her paw up to her mouth, secret-agent style, and, speaking into an imaginary hidden device, had whispered furtively, "I'm in!"

I included this story in this section because it began with a visitation from the Lord. However, this entire experience of Melissa's death, from beginning to end, was remarkable in that it also combined words of knowledge, words of wisdom, great comfort, and divinely directed circumstances, as well as a visitation from a little creature who was enlisted into the Lord's service. It was a powerful illustration to me of the fact that the Lord cares about what we care about, and that He loves us and the living things He has placed in our care. However, in the midst of it all, He also soberly reminded us, "People come first." This is His incontrovertible will for the created order, but to all who love their pets and all the other creatures in God's world, I will give Scripture's amen. From Genesis to Isaiah, from Romans to Revelation, God's Word resounds with the glorious theme that the fallen creation, sub-jected by the Creator to death and decay, will one day be restored. *"How could anyone who knows Me.... ?"*

I have also been visited by the Lord in dreams, where He has typically been seated at a short distance from me, robed and with sandal-clad feet. I am never able to see His face, but He always gives a short teaching or instruction which I receive as audible or inaudible words, communicated Spirit to spirit. I shall give an astonishing example of one of my most memorable experiences of the latter. Below is my journal entry from 5-16-97. Perhaps it will also give some further insight into the whole process of hearing, recording, praying, discerning, corroborating, and interpreting:

"I should try to record a short dream I had last night shortly after I went to bed. I don't remember the earlier part, but all of it seemed to involve Jesus giving me some sort of instruction. The part I do remember related to the issue of the Rapture. (Note to reader: This term refers to the Lord's revelation to the Apostle Paul concerning what would happen to those believers who were still alive at the time of Christ's return at the end of the Age. (Please see I Thessalonians 4:13-18). The message seemed to be that we wouldn't simply 'come to' in heaven, but would be conscious during the process [of being caught up to be with the Lord]. At the moment of being changed (see I Corinthians, chapter 15), there would be a flash of pain, though I don't think it would be severe. It would be largely in the physical, though perhaps not totally so. (I should add here that while Jesus was speaking to me, I actually experienced the intensely realistic sense of being lifted up, caught up, of rising through a layer of cloud. As I did so, I felt an intense, crushing pressure being exerted upon my body, as though my mortality and my old sin nature were literally being squeezed out of me. Though not intolerable, this brief experience was painful enough that there was a serious question as to whether or not I wanted to or even could go through with the process, and I understood that if, in exercising my free will, I chose not to continue, to go back, that I would be allowed to do so). [However,] we were to be encouraged, perhaps because it was necessary to accept and say yes to that pain. At that point, the Lord, who was seated, leaned forward towards me and said something further about the pain, about its being 'right,' or needed, or something, at the moment when we broke through the clouds. I wish I could remember the exact words. Lord, [I continued,] I ask you to confirm with a Scripture if that dream was from you at all. (I immediately thought I got Genesis 37:9, which begins), 'Then he [Joseph] had another dream, and he told it to his brothers.' I then asked, 'Lord, why would it be valuable for me to know this?' This Scripture followed: 'Look! It is Solomon's carriage, escorted by six warriors, the noblest of Israel..."' (Song of Songs 3:7)

In interpreting this beautiful love poem, many agree that King Solomon, the Lover, the Bridegroom, may also be viewed allegorically as a symbol of Christ, coming for His bride, His Beloved, the Church. That same morning, Allen and I prayed together about the dream, and here is what he wrote:

"Jan related an unusual dream that she had last night about the Rapture, and we talked about that. Jan asked this: if the dream were instruction, how could it help unless the Lord told everyone the same thing? I thought I heard, *'I do tell everyone, but not all are listening— in fact, only a few. Those who hear, receive the message processed through their own history, so the form may be quite different for each of them.'*"

I continued, "Lord, Is the message that we need to accept the positive value of pain?" The next day, Allen and I prayed about this matter again. Allen wrote, "Jan asked about the message that some pain must be accepted when the Rapture occurs. I thought I heard, *'Pain is necessary for growth. It must be so.'*"

I feel that I must be clear that I do not necessarily see this dream as a promise of personal Rapture, though of course I can't exclude its possibility, either. The times are in the Lord's hands.

VII. Illustrations from (or Observations of) Life or Nature

Psalm 19 begins, "The heavens declare the glory of God." Romans Chapter 1 also tells us that there is no excuse for not recognizing the Creator in His handiwork displayed in the physical world. In addition, day by day, as we are listening, the Lord reveals Himself to us in the things around us in our world. Following are some examples from our own experience.

We have what might arguably be described as the world's most affectionate dog. A black and white cocker spaniel mix, Lydia craves attention and adores being petted, as well as being rubbed on her stomach. In order to get her needs met, she will go so far as to demandingly position her head under one's hand, or her stomach over one's foot, accompanied by a comical expression of imploring, ingenuous determination. While she is being petted, her eyes glaze over, and a look of utter, unabashed bliss comes over her, which is funnier still.

If one stops this ritual before she has had enough, which is usually never, Lydia persistently paws the person's arm or leg until the petting is resumed, all the while gazing imploringly into his or her face. Though it's always good for a laugh, the truth is that sometimes the whole thing can get a bit annoying. One evening during our home fellowship group, as Lydia was again relentlessly pestering one of the women with this routine, I suddenly thought that I heard the Lord speaking to me about it: "This is how I want you to be with Me." I knew that He meant that we were to bring our needs and requests to Him boldly, unashamedly, and with (forgive the pun) dogged persistence.

Scripture agrees. In the parable of the man who goes to his friend at midnight to borrow some bread to feed an unexpected guest, Jesus explains, "I tell you, though he will not get up and give him the bread because he is his friend, yet because of the man's boldness he will get up and give him as much as he needs."(Luke 11:8)

We also learn a great deal from observing our children. Some time ago, we were struggling with a spate of turbulent behavior from our kids—the constant bickering, fighting, and arguing with which every parent is all too familiar. We were at our wits' end, and sought the Lord as to how to deal with it. Sitting in silence, we waited for Him to give us some profound and lofty advice which would bring us some resolution and relief. Instead, to our chagrin, He only said, "That's how *you* (I had a sense that He was including all of humanity here) look to *Me*." Oops. The sudden glimpse we got of ourselves in the mirror of our children was worth a thousand words. How like the Lord. He didn't condemn, but, instead, skillfully pointed us to an illustration with which we could all too painfully identify.

Several years ago, Allen and I had taken a group from our church on a tour of Israel. It was early January when we arrived in Jerusalem, and the weather was unrelentingly cold, windy, and wet. The streets were filled with deep, icy slush, and nothing seemed to keep our feet warm enough. We were cold to the bone. We longed to get settled into our room, and we were especially anxious for a nice hot shower. The next morning I arose early and eagerly stepped into the shower stall, only to find that in our wonderful but older hospice, the water pressure was negligible. The shower head was close to the wall, and the small stream of water which emerged backed itself down the handle and trickled down the tile wall. I did my best to get my hair wet, but trying to get it rinsed after shampooing was a comical exercise in futility. I stood for some time with my nose pressed tightly against the tile, alternating between laughter and complete frustration. Allen was next. As I dressed, still complaining under my breath, he called out from the shower, saying, "I think I just heard the Lord say, very softly, 'Some people don't have any showers.'" Oops.

VIII. Signs

Some attention must also be given to the fascinating topic of signs. While this subject deserves much time and study, I will simply say here that a sign may be described as something which gives evidence of something else. It may be divinely manifested for the occasion, as with the Star of Bethlehem. It may be rooted in past, present, or future events: "You will find a baby wrapped in cloths…."(Matthew 2:12) It may also be derived from an observation of something in the natural world: "See how the lilies of the field grow."(Matthew 6:28b), or expressed in the symbolic activities of a prophet, as with Jonah's three days in the belly of the great fish.(Matthew 12:40) Scripture is replete with God's use of signs to underscore His wisdom, power and authority. The rainbow was a sign, as were circumcision, the Sabbath, and the miracles of Jesus.

God, being the same yesterday, today and forever, continues to employ signs in order to underscore His Word, both Scriptural and personal. In late July of 1996, not long after we moved to Alabama, I had an amazing dream. I wrote:

"I was perhaps in a room looking out a picture window, although that part is vague. It was nearly but not fully dark outside. I looked up into the sky and saw a pale white horse approaching from a distance. Its legs seemed to be in a galloping position, although I did not see them moving. I was with a small group of people. The horse kept coming until it was in the sky above us, and it seemed to move about in that area for a while. Then, it began to move away again, and I commented to someone that it was going back to where it had come from."

During prayer the next day about this dream, the Lord referred Allen to Psalm 2, a warning to the arrogant rulers of the earth of the coming reign of the true King, Christ. On an early spring evening nearly eight months later, Allen and I found ourselves standing out in the backyard with another couple from church. We were all gazing intently up at the Hale-Bopp comet, its long, pale tail streaming behind it. On March 31st, 1997, I noted this in my journal:

"I am looking back at my 7-31-96 entry of the dream of the pale horse. It strikes me now that it may well have applied to the comet. Psalm 2 was also given us at that time. When I had prayed last week about the meaning of the comet, I felt that I had heard these words from Handel's Messiah ringing in my head: 'For He cometh, for He cometh, to judge the earth.'"

Allen had also heard the Lord say, in response to my question as to whether or not the comet had any significance, "Everything I do has significance." We again both had the sense that this sign in the heavens was a warning. Some years later, we were treated to a spectacular display of Leonid showers, and, being now more attuned to the possibility of some spiritual meaning behind these celestial phenomena, I remarked to the Lord that it was fascinating that these meteors were all shooting outward from a radiant in the constellation Leo. Since Christ is also called the Lion of Judah, I asked Him if these meteors had any spiritual import. He replied,

"All things have significance in My plans, since I am a God of the details as well as of the great things of the universe. I have planned all of these things so that you will know more of who I AM.

These are some signs in the heavens, and you know that I do nothing lightly. All of My works and all of My signs have meaning, though you cannot fully understand the depth of all that I am doing. The signs in the heavens are not meant to give direction, but they do point to Me and to My power and My ongoing and imminent action."

All things indeed have significance. The celestial examples above are observable to the world and point to the unfolding of salvation history. However, the Lord may also use even the most mundane objects and events in everyday lives to verify His personal words to us. For example, our adoption story, at the end of this book, pivoted on the appearance of a double-yoked egg in a frying pan.

On an equally humorous note, while at Trinity I was struggling to do some necessary writing, my problem only aggravated by my tendency to perfectionism. The Lord spoke through a writer friend who counseled that the best course of action was to sit down, pen in hand, "vomit" something out on the paper, and "clean up the mess" afterwards. The very next afternoon, I stepped outside to speak with a neighbor who happened to be holding his infant daughter in his arms. We had barely begun our conversation when the child unexpectedly threw up. Over the course of the next two days, I was treated to two more incidents of people vomiting. I thought the experience quite odd until I suddenly recognized with a grin that the Lord was simply "signing" His message to me about my writing. I don't think He made people sick for my sake, but rather took advantage of some timing.

I do believe that it is quite acceptable to occasionally ask the Lord to verify a word with a sign, especially if the matter is of great import in our lives. Jesus chided the Pharisees in this regard because they were insincerely demanding repeated signs to supposedly verify obvious works of God.

IX. The Arts and Architecture

It is utterly impossible to do justice to the ways through which God speaks in the visual, structural and performing arts. However, we *can* say that, in most instances, the messages will tend to be general rather than specific as regards our own individual needs, situations, or questions. Nonetheless, we can learn much about the nature of God and His work in the world from man's creative response to it. Here is a brief overview.

A. *Music*

To me and, as surveys attest, to much of the rest of world as well, the most profoundly inspired and inspiring piece of Christian music is Handel's Messiah. Each time it is played or performed, the Gospel message rings gloriously forth. Also enormously appealing to me was the performance of The Young Messiah which Allen and I were fortunate to attend in Pittsburgh in 1993. However, as much as we were enthralled with the worshipful skill of the singers and musicians, it was perhaps more thrilling to see thousands upon thousands of young people being moved by this marvelous rendition of God's Word written.

Likewise, we have also been continually amazed by the impact that good contemporary Christian music has had upon our kids. Lera, our then 15-year old Russian house guest, though self-admittedly not a believer, quickly became enamored of our Christian music CDs, and she took some of her favorite music back home with her. The song she loved most was Buddy Greene's beautiful Mary Did You Know? , and, once back home at school, she eagerly shared it with her classmates and her favorite teacher. Shortly afterwards, she excitedly called to tell us that many of her friends were singing the song in the halls between classes! An evangelist despite herself, she was awed and bemused by the effect the music was having upon its listeners.

A while ago, a friend was expressing her anxiety about the uncertainty of her elderly father's salvation, since he had always manifested a combination of confusion about and resistance to the Gospel. Allen and I offered to pray for him, and, as we did so, Allen got an immediate sense from the Lord that some Christian music geared to his own musical taste might be helpful. The reason, Allen thought he heard, was that the music would speak directly to the subconscious, to that God-shaped hole at the center of his being, bypassing the blocks and filters of the conscious mind.

B. Visual and Performing Arts

Several years ago, while shopping for boxed Christmas cards, I came across Luc Merson's 1879 painting Repose on the Flight into Egypt. It was my first introduction to this painting, and I was deeply moved by it. Set against the background of a starry desert night, and ludicrously out of scale for purposes of illustration, it depicts Mary cradling Jesus on her lap, herself peacefully asleep between the front paws of the Sphinx—itself the ironic symbol of all that opposed Christ. If an image is worth a thousand words, this painting speaks volumes.

Included in the category of visual arts would, of course, be theater and films, and these can be a powerful means through which God may speak, particularly due to their ability to reach mass audiences. The ability of The Jesus Film, for example, to touch millions of people with the Gospel has been extraordinary, and we could mention the impact of The Passion of the Christ, Lord of the Rings, and The Lion, the Witch and the Wardrobe.

I believe that the Lord is currently using these latter two films to speak to a new generation and a culture that have otherwise grown dangerously indifferent to the spiritual battle between good and evil. In our own case, they have provided many good opportunities to talk about these crucial issues of spiritual warfare with our children. They were especially intrigued by Tolkien's depiction of the tormented Golom, and their insightful questions enabled us to discuss with them critical issues surrounding the nature of free will and the moral struggle within.

Films (or anything else, for that matter) do not have to be overtly Christian in content to convey a message from the Lord. Several years ago I was drawn to watch the new Ann of Green Gables movie, starring Megan Follows. In addition to reviving my childhood memories of the book, I was deeply moved by the themes of love, courage, loyalty, friendship, faith, perseverance, imagination, and reconciliation with which the film resounds. I was so strongly impacted by the movie that I finally sought the Lord as to the reason behind my response. He replied from Philippians 4: 8 and 9: "...whatever is true, whatever is noble, whatever is right, whatever is pure, whatever is lovely, whatever is admirable—if anything is excellent or praiseworthy— think about such things....And the God of peace will be with you." Likewise, a visit to the Chattanooga Children's Theater to see a performance of Charles Dickens's A Christmas Carol provided a good opportunity to be reminded of the brevity of life, the dangers of self-absorption, and the need to have a servant's heart.

C.   *The Architecture of Worship*

Sacred space is meant to speak to us of the work, the purposes of, and the attributes of God. As with the other categories I have mentioned, this one deserves vastly more space that I am able to afford it here. I can only touch on some aspects of the subject of sacred architecture that have been helpful to us in hearing the Lord.

While at Trinity, for example, Allen and I had the opportunity to take a class on the history of the relationship between theology and church architecture, given by Arnie Klukas, a priest with a doctorate in art history. Since then, our visits to church buildings, both historic and contemporary, have had an added dimension of insight, and we have also been better able to distinguish between what in their design expresses enduring Scriptural truths, and what has developed and changed as a result of human tradition and the historical process.

More recently, I have been reading a book by David M. Levy entitled The Tabernacle: Shadows of the Messiah.[vii] In it, Levy systematically examines the priesthood and the sacrifices, as well as each article and feature of the tabernacle itself, wonderfully explaining how their typology is fulfilled in Christ. In his introduction, he points out that a full fifty chapters of the Bible are devoted to detailed descriptions of the tabernacle and the sacrificial system. No other single subject in Scripture has been granted so much attention and emphasis, he reminds us. God spoke His plan of salvation history into the design and furnishings of the tabernacle and, later, the temple, and we would do well to study their forms and sacrifices. As Allen Ross, our Old Testament professor at Trinity, repeatedly stressed, it is impossible to truly understand the theology of the book of Hebrews without a solid grasp of the book of Leviticus, including the physical descriptions of the tabernacle.

The architecture of worship, it would seem, also has a highly significant role to play in the age to come, for chapters forty through forty-six of the book of Ezekiel are devoted to a meticulously detailed description of the millennial temple, its appointments and its rituals. Here again we see much space devoted to a deliberate connection between architectural features (and dimensions) and theological content. Just as the tabernacle and the temples of the Old Covenant were concrete, visual expressions of Israel's relationship with the Lord and of His presence with His people, so too it will be with this new temple, into which, Ezekiel tells us, the glory of the Lord will return.

X. Humor and Word Plays

Since God invented humor, I thought it would be fun to close this chapter with some illustrations of God's use of it. Humor, God knows, is a great device for getting people's attention and making the point hit home and, also, a wonderful means of reminding us that we tend to take ourselves far too seriously.

We have been astonished and fascinated to find that the Lord loves puns and delights in playing with language, and I am convinced that entire books could easily be written on this subject alone. One can scarcely begin to examine Scripture itself in its native Hebrew or Greek without unearthing astonishing instances of this, but we have also found that He frequently springs His humor upon us in His daily communications with us.

One funny experience of the Lord's humor occurred while Allen was at Trinity, preparing to take his general ordination exams. These exams are the seminarian's equivalent of medical or law school boards, and Allen was exceedingly nervous. His anxiety increased daily as the dreaded exams approached. One night, just as he was going to sleep, he suddenly sat up again and said, somewhat hesitantly, "I just heard the two strangest words." "Well, what were they?" I nudged. "Helium" and "Arctic," he replied. Naturally, we had absolutely no clue as to what the Lord may have meant, and we were so exhausted that we soon fell asleep. However, being the curious person that I am, this enigmatic message continued to tease at me.

Over the next few days, I asked the Lord about the words several times, but there was no response. Finally, two weeks later, as were again about to go to sleep, I tried once more: "Lord, what did you mean by "helium," and "Arctic?" Suddenly, Allen heard: "Lighten up and chill out." We both nearly fell out of bed laughing. Interestingly enough, sometime later during that same week, I happened to note in the newspaper that someone was attempting an Arctic crossing in a helium balloon! If the Lord had simply said, "Relax!" we would have missed all the fun of the word plays, the imagery, the multiple meanings, and the timing of the word.

Again, one night while at Trinity, Allen received a vision of a goal post. He even drew a little picture of it. Pondering the image a bit, and playing with the symbolism, I asked, "Lord, do you have a goal for us?" Knowing in advance what my question would be, for I had obviously been set up, His response was, "My goal is the same as it has always been." I had been taking Hebrew reading that semester, and we had been studying the Book of Ruth in which the key word is the verb *ga'al,* meaning "to redeem." The participle describing Boaz, Ruth's kinsman-redeemer, is *go'el.* Here was an intriguing play on words, for the goal of Jesus, our Redeemer, was and is redemption.

Scripture itself is replete with examples of Jesus' sense of humor, though I think we often miss the subtlety of much of it—first because we have lost its Jewish context and second because we may erroneously presume that He was always serious and stern. Serious about His mission, He of course was. Surely, however, He intended some humor when He suggested to people that they take the logs out of their own eyes before addressing the specks in another's'. Perhaps my favorite illustration of Jesus' sense of humor comes from the story of His Resurrection-eve encounter with two of his disciples on the road to Emmaus in Luke, chapter 24. The men, we recall, were vigorously discussing the momentous events of the past days when Jesus came alongside and engaged them in conversation. He asked them what they had been discussing, and, when they replied by asking Him if He was only a visitor to Jerusalem who did not know the things that had been happening there, Jesus asked, *"What things?"* I have often wondered if it was difficult for Him to keep a straight face. Behind the tongue-in-cheek question, of course, was the earnest matter of the testing of hearts.

God has also woven His sense of humor into the natural world which He created. One needs only to watch kittens playing, or a pair of otters cavorting in the water, to know that God enjoys fun. Even more intriguing is the serious message behind it all: that our ability to play is inextricably entwined with our freedom to *be*. The antics of animals are, at least partly, so appealing because, in them, we sense an aspect of what it is to live by grace: to receive our being freely and joyfully as a gift from God.

Finally, God may even use the humor hidden in the most common everyday situations to speak to us. For example, our friend Sarah Earley tells me of a woman who felt led to go to a Faith Alive Conference after noticing that a cross had been formed by the chocolate dribbled into the center hole of the Keebler Fudge Stripe cookie she was eating! On any given day, there are likely untold thousands of people who bite into Keebler Fudge Stripe cookies. On this day, one saw a message from God.

Having ended on that deliciously silly note, we shall now move on to a more serious matter, as we examine the important questions regarding discernment in the hearing process.

Chapter 5:
Discernment

Issues of discernment have primarily to do with the presumed source of what we think we are hearing. How, in the midst of these efforts to hear God, the reader should rightly ask, does one manage to distinguish between what comes from God; what might come from one's own mind, emotions, preconceptions, prejudices, and desires; or, worse yet, what could be coming from the Enemy? There is no perfect answer, but let me say several things with regard to that sorting process:

1) The cardinal rule of discernment is that any word or image received must, as already emphasized, be in accordance with the written word of Scripture. If it conflicts with Scripture, it's not from the Lord.—period. Recent history has been filled with examples of people who decided they knew when the Lord was returning, all despite Jesus' plain words that no man knows the day or the hour. As a corollary, the word must, in its pronouncement, application, and outworking, glorify the Lord. Anything, however right it may seem, which takes the glory or the focus from Christ is not from God. Revelation 19:10 tells us, "For the testimony of Jesus is the spirit of prophecy." We must always be careful to confirm that what we receive agrees with God's Word written.

2) Our own general pattern has always been that Allen and I would share any words we felt we had gotten with each other or with our prayer group, testing them against the truth

of Scripture, and allowing ourselves to be subject to one another's prayerful discernment. This is the second corrective which Scripture prescribes.

3) The process of learning to hear, though God-given and guided, takes, as with the exercise of the spiritual gifts, practice and training. The ability to hear does not emerge full-blown. Let no one kid himself. In our own case, we are talking about years of weekly meetings in addition to other prayer times, individual and group, and countless hours spent praying and listening, praying and listening—all the while keeping a written record. However, lest the reader be discouraged, let me quickly say two things. First, one obviously must begin *somewhere,* and, as the old saying goes, beginning is half done. Secondly, much good fruit can be born right from the beginning. Some of the most crucial guidance we have received came very early on. Assuming prayerful discernment, one's incipient hearing is valid and can be trusted. The broader issues have rather to do with an ongoing process of maturation, both in terms of internal comprehension and external action.

This whole process is a training ground. As I described earlier, for a long time after Allen first received his prophetic gifting, the Lord would prophesy through visions concerning events which we later saw fulfilled. This process was repeated dozens and dozens of times. I am convinced that we were being trained in interpretation skills, in trust, and in discernment. Why? In part, at least, I believe that God does this so that when the times come that it is crucial to hear and act on what we are hearing, we will be prepared, having the confidence born of past experience. We will have learned how to recognize His voice.

4) With regard to heard messages, we discovered almost immediately that there is a peculiar combination of depth and pithiness to the words which the Lord gives. This has always helped us to distinguish His voice from anything that might originate in our own minds, for the tone of authority, choice

of words, syntax, turn of phrase, and brilliant sparsity of language, though filtered through our sin nature and experience, always bear His unique stamp. The reader will hopefully see ample evidence of this in the illustrations I have given throughout this book. I suspect that this characteristic is a good part of what the Lord meant when He said that His sheep follow Him because they know His voice.(See John 10:2-5) As I have often remarked to people, "Left to our own devices, we are simply not that clever, well-reasoned, or insightful."

5) Similarly, we have so often found that the Lord's input on a matter will be profoundly contrary to our own, producing in us an odd but simultaneous mixture of resolution and conviction. Declares the Lord, "As the heavens are higher than the earth, so are my ways higher than your ways, and my thoughts than your thoughts."(Isaiah 55:8) Our experience with people who always seem to receive comfortable words which only confirm what they already wanted to hear is that they are probably not hearing from God. The peace that *passes understanding* is so precisely because it is not what our fallen nature expects or desires, and it is often conjoined to a stretching, painful, and holy *dis*comfort which leads us to a new place in our spiritual walk.

6) We must also remember that, because we are imperfect and see through a glass darkly, our hearing is imperfect. It will be so until the Lord returns. Mistakes in hearing will be made. The Lord knows this and understands our weaknesses. As a funny example of this, some years ago I prayed to the Lord for relief from a persistent scalp irritation that did not respond to the normal treatments. Allen thought he got the word "fudge." Of course, that made no sense, (although I might have liked it to!) but, quite some time afterwards, I realized, due to some other problems I was having, that the Lord had more likely said "fungus." We have always found that if we keep listening, He will graciously repeat critically important material, sometimes in varying forms,   until we

hear Him correctly. This, again, is part of growing and learning. Of course, He always makes available to us the correcting influence of other believers.

7) First Corinthians 12:10 tells us plainly that "distinguishing between spirits" is a spiritual gift, given by the Holy Spirit for the common good of the Body. This gift serves to protect the Church and the individual believer from the intrusion of false prophecies, and it helps to assure us that, when we pray, we do not get a snake for a fish or a scorpion for an egg!(See Luke 11:11-12) However, there is a strong warning here. If we persist in willful and unbiblical thinking or prayer, it *is* possible to begin to hear other voices—either our own, arising from our fallen nature, or worse. Satan is all too willing to step into this kind of opening, and it is a lot wiser and easier to keep him out in the first place than it is to try to get him out once he has gained entry, since we may temporarily lose our discernment. We have sometimes felt it advisable to begin our prayer time with a request for the Lord's protection against attacks from the Enemy and have sometimes halted prayer to do the same, sensing that it was necessary to do so.

Ultimately, one can only learn this process of discernment through practice, group accountability, and the test of Scripture. In the end, all I can say is that there will develop a knowing in the spirit, for this is where the communication with the Lord happens: Spirit to spirit. "My sheep know My voice."

Chapter 6:
Blocks to Hearing

Another critical area needing attention involves the issue of blocks to effective praying and listening. Among these I would list the following:

> 1) *Unbelief in God's good nature, His love for us, His ability or willingness to speak to us or, conversely, in our ability to hear Him.* Generally, these arise from wrong, ineffective, inadequate or misunderstood teaching, often reaching back into childhood. Given any of these unfortunate preconditions, one is not likely to even attempt to engage in the process of hearing. The seeds of these blockages were sown with the first lie of Satan in the Garden, for he first caused Eve and then Adam to doubt God's good purposes, and the history of man's resultant separation from God reflects the sad results. Two simple but crucial points bear repeating here. First, to listen, we must believe in the *goodness* and *faithfulness* of God. If we struggle in this area, we must appeal both to the testimony of Scripture and to the ministrations of the Holy Spirit and the Body. Second, we must have the seed of faith that He *does* speak and that it is, at least, *possible* to hear. We are saddened, astonished and dismayed at the number of Christians we regularly encounter for whom that second point is either foreign or worse—offensive.

2) Unwillingness to take the required steps of discipline in its various forms. Productive hearing comes out of long-standing submission to both self- and corporate disciplines. These include quiet time, Bible study, small group fellowship, and a determination to press in until we understand, if only in part. With regard to the latter, it has been our consistent experience that God often chooses to speak to us in parabolic and veiled ways that drive us to study, ponder, confirm, wait, and, in other ways, work at our hearing. Apart from needing wisdom in a crisis, interpretation and discernment are rarely handed to us on a platter, even when we deem ourselves unable to rise to the task. Hearing and listening are hard work and are rewarded as such.

Last week, our oldest vehicle suffered a blown head gasket and expired. We decided that my car would be the one replaced, but, with five drivers and now three vehicles, we were in a time crunch. I needed to find another vehicle in reasonably short order. I was already tired, and a long, cold Saturday spent walking used car lots and doing test drives produced several decent choices but, also, much confusion and further fatigue. I was sorely tempted to simply select from one of the cars we had deemed acceptable. As we prayed and pondered, however, I had the growing sense that we needed to wait and continue to seek the Lord.

When our friend Cindy came for our regular weekly prayer meeting, the Lord gave her the intriguing image of a papoose, so wrapped that only a very small portion its face was visible. Allen, meanwhile, was given the image of a nicely made steel pipe, as well as Acts 10:12, from the story of Peter and Cornelius. The images were baffling, but I got to work studying and pondering the Scripture passage. In it, Peter has been sent to witness to this Gentile centurion, but, as he is on his way, he stops to pray, becomes hungry and, while waiting for the meal to be served, has a vision in which unclean animals are lowered down from heaven in a sheet. Three times, the resistant Peter is told to kill and eat what has previously been totally out of consideration for him. What, we wondered, was the application for *us*? Though there was much in the story to contemplate, I keep going back to the thought that the vehicle make/ model/dealership/age/price or some combination thereof to which the Lord was pointing might be things which we had either ruled out or had simply never thought of as possibilities. The nearly hidden papoose seemed to echo the message of something not only new to our thinking, but something scarcely even seen in our earlier searching. Though low on energy, we set out again the next day, the words and images from the Lord playing in our minds. Since we hadn't previously thought about going there, our first stop was at the local KIA dealership where, to our surprise, the salesman immediately led us to a low mileage used Chrysler Sebring which turned out to be perfect for me in every respect, though two or three years older than cars we had already been considering. Best of all, the price was nearly three thousand dollars less than that of any of the vehicles we had almost purchased instead! The salesman informed us that, for some inexplicable reason, this great car had been on the lot for three months, and they had dropped the price to below wholesale value shortly before we appeared!

In every regard, the car and its location were things we had not considered at all. The salesman at the first dealership to which we had gone had mentioned Sebrings in passing, but the idea had simply not registered with us, and, though we had walked right past one that he had suggested, we had never so much as opened the door to look inside. This salesman's background was Lakota Sioux! Just as amazing was the fact that, when I later checked a Wikipedia article on KIA, I found that they had begun as a manufacturer of bicycles and *steel tubing!* (Please note that I am not singling out Kia or Chrysler for endorsement, but only sharing a story for purposes of illustration).

As I have said, I was tired when I began the whole search process and, frankly, frustrated with the Lord for asking me to spend several days wrestling with words and enigmatic visions. He, of course, knew that I was weary and seemed to be asking me to persist anyway. When I saw, in retrospect, where it had all been leading, I was not only excited about my car but, also, happy to be able to relate the story of God's guidance and blessing. Waiting and wrestling are disciplines.

3) *Undue dependence on others to do the hearing.* For years, I relied on Allen to do most of the hearing. Finally, the Lord pointed this out to me, and I began intentionally trying to hear better on my own. The Lord even gave me some incentive to practice. On one occasion when I really wanted an answer to something that was troubling me, He told me to persist in prayer and listening until I heard for myself. He would not speak it through Allen. Based on my own experience, I would say that this particular block to hearing comes, not so much from laziness, as from insecurity, and it can only be overcome by stepping out and trying, despite the anxiety—admittedly easier said than done.

4) *Worldly distractions, busyness, fear and worry.* If our minds and spirits are anxious, fearful or distressed about something, we may find it extremely difficult to hear or, sometimes, even to pray at all. This is because divine impartation is nonetheless borne through the medium of human flesh. Allen has found that, if he is tired, distracted, weary, or in some other way spiritually blocked, the visions he sees may be indistinct, confused, or so fleeting as to be unintelligible. They may actually appear to have lines of static in them, like an old TV, as if his "receiver" were working improperly! To me, all these things are further clear indications that these images do not come from our own imagination but, rather, are being literally transmitted to us from the Lord. If these challenges to hearing are *temporary*, the remedies may center on the obvious: disengaging from excessive activity, deliberately getting more rest, seeking godly counsel from other believers, offering to God the sacrifice of praise, and giving our cares over to the Lord. If the above issues are *on-going*, however, the implication may be that our entire lives may need restructuring and redirecting, and our hearing may guide us first and foremost to this task.

5) *Lack of ongoing repentance and confession in the local Body.* In James 5:16, we read, "Therefore confess your sins to each other and pray for each other so that you may be healed. The prayer of a righteous man is powerful and effective." This verse makes it clear that the effectiveness of our prayer life in its corporate context, including our ability to hear, is connected to our right standing with God, based on regular confession and repentance. God asks us to keep short accounts with Him. It is often assumed that the healing mentioned here is strictly physical, but the Biblical concept of healing always involves the total person: body, soul, and spirit.

6) *Unresolved guilt relating to a specific situation from one's past.* On the simplest level, this subconscious guilt may be due to a lack of repentance, but, more sadly still, it may be the false guilt which comes, as mentioned earlier, from a wrong understanding of the Lord and of His forgiveness. If the latter is the case, the individual may need to delve into God's Word, perhaps with the help of other believers, to learn and to internalize the truth in these matters. If this fails to bring resolution, the person may require some deep inner healing work.

7) *Continued, willful disobedience in some area of one's life.* Psalm 66:18 tells us: "If I had cherished sin in my heart, the Lord would not have listened; but God has surely listened and heard my voice in prayer. Praise be to God, who has not rejected my prayer or withheld his love from me." Scripture is abundantly clear that a persistent state of disobedience and rebellion will separate us from fellowship with the Lord, and consequently block our ability to hear His voice. The message, again, is that of confession and repentance.

8) *Unforgiveness of others, which also leads to broken fellowship with God.* The words of the Lord's Prayer say this most succinctly: "Forgive us our debts, as we also have forgiven our debtors."(Matthew 6:12) We have already dis-

cussed our human tendency to have an unbalanced and unhealthy view of the nature of God, causing us to doubt His good purposes and thus block our hearing. At the opposite end of the spectrum, however, lie our equally destructive attitudes of self-righteousness and self-justified refusal to forgive. Unforgiveness is, in fact, so ingrained in our fallen human nature that we may often not be consciously aware that we are harboring it. Even when we are aware, we grasp at reasons to excuse or vindicate ourselves, particularly in our post-modern, self-centered age. Of course, we are, in reality, objectively incapable of *self*-justification, and this is precisely what Jesus was teaching in His model prayer. Relationship is grounded in a divinely ordained, interactive circle which binds together God, self and others. The sin of unforgiveness will hinder not only our fellowship with others and our own pardon but also, ultimately, our very relationship with the Lord. This is yet another reason why I appreciate the historic liturgy of the Church, because confession, forgiveness and absolution are at the center, in every way, of worship. Not by coincidence, it is, as I write this, Ash Wednesday.

9) *A mocking spirit present in some member of the prayer group.* In such cases, the only solution is to follow the guidelines given in Scripture: that is, to first talk with the person involved and, barring further resolution, to cease praying in the presence of that individual. Not surprisingly, this mocking spirit is often most evident in those to whom we are closest, and the stronger our hearing and giftings become, the more it may manifest. Even Jesus could do few miracles in Nazareth.(See Matthew 13:58)

10) *Inappropriate fear of God stemming from a misunderstood experience in one's personal history.* Speaking for myself, it took me years to realize that I was subconsciously avoiding and sabotaging my own quiet time and, thus, my ability to hear the Lord because, at heart, I was afraid to be alone with Him, afraid of what He might say. I saw Him as harsh and judgmental—just waiting to criticize, punish, or

condemn. Yet, at the same time, I complained because I always felt that I couldn't hear Him for myself as I wanted and needed to. Finally, through Allen, the Lord seemed to say, "You'd be a lot better off if you'd just realize that I'm not your mother!" Again, after a dream I once had which warned of God's coming judgment, Allen thought he heard, "You are too ready to assume that everything is directed at some fault in *you*. That is why you don't hear me more of the time." It is my sincere hope that others will, if necessary, recognize themselves in this paragraph and take the steps of inner healing necessary to correct this particular source of spiritual blockage. In my case, the Lord's instructions to me were, "You need to write one hundred times a day, 'God is not my mother!'"

11) *Our own human inadequacies.* These we must live with for, as the saying goes, God is God, and we are not. He is Creator, and we are creature—and fallen at that. The fallen and finite simply cannot fully comprehend the holy and infinite, and so we see as through a glass, darkly. What Adam and Eve thought they were gaining when they ate the fruit of the Tree of the Knowledge of Good and Evil, they lost instead. That said, we can and must rest in the Lord's assurance that, if we remain in Him and continue to seek, we will hear well enough for His and our purposes. God's intention is to bless, not punish!

12) *Blocks coming from Satan.* We scarcely need to be reminded that we have an adversary, and that he is the enemy of our souls. Nothing is more threatening to Satan than our intimate, personal relationship with the Lord, and many of the blocks listed above are, hence, either caused or vigorously encouraged by Satan. It is therefore no accident that Jesus speaks in such strong metaphors of our hearing-centered connection with Him. He is the true vine, in whom we must abide, the good shepherd, whose voice we must follow, the way, the truth, the gate, the light for our path, our daily bread, our very resurrection and life. Our protection from the

enemy must come from our listening and obeying, and they in turn can only come from our abiding.

13) *Blocks coming from the Lord Himself.* We have periodically been bemused upon discovering that the Lord *Himself* may give a message in such a way as to lead us to a course of thinking or action which we might not so readily follow if we grasped the full picture from the beginning. In other words, the block may actually be divinely engineered. We need look no further than God's directive to Abraham: "Leave your country, your people and your father's household and go to the land I *will* show you."(italics mine) (Gen. 12:1)

Let me give a personal illustration. Having done home church for several years, the word came from several different directions that we were to seek out a local fellowship through a systematic process of visiting churches. We enthusiastically made a list of desired characteristics and began our search for the place that would meet our needs. Now, mind you, the Lord does not deliberately mislead us, but He doesn't say all He knows, either! It's for our own good. As is generally the case, He here combined partial information with a knowledge of our human foibles, for with typical short-sightedness, we thought it was all about us. However, as time went on, it became evident that in each instance we were to discern needed areas of change and address them prophetically with the pastors or leaders. If that word had come in its fullness, I do believe that we would have tried to be obedient, but our enthusiasm in starting the process would likely have been replaced with considerable anxiety and delay.

14) *Inability or unwillingness to praise God.* In addressing blocks to hearing, I have chosen to save for last what is beyond a doubt the most critical issue of all—the inability or unwillingness to praise God for who He is as evidenced in Creation and in salvation history, and for what He has done and is doing in our lives. It is not possible here to adequately delve into the profoundly significant subject of the relationship between praise and hearing, and thus it is my intent to

examine this connection in some depth in the companion to this book entitled <u>Hearing and Healing</u>. For the moment however, and, as a foretaste, I will pass on two words on praise which we have received in recent days.

"A little humility does wonders for the soul, and a good dose of praise puts many things in perspective. Praise also opens up the pathways to hearing Me, for those who cannot truly praise will never be able to hear unless I use them as a temporary agent for some larger purpose. Even in your own lives, the gates will open to hearing if you discipline yourselves to praise even when you don't feel like it. Those who implore Me to heal do not take advantage of the powerful healing of praise, and, because they don't praise, they are also unable to hear the words that I speak to them about their distress. Indeed, it is very much a matter of prideful hearts not being able to turn away from focus on self or self-comfort. These are surely hard things to deeply understand, but I have made living things to function in ways that go far beyond the understanding of physicians and scientists."

And again,

"I AM far more in every respect than you might ever imagine. This is why I have made so much of the theme of praise, for it truly gets to the heart of humble discovery. The more that you are willing to find out about what I have done and what I have made, the deeper is the true, unshakable core of belief which then wants to praise more and more. Many Christians have so limited and structured what they think that they are really unable to praise in terms of pondering the truly incredible things I have done. I AM not at all tame, and I don't like the presumption that My job is to provide material blessings and comfort to those who claim Me. Indeed, it is astonishing, but praise is one of the most difficult things for most to do because it takes them out of control. If they really recognize who I AM, and the vastness and depth and breadth of My work, then they must come to grips with their own sin, pride, lust, greed, and, of course, death, and they must respond to My call. In the end, praise is the utterly essential ingredient— more than anything else."

I feel I must address one other important issue in this chapter, for I suspect that some readers may be wondering about it. Everything I have been discussing thus far presumes a relationship with Christ as Lord and Savior, and this begs an obvious question: Can *unbelievers* hear and be guided by the voice of the Lord, albeit unwittingly? Obviously yes, for otherwise how could they hear the Holy Spirit wooing them to conversion in the first place? And how could they recognize the truth of Scripture when they encountered it? Further, we have all heard of examples of people who, in an isolated instance of hearing, escaped accidents or disasters because they had a strong sense at the last minute that they were to avoid a flight, get off the train, or travel by a different route. History itself is filled with examples of unbelievers who heard and followed a direction from the Lord which served to advance the kingdom of God. Consider, for instance, Rahab, who hid Joshua and Caleb as they spied out the land they were entering or Cyrus, who gave the decree which allowed the Babylonian exiles to return from captivity, though he himself gave the credit for his guidance to the god Marduk or Pharaoh, who appointed Joseph as the second most powerful man in the world, saving Egypt and the surrounding lands from starvation during the seven years of famine or those Chaldean astrologers, the Magi, who followed the star to Bethlehem, there to become the first Gentile worshipers of Christ.

We asked the Lord to give us some further insight into the issues regarding hearing and the unbeliever, and I will relate what we thought we heard. The word also gives some further understanding of the nature of hearing in general:

"I do not exclude unbelievers from hearing, but it is quite a different kind of hearing. I communicate with them at My initiative when I am working out My plans. I do not have the sort of relationship with them which I make available to all who believe in Me, and who are willing to pray and listen and obey. My communication, then, with those who do not believe is functional, to accomplish some goal or to seek to draw them into relationship with Me if they cannot otherwise hear of Me. Believers, on the other hand, can have an open line for guidance, wisdom and all else I offer, whenever they are willing to have the conversation. Of course, sin still distorts the conversation to a degree because a direct word would be so over-whelming that most could not bear even a bit. Yet, I do speak, and My message does get through to those who seek, for they will find. Though sin is a wall, I can still be heard through the wall. That is why healing in the largest sense is so important because it is the damage caused by sin, either your own or that of others, which causes the wall to be built, and I make dismantling the wall a high, high priority. But, too often, even My people are fond of their wall, so they have to hear Me in muffled tones. The good news is that I do get through to all who are willing to listen. Actually, this is why praying with others is so necessary, for they will hear differently through their wall, and the message will become clearer more quickly. Of course, I could just shatter the wall, but humans could not stand that in their present state—even the most committed believers—though a few have come close to hearing My unmuffled voice. I AM far beyond anything you can imagine or comprehend, and your limited vision is both necessary and challenging. It is necessary because your mind would burst if it tried to hold all that I AM, but it is challenging, because you are unable to fully see, and, until I return, you will not really understand. Just know I'm at work; I'm talking; I'm with you."

The joy in hearing for believers is when Jesus, in His Good Shepherd discourse, described being in relationship with Him as hearing and knowing His voice. He added that it was that ongoing, moment-by-moment, Spirit-filled, personal relationship that was meant to lead to life—eternal, of course—but also life in the here and now—abundant, full, overflowing. The Lord explained it to us this way:

"I am about great things in the world. All who believe and are willing to listen and follow will have a part in My plan, but, as you have come to know very well, there are many who ardently believe in Me, yet steadfastly hold that I speak only through My Scriptures. How odd that a living God should be confined that way! I surely do speak through My Scriptures, and they are inviolable, but I surely also speak to anyone who will listen with the application of the Good News to each life. The Gospel is not only a principle of salvation, but it is life to each particular human being, and I come to bring life—abundant and rich."

Lastly, I will pass on this general advice which the Lord gave us concerning the blocks to hearing:

"You can continue working on hearing Me. You know that I desire that all of My people hear Me, but you should also know that there are major barriers to hearing. All of the 'noise' generated by relationships past and present, by circumstances, by unfilled needs and desires, and, yes, even by the Evil One, can block the process or confuse it. However, when My people make a choice to listen and obey, I will make a way. The 'noise' is still there, of course, but it cannot fully block My voice, and the more obedient My people are to the things they understand, the more they will understand."

Chapter 7:
Challenges with Interpretation and Application

Ultimately, of course, the two thorniest issues with regard to prophecy and guidance involve right *interpretation* of what we receive from the Lord, followed by correct practical *application*. For us, these have been by far the most challenging and frustrating aspects of the process of learning to hear and respond to God's voice.

Our Lord delights in the use of rich and complex verbal and visual symbols, and Scripture, our own experience, and the experience of others all confirm that the prophetic word very often comes wrapped in enigmatic packaging. Nonetheless, I believe that the challenges with interpretation and application are definable, and this chapter, while it cannot provide answers to any one person's specific questions regarding these issues, may at least offer some comfort, since all who engage in attempting to hear the Lord seem to wrestle with these same things. I will deal with visions and dreams first.

Visions and dreams, by their very nature, are surely the most difficult to interpret and act upon, since they come couched in such highly symbolic picture language. Scripture testifies to the fact that the prophets, in both the Old Testament and the New, struggled to grasp the meaning of what they were seeing. Daniel was flatly told to seal up his book: his dreams and visions would not be truly understood until the time of the end. I can't help but wonder if he didn't experience the same odd mixture of frustration and curiosity that we so often have!

Allen and I have fared no better than Daniel and countless others, for we have understood but a small percentage of the host of images we have received. Moreover, as regards those dreams and visions which we *have* thought we understood, we have in reality discerned only a tiny fraction of their full meaning. As with Scripture, the depth of the images is unfathomable, the number of facets innumerable.

With time, more insight is often gained into the significance of a vision, dream, or word, though we will not, as Paul says concerning the gifts, discern fully until the Lord returns: "Now I know in part; then I shall know fully, even as I am fully known."(I Cor.13: 12b) Partial revelation, however, despite its challenges, has its charms, for I am frequently fascinated and astonished on looking back at an image or word to see a nuance or a teaching in something hitherto completely hidden. Then, over time, that same process happens again and again with the same message, revealing layer upon layer of meaning. Each time I go through the journals, I find a few things that make me say "Aha!," and I am convinced that God relishes our delight when an understanding, in His timing, is discovered, as though a precious jewel had been unearthed, or a veil suddenly lifted from our eyes. Many visions, dreams, and even words do continue to remain largely a mystery, though as with the prophets of old, the Lord has, on some occasions, graciously illuminated their meaning. The following is an example:

Some time ago, while praying in a small group setting, I suddenly saw just above my head a bunch of wonderfully ripe, purple grapes, and I also had the sense that I could just open my mouth and drink the sweet, refreshing juice which was coming out of its own accord. The Lord explained,

"The grapes demonstrate the abundance of what I have, and they also are one thing with many parts. You must be ready to drink and be refreshed, for I have already told you there will be challenge as well as blessing. The nature of human life is struggle, for sin is rampant, but I provide blessing and provision, and I am an oasis filled with rich grapes pouring refreshment into you in a time of need."

As usual, there were some intriguing interconnections and a depth of other meanings going on here as well. We had just received a copy of <u>Christians for Israel</u> magazine, and, in it, there was a great study on the Hebrew letter *alef*—not only the first letter of the alphabet, but also the letter used to represent the numeral "1." Not by coincidence, of course, I happened to read the article just a day or two after receiving the vision. In it, the author, Pat Mercer Hutchens, notes that *alef*, the first letter of the Hebrew word "echad," is also the word used for "one" in the Shema of Deuteronomy 6:4: "Hear O Israel, the Lord our God, the Lord is One." She writes,

"But what does 'echad' mean? The word begins with alef, the letter for number one. Therefore, does it mean an absolute unity, a unity of essence bonded so tight that any multiplicity is impossible? Traditional Jewish theology says yes. Ben-Yehuda's dictionary lists the root word of 'echad' as meaning 'to unite, or join.' Adam and Eve were said to be one (echad). It takes more than one absolute unity to be united or joined. When Joshua and Caleb came back from spying out the land of Canaan, they brought back *a bunch of grapes* (italics mine), called 'echad.' They were one in unity, yes. There was one bunch of grapes. But, there was a multiplicity of units within the oneness, within the echad. As a person made in the image of God, I have a body, a soul, and a spirit—all bonded into one me, an 'echad.' This supports the Scriptural basis of belief in the unity and oneness of God—yet with different manifestations of that oneness in the Father, Son and Holy Spirit."

Apparently, in the midst of the word of comfort that I received from the Lord, he had decided to provide me with a fascinating little teaching on the Trinity as well!

We thank the Lord for these gracious gifts of insight when we receive them. Nonetheless, our thinking is finite, fallen and tainted by sin, while God's is inscrutably infinite and holy. Hence, I do not believe that we are able to, nor indeed are we meant to, understand everything in this life. Mystery is intrinsic to God's nature, and, in His wisdom, He has chosen to keep much hidden from us. Once, while going through the journals to select material for some writing and agonizing over the decision-making process, I complained to the Lord that I understood so little of what He had given us. He pointed out that that was deliberate and a great blessing, since I could scarcely deal with the sheer volume of what I *could* understand! I already had more than enough material to work with.

Timing, as I have said, also plays a major role in interpretation: for what we *are* meant to understand, we are not necessarily meant to understand *now*. In our experience, certain things have become clearer with the passage of days, months, or years, while others have not been understood at all until illuminated by hindsight. Still other words have been understood well enough to be acted upon but were more strongly confirmed after having done so. Allow me to relate our most recent example of the latter.

This past summer we began to have the sense that we were to take a family trip to Hawai'i to visit old friends there. Naturally, since there are five of us, we were pondering a fairly sizable undertaking. Nonetheless, through confirming words and circumstances, we did have a clear sense of being called to make the trip. We had a delightful reunion with our friends and, also, learned much about the culture and history of Hawai'i. However, while in prayer about the trip a few days after returning, a most astounding thing happened: Allen thought he heard the word "Arcturus."

Remembering that Arcturus is a star, I went to the internet to gather more information, wading through several articles full of astronomical data, none of which seemed to be to the point. Finally, I found a Wikipedia article on Arcturus and, skimming past the math and science sections, was immediately drawn to a paragraph entitled "Cultural Significance." I gasped when I read that Arcturus is the Zenith Star of the Hawaiian Islands and that the Polynesian navigators who settled there had used the star to guide them! The Lord then explained, "I AM Arcturus for your journey. If you stay fixed upon Me, I will lead you to the places you are to go, and also, of course, to your final destination."

How incredible to have gotten not only this stunning confirmation but, also, a renewed awareness of a God who knew our thoughts, heard our prayers, planted the idea and the desire to go in our hearts, and directed our path! As often as this sort of thing happens, it never gets old, but fills us again and again with fresh awe and wonder.

Why then, in nearly all instances involving interpretation, do meanings continue to unfold over time? First, God may be withholding a fuller revelation because we are in some way unprepared for it. Sometimes, the reasons here may be related to *kairos*, or opportune time, meaning that other persons or circumstances need to be moved into place or taken into account in order to enable His plans, in which case premature action on our parts would be counterproductive. At other times, the reasons could be spiritual or emotional, indicating that our *own* hearts or minds are not yet capable of receiving and processing the fuller picture. In this case, a lack of greater understanding could either serve to keep us from acting unwisely or protect us from carrying the burden of a message for which we are not yet ready. In both of these instances, then, timing could also be considered to be another form of divine blockage. Indeed, as regards prophecy, the Lord has indicated to us that man could not bear the weight of knowledge and responsibility which would accompany complete and unhindered revelation. Then again, the reason for delayed or blocked understanding could simply be that we are being called to walk in faith, receiving the stronger confirmation after the fact, as with the Hawai'i trip. Finally, in the broadest sense, interpretation will be blocked, delayed or partial, simply because God is God, and we are not, and, in His wisdom, He has determined not only that we shall see in part but that we shall seldom see the end from the beginning.

The amusing thing, of course, is that, when seen from God's perspective, we might better call the whole process of hearing—gradual or progressive revelation. (Scripture itself being the premier example) Terms like "blockage" and "delay" may more accurately reflect our own human impatience and frustration than God's activity. God is simply about His work in the way He sees fit, and He is not only sublimely enigmatic but rarely, if ever, in a hurry. "My ways are higher than your ways....."

In the midst of it all arises that old dilemma. Given partial revelation, do we take a tentative step in faith, trusting that illumination will come as we do so, or do we hold back, sensing that it would be unwise to presume an understanding and, therefore, the path? *Assuming that our hearts are right,* and allowing for exceptions, I believe that the question is strongly weighted in favor of an *active* but humble seeking: pushing on doors, experimenting, and, even or maybe especially, learning by honest failure. Veiled understanding, then, is not meant to squash our energy and initiative, dampen our spirits, or curtail the learning process, all of which are God-given, but, rather, to submit them all to divine direction. "You pedal, I'll steer."

As another example of hearing in relation to timing, some years ago we spent a year in close relationship with a foreign student who presented himself as the victim of lies, threats, and persecution from wicked people back at home. We regularly prayed with and for him and consistently received Scriptures, words, and visions which seemed to support his testimony. Our affection for him, and his unfortunate skill at deception, blinded us to the truth. When things finally began to unravel, we asked the Lord about His messages to us during that year. He replied, *"Re-look at the prophecies."* I did so, going back through the journals and carefully studying everything the Lord had said about our friend and his situation. What I suddenly realized was that the words and images regarding the lies and deception were all true, but they had, in fact, applied to our friend himself! We needed to reinterpret their message in the light of our new insight. Why were we allowed to be deceived for so long? I can only surmise that, perhaps, our friend needed a year in which he experienced our unconditional love and friendship.

This story of our friend raises the larger issue of being willing to be made fools for Christ. Here is a funny example from our own experience in that regard. Years ago, while at Trinity, we received a name one night while praying about a possible further connection with some Indonesian evangelists whom we had recently met. The name was "Murray Fishbein." Go figure. Along with the name, came the instructions, "Invest overseas." I reasoned that Murray was probably Jewish, and we later got a further sense that he had some connection with New York City. The reader, by now acquainted with my curiosity, shouldn't be surprised to read that I spent some time going through the Pittsburgh and New York City phone books looking for Murray. He wasn't there. Some time afterwards, I did discover, on doing a bit of research, that a man named Fishbein had, in fact, written a book on international investments! So, what was I to make of it all? Were we to do some overseas investing? We scarcely had enough money to get through seminary. Then again, was there some tie-in to evangelism, since that had been the subject of our prayer? And, after all, when you think about it, isn't investing overseas exactly what sharing the gospel in other lands would be?

After we moved to Alabama, Murray's name came back to me one night and, armed with recently acquired internet access, we decided to do a nationwide search. The only Murray Fishbein we found was in Sun City, Arizona, and, well you guessed it, I mustered my courage and gave him a call. Murray answered the phone and, with sweaty palms and quavering voice, I tried to explain about the word we had gotten from the Lord. Murray's demeanor was, as would be expected, distant and not-a-little suspicious. "What are you selling?" he demanded. I earnestly insisted that I *had* nothing to sell. Finally, I ventured, "Did you ever live in New York City?" After a stunned pause, he replied that he had. In the background, I could hear his poor wife repeatedly asking, "Murray, who is it?" I don't remember if I ever managed to ask him about investments, nor do I know what I would have done if he had said that he had actually been involved in investing overseas. I was beyond embarrassed and afraid that they might be starting to think about having the call traced, so I apologized profusely for bothering them and got off the phone.

When we later sat down to pray about the experience, I complained, "Lord, I felt so foolish." I expected empathy, not to mention a pat on the back for my bravery, but His only reply was, "Many times I have asked My people to be foolish." Comforted by the reminder that I was in good company and that there had to be some worthy purpose behind it all, I put the whole matter of Murray to rest, hoping that I had at least witnessed somehow to a relationship with the Lord. It was only two or three years later, when we were in the process of adopting our three Russian children, that the meaning of the message suddenly hit home. We were indeed "investing overseas"—financially surely, but infinitely more importantly, in the lives and destinies of our three children-to-be. Of course, our exchange students also came to mind. *Experience* informs me, however, that the rich layers of meaning in this word will undoubtedly continue to unfold for years to come, and *wisdom* tells me that the returns on our investments will reverberate through all eternity. In recalling this story, I trust that the reader has also enjoyed seeing how intriguingly complicated the threads of such words can get. "My ways are higher than your ways....."

One other example of the challenge involved in interpreting a word or dream or vision concerns determining whether the message is to be taken literally or figuratively, or both. This issue is often raised with regard to dreams or visions of cataclysmic natural phenomena such as earthquakes, fires, tornadoes, and volcanoes. In these instances, the Lord may be simply speaking of a literal event, in order that we might pray that warnings be heeded. Often, however, the message may also be seen as symbolic of economic, political, social, or spiritual upheaval, since a natural event may either reflect or predict its more figurative counterpart. Thus, in ways that are beyond our comprehension, there is a profound spiritual connection between what happens in the spiritual realm and what happens in the natural world.

In January of 2001, I had a dream one night in which I had a sense of feeling two earthquakes which occurred within a short time of one another. Shortly afterwards, I read in the news of two real earthquakes—one in India and one in Pakistan. When we prayed about this, Allen heard the Lord say, "These are symbolic of political and spiritual uprisings in these countries. Natural events often fore-tell the other events of history."

Our human tendency is to think one-dimensionally, yet even a symbol itself can have double meanings. For instance, does fire suggest judgment or revival? Doesn't judgment often and of necessity precede revival? Is the image of a roaring lion a symbol of Satan looking for whom he may devour, or is it Jesus, the Lion of Judah, fierce in His protection of His people? Does a vision of a serpent represent a warning of Satan's deception or, as with the serpent on the pole in the wilderness, healing and salvation? Only further prayer and discernment can sort these things out, and of course, sometimes both meanings may apply.

I will relate one other personal instance of struggling with inter-pretation and application. While we loved Ambridge, summers in our old row house proved to be suffocatingly hot. Sleeping in our second-floor bedroom was sometimes well-nigh impossible, and cooking meals often left me drenched with sweat. We were hesitant to have air-conditioning installed, especially since our funds were low, but we prayed about the matter, and Allen received a Scripture verse relating how Simon of Cyrene had been pressed into service to carry Jesus' cross. (See, for example, Mark 15:21)

The basic interpretation was pretty clear: Simon's conscription had allowed Jesus some relief from His suffering. The problem was, from whose vantage point were we to operate? Like Simon, were we to accept some suffering as a part of our service to the Lord in that place and at that time? Or, like Jesus, were we to graciously receive the help? In the end, we opted for suffering, partly because we were concerned about spending the money, but, also, partly because we chose to err on the side of suffering rather than comfort. I find it interesting that the decisions we make in these circumstances often say a lot about where we are in our relationship with the Lord at the time, and we, perhaps particularly I, being still in recovery from my cancer surgery, were zealous not to cause offense. From our present vantage point, however, I think we would be more likely to accept the relief and also to believe that God would provide in the midst of it. Thus, as usual, the issues often seem to reach beyond the immediate situation. The Lord could have simply said: "get" or "don't get an air conditioner." By being more enigmatic, I suspect that he was probing our hearts with regard to issues of receiving and trusting.

Finally, as concerns interpretation, I find myself periodically forced back to this most basic question: "Lord, are these things we are seeing and hearing *really* from You at all?" Assuming that we are in right relationship with the Lord and seeking His protection, I believe that the visions and words themselves *are* from Him. At one point in our early learning process when we doubted the validity of what we were receiving, Allen thought he heard the Lord say, "Accept the images. The meaning will become clear." The challenges, the Lord seemed to be saying, do lie with our efforts to interpret, and it is here that error is apt to creep in. As illustrated above, there have been times when I was absolutely certain that I understood what the Lord was saying, only to eventually discover, to my chagrin, that the meaning was quite different than what I had thought. Often this was due to my own preconceptions of what I thought a vision, dream, or word should mean, or what I wanted them to mean. Here, again, is one way in which the Lord keeps us humble: He will never allow Himself to be fully figured out! In the case of our friend from seminary, I feel that our year of blindness provided a safe haven for him, a secure place in which healing could be possible, and while, to our eyes, that healing did not appear to happen, I pray that it yet may.

Scripture itself shows that validity and right interpretation have always been thorny issues. It is interesting to read that King Nebuchadnezzar needed help in knowing the content, origin, and true meaning of his prophetic but forgotten dream of the colossal statue. Daniel related the dream, confirmed its divine source, and applied his own correct interpretation of it through the Lord: "The great God has shown the king what will take place in the future. The dream is true and the interpretation is trustworthy."(Daniel 2:45b)

We observe two things in this story. First, since Nebuchadnezzar was an unbeliever, Daniel was called to affirm that his dream was in fact from the true God—in other words to validate it. Second, it is clear here that the validity of the dream and its right interpretation are two separate yet connected issues. Though the dream had been from God, the king still awaited a right interpretation. *"Accept the images. They will become clear."*

As long as we are clothed in earthly flesh, right interpretation and application will remain challenging. However, we are only called to be faithful in prayer, as well as humble and honest before the Lord. He knows our frailties, and He is more than able to make clear what He needs to, when He needs to.

Chapter 8:
Teaching Others to Hear

The Lord has consistently reminded us that the ability to hear for personal direction and guidance, as distinct from the office of prophet, is something that He intends for *everyone*. It must be so. The logic is inescapable. If Jesus is the Bread of Life and, if man does not live by bread alone, but by every word which comes from the mouth of God, and if it is He who commands us to ask for daily bread, then that bread cannot be physical provision only, but it is the very life of our communion with God.

If the Lord's sheep are those who know His voice and follow, there should be no reason for believers to be in the dark about the Lord's specific will for their own lives. That so many Christians have gone to their graves never knowing and applying this simple truth is a tragedy of profound proportions and eternal consequences. It is therefore my highest prayer that this book (and others like it) will provide the necessary tools and incentive, the concrete practical instruction and example necessary to assist in the nitty-gritty process of finding and following the unique path which God has ordained for each life.

My purpose in this chapter is to emphasize that, though this process is far more art than science, it is an utterly and easily duplicable process. The best and, frankly, the only way to teach others to hear is to tell about it, teach about it, demonstrate it, and live it—witnessing consistently to the results. I have already laid out the basics required for effective hearing, but I will reiterate them here.

1) The fellowship and accountability of small prayer groups

2) Consistent discipline in terms of personal quiet time and Scripture study

3) Faithful journaling with respect to one's prayer life, daily experiences, and what one thinks he or she may be hearing from the Lord, as well as a good system to keep it all organized

4) Inner receptiveness to the Lordship of Christ and the baptism and leading of the Holy Spirit

5) Understanding of the processes and parameters outlined elsewhere in this book with regard to such issues as blockages, interpretation, application, discernment, and alertness to ways in which God may be speaking, and why

Since my emphasis here is on modeling the process of hearing, I will offer some illustrations of how that has worked for us. Some time ago, we announced, among some friends, that we had decided to meet once a week with anyone who wished to learn more about the topic of hearing God. Our friend Cindy took us up on the offer. She sat on our sofa as we related the same things which I discuss here, and we asked her if she desired to receive the baptism of the Holy Spirit. She said "yes," and we laid hands on her and anointed her. Later that very same evening, as we entered into prayer about a concern in her life, she matter-of-factly announced that the Lord had given her a picture, a vision, concerning the particular issue with which she was struggling. I asked her if she had ever had a vision before, and she said "no." Before the evening was over, the three of us had each been able to share and discuss the words and images which the Lord had given us for her situation, providing her with the wisdom, peace, comfort, and direction which she needed. She was thrilled and excited, and returned week after week, now confident that she could begin to hear the Lord's answers to those areas of her life which troubled her. She would regularly exclaim, "Why wouldn't anyone want to do this?" Why, indeed?

Some months later, she invited two co-workers to join her in a small lunch-time prayer group at her office, and she simply duplicated what she had learned and experienced with us. To her delight, when she laid hands on and prayed for these believing Christians, they too immediately began to receive the Lord's ministrations. These occurrences are not aberrations. A study of the New Testament shows us that this was designed by God to be the normative pattern for the Church.

In like manner, our then seventeen-year old daughter Alicia astonished Allen by asking him some pointed questions. She had been observing our prayer life for a year-and-a-half, watching as we prayed and listened, notebook and pen in hand, and she was increasingly curious. It had become clear to her that we were listening to God, as we prayed, and writing down what we thought we were hearing. Now, with enough English skills to express herself, she began pumping her father for information. Could we teach her to do what she saw us doing? Would we pray with her and show her how to hear? She had grasped the obvious: *isn't it a lot more fun to talk to God if you can hear His side of the conversation?* Two nights later, she sat with us as we laid hands on her and baptized her in the Holy Spirit, asking the Lord to give her spiritual gifts for ministry, to speak to her, and to help her to learn to hear His voice. Almost immediately, she began receiving prophetic dreams and visions which continue on a regular basis to this day. "And afterward," says the prophet Joel, "I will pour out my Spirit on all people. Your sons and daughters will prophecy, your old men will dream dreams, your young men will see visions. Even on my servants, both men and women, I will pour out my Spirit in those days."(Joel 2, vs. 28, 29)

Likewise, some years ago our son Max told us of a dream he had which we understood to be clearly prophetic. When we offered him the in-filling of the Holy Spirit, he responded positively and, almost immediately afterwards, had another obviously prophetic dream. We suggested that he begin to write down his dreams, but I wondered to myself if he really would, His high-energy, thirteen year-old brain was, as one might expect, typically far more focused on basketball and computer games than it was on matters requiring spiritual discipline. However, on inquiring, I was surprised to find that he had in fact at least tried to record his experience.

Again, not long ago, both of our daughters began having dreams urging them to share the Gospel with one particular person. In one instance, these dreams occurred on the same night! Since Scripture says not only that a thing is confirmed by the testimony of two or three witnesses (Matt. 18:16), but also that the divine source of dreams is confirmed by repetition (Gen. 41:32), we felt that we needed to strongly encourage and assist them in following through.

These and other experiences with our own kids lead us to the reminder that *children* also want and need to be in relationship with the Lord, and to hear His voice and be guided by Him. Hence, below are some guidelines for others with regard to the issue of children and hearing:

> 1) Do not assume that children and teenagers are too young to begin to hear and follow the Lord, for they can do so, and should be gently encouraged in this regard. They may, in fact, be more receptive to hearing than adults, as their spirits are more ingenuous and less skeptical. The prophet Samuel was probably about twelve years old when the Lord called to him in the Tabernacle, and he responded; likewise Jesus, at twelve, was found by his parents in the Temple where He was already "about His father's business." However, Scripture also reminds us that they each necessarily continued to grow in wisdom, in stature, and in favor with God and with men. (See 1 Sa. 2:26 and Luke 2:52)

> 2) The Lord will speak to each child in ways that are age-appropriate, suitable for that child's situation, and unique to his or her personality and nature.

> 3) Younger children may indeed be hearing from the Lord, but they may or may not recognize it as such, nor do they yet have the discernment which comes with emotional and spiritual growth. A wise parent, trained in the hearing process, can provide gentle input and guidance.

> 4) All children should be encouraged to hear and experience the Lord through the reading and studying of Scripture, as well as through the wonder of what God has made. Some years ago, as I was putting our son Max to bed, he enthused, "Mom, did you know that humans have six hundred muscles? God did that." He had heard God speaking of Himself through His creation.

5) Recognize that, as with adults, learning to hear for children is a process which matures over time. Moving too fast with them would be frightening and disconcerting, and younger children, especially, should not yet have the responsibility which comes with hearing. Children need the opportunity to be children, under godly guidance. God will work by appropriate degrees in each of their lives, teaching them what they are ready to hear. In the midst of this, recognize that one of the hardest things for kids, even harder than for adults, is learning the lesson of waiting for God's timing. They want everything *now.*

6) As children grow into their later teen and early adult years, they should be encouraged to grow into their hearing as well. As mentioned earlier, we are seeing that our two teenage daughters, and now our son as well, are already hearing God speaking through dreams and visions, as well as in other ways, though they still very much need our wisdom, discernment, guidance, prayer, and oversight to help them sort out and understand what they are receiving.

Speaking of wanting things *now,* I will remind the reader again of one other indispensable element when teaching others about hearing—that of waiting on the Lord during prayer. In our experience, we have observed that this simple discipline of waiting seems to be one of the hardest for people to accept and adapt to. I believe that there are several reasons for this. First, we are hampered by our Western mindset, which tells us that we must always be in control, always accomplishing something through our own initiative. Second, we are constantly pressured by our hectic schedules. Third, those of us who have grown up in the Church are the recipients of much unfortunate conditioning. I, for one, had never been taught, or even exposed to, the concept of listening prayer. Last, most people find it excruciatingly uncomfortable to abide a space of silence in a group setting. Something within us feels compelled to jump in and fill the void, and, almost inevitably, someone will break the silence simply out of distress or embarrassment. (This, by the way, is another good argument for small groups, for it takes some time for people to become comfortable enough with each other to tolerate the silence.)

Despite all of these impediments, however, I cannot emphasize enough that part of teaching others to hear is an insistence upon allowing adequate space for hearing the Lord's response to our prayers. It doesn't matter how many questions we ask of God if we don't stop long enough to hear the answers. It strikes me as both amusing and sad that the same folks, who would never think of being so inconsiderate in human conversation as to talk endlessly without letting the other person get a word in edgewise, have no qualms about doing that very thing with the Lord of the universe!

That Jesus' disciples often fell asleep (and got scolded for it!) while they were in prayer with Him suggests that He both engaged in and modeled lengthy periods of silent waiting and listening. "Could you men not keep watch with me for one hour?" He asked Peter in Gethsemane. (Matt. 26:40) Waiting is a discipline that God both expects and honors. Waiting, of course, does not guarantee that He will choose that *particular* time to address the matter we have raised. In our case, we sometimes discern, after a period of quiet, that the Lord is not ready to speak to that concern, and we go on to the next one.

I will close by encouraging the reader, once he or she has begun the process of hearing and has gained a little confidence, to pass on the blessing by teaching others to do the same. In my opinion, there is no greater gift.

Chapter 9:
Lessons Learned from the Journals

Some time ago I made an inventory of the spiritual lessons I had learned from rereading our prayer journals over the years. They are as follows:

> 1) I was embarrassed to realize how much of what we were concerned, or even panicked about, at any given time was at best silliness and at worst a serious lack of trust. I became painfully aware of all of our petty thinking, misguided concerns, and self-centeredness, and I had ample opportunity to see how *patient* the Lord is with our human frailties.

> 2) On the other hand, I did see a lasting record of our intercession for others, the Church and the world, and I was astonished at how many prayers, both for ourselves and for others, had been answered. I was able to see how *faithful* the Lord is.

> 3) I was acutely aware of our constant agony of waiting. In some ways, it seems that we spent ninety percent of our time in the hard process of being made ready for the work to come, and in waiting for answers, instructions or direction. In the end, we found that God had always done more than we could ever possibly have hoped or imagined, but He did it *His* way and in *His* time. How seldom are our ways God's ways. We saw how *wise* God is. In his insightful manual, According to the Pattern,

Father Ed Stube, founder of the Holy Way, said this in speaking of Jesus' time in the wilderness:

"We too, when we receive the power of the Spirit, must spend some time in the wilderness. We do not simply live happily ever after. The Lord has to break down some old attitudes, ego-trips, and tendencies to misuse the Lord's gifts. The chaff in our lives needs to be burned up in a baptism of fire. In fact, those whom the Lord really uses will spend considerable time in the wilderness or in the fire, getting purged and reconstructed according to His specifications and made ready for His use. My own experience has been that long periods of preparation, seeking the Lord and being worked over, are interspersed with short and glorious intervals of seeing the Lord use me in ministry."[viii]

4) I realized how little we truly know and understand of the mind of God. Each vision, each word, each page of our journals, reveal volumes of Biblical theology. I saw how *great* God is.

5) I saw, in retrospect, that *everything* we had experienced was only for our growth and blessing. Despite my anger, fear, frustration, and complaint at the way that it seemed that God was or was not working at any given time, in the end I saw how *good* He is.

In closing, if I were asked to distill what I understand to be the essence of God's heart from all our years of seeking to communicate with Him in listening prayer, I would answer by way of two fundamental *questions*. The first is, "What does God want *from* us?" I submit that He wants obedience, for our sake, and our fellowship, for both our sakes, because He loves us and made us for Himself. The second is, "What does God want *for* us?" I believe that, above all, He wants our redemption, followed by the abundant life of joyful service which results from hearing and acting upon His specific instructions for our lives.

Having said all of this, it is my hope that, as I now relate this longer example of listening from our own journey, the reader may be better able to picture how we prayed and heard, and how we lived out that hearing. Beyond that, it is my earnest desire that the reader may gather the courage and enthusiasm from our own experiences to embark on a great spiritual adventure of his or her own!

PART THREE

AN EXTENDED LIFE EXAMPLE

Two Eggs, Three Yolks:
A Story of Adoption

The story of how we came to adopt three Russian siblings begins on the scorching July afternoon in 1995 when Allen, on arriving home from his Clinical Pastoral Education class at the VA hospital in Pittsburgh, reported, with a mixture of awe, trepidation and bemusement, that he thought the Lord was calling us to adopt a child.

We were already completely absorbed in fulfilling requirements for graduation and ordination to the priesthood, overseeing the care of my elderly parents back in Connecticut, and beginning the search for a full-time rector's position, when the Lord chose to interject this startling new thought into our plans. What's more, I received this message of potential parenthood with mixed emotions. As all who knew us so poignantly recalled, our seminary adventure had been preceded by and, in fact, prompted by, my hysterectomy. While I had had a few bouts of tearful self-pity over our lack of children, adoption had, for some reason, never been a serious consideration.

We immediately began to ponder this unsettling new word and to pray about it. However, we knew that our job search was likely to call us away from Ambridge and, probably, from Pennsylvania as well. So we decided to wait until we had relocated in another state to follow through with a home study and other concrete adoption efforts. Our lives were further complicated by the situation with my parents since my mother, now in a nursing home, was suffering from dementia and failing rapidly, while my father, still living at home alone, was beginning to show early signs of Alzheimer's. Our weeks were soon to be consumed with lengthy drives between Ambridge and Illinois to prepare for two ordinations, and Ambridge and Connecticut to check on my parents. At the same time, we were diligently applying and interviewing for the rectorship of a parish.

Despite these obstacles and distractions, from the time that we received the word to adopt, we determined to be diligent in prayer about the matter. Though we prayed regularly over the next few months, we got no specifics at all concerning the course we should pursue. The only thing that I did have an initial sense about was that I wanted a girl. Who would this child be, and where would we find her?

The Lord's early words to us concerning this adoption were always enticing, yet always enigmatic enough to keep us guessing. The very first thing we thought we heard was, "A child is part of your healing." "How would that be?" I mused, as I turned the thought over and over in my mind. The notion was both strangely attractive and not a little intimidating, for, having recently gone through a lengthy and difficult period of inner healing, I wasn't sure how much more I could endure!

At various other times in our prayer, the Lord would refer us to Scripture verses on the desperate plight of the fatherless and orphans, and this certainly gave us a general sense of our call, but beyond this, in response to our anxious questionings, the Lord simply said, "Be still and know that I am God."

Our first concrete instructions were to begin to talk to some people. "Begin seeking," the Lord said. "You are free to do that." We soon found ourselves in conversation with numerous adoptive parents. Many of them were classmates and associates—people with whom we had been in daily contact for several years. Yet we had never deliberately discussed this most significant aspect of their lives with any of them. These conversations encouraged us and spurred us on, yet gave us little sense of definite direction.

The Lord further reminded us that the adoption process was much like the process of finding a rector's position. "You have to push on doors, and I'll open them," He urged. Through it all, we had a beginning sense of being moved along by the Lord's unseen hand, but we seemed to be walking through a vast gray haze, for clarity eluded us.

As I now began to think seriously about the realities of an adoption, I started to experience some anxieties about the inevitable changes which would result in my life, and I would periodically bring these up to the Lord. On one occasion, I asked Him how I would have the energy to take care of a child. He replied, "It won't make you too tired, and it will keep you young." This truth left me dubious, but it certainly was a well-calculated appeal to self-interest! In hindsight, I can say that He was absolutely right. On another occasion, I asked the Lord how I could possibly do the writing I felt I was being called to do and still take care of a child. I wonder now how it was that it never occurred to me that it was precisely the adoption that I would be led to write about!

As might be expected, however, we spent most of our prayer time intensely focused on the choice of this child who would be ours. The Lord, well aware of my consistent and determined need to try to figure things out, cautioned, "Let your heart choose, and not your mind." Since my natural inclination was to trust my mind over my heart, I should have recognized that the Lord was using even this process to work a bit of healing in me, for the need to know was in reality a need to control. However, by far His most intriguing word on the choice of our child was this: *"Even if you think you've picked, I've picked."* Contrary to the Lord's advice not to think too much, we pondered this divine mystery until our heads hurt, but we could never succeed in unraveling its threads! Nonetheless, this was to be the word that would ring in our ears throughout the challenging months ahead, and the one on which the entire adoption would hinge.

Our ministry call, as it eventually turned out, was to a parish in Mentone, Alabama, and we arrived here in June of 1996. With the Lord's exhortation still in mind, we shortly thereafter applied to the Department of Human Resources to do a home study. Our initial desire was that we focus on a girl child, perhaps of infant to toddler age. Since we had few financial resources after four years in seminary, a state agency made the only sense as a place to start, because their home studies were done free of charge.

The home study process was finally completed, and we began to wait for news of an available child. Meanwhile, we also talked with both our family physician and my gynecologist, in the hopes that they might lead us to a young girl who had chosen not to keep her baby. While out shopping in Ambridge one day, I had even purchased a toddler's Peter Rabbit cup and plate set! I was acting in faith, and this was my down payment on the adoption.

Several months passed by most uneventfully as we waited to hear something from DHR. We made a few periodic calls to attempt to jar them into some action, but to no avail. On two occasions, we did get a copy of a general mailing offering large sibling groups of older and severely abused children, but, while our hearts went out to these kids, this seemed far from our vision of adopting one infant girl. We seemed mired in a strange admixture of waiting, urgency and massive confusion, and we often wondered if we were on the right track at all.

At times, we thought of international adoption. In fact, we had gotten several Scriptures from the Lord over the previous months of prayer which seemed to point toward care of the foreigner and the alien, but two things always stopped us. The first was the obvious lack of the financial resources necessary to undertake an international adoption. The second was the firm instruction we had gotten from the Lord regarding doors: we were allowed to push on them but not to batter them down nor decide, in advance, which ones would or should open. Further, we were not to close any doors ourselves, as that was to be the Lord's prerogative. Hence, amidst great uncertainty and with gradually dimming hope, we continued to stick with DHR and to wait. At one point, when we asked the Lord if we were really to have an infant, he obliquely replied, "DHR is a doorway to begin the process. I will manage the circumstances; you keep pushing on doors."

The Lord, of course, knew our confusion, and at one point He gave us this reassuring Scripture: "Though I have been speaking figuratively, a time is coming when I will no longer use this kind of language but will tell you plainly...."(John 16:25) We may not have known what we were doing, but we were consoled with the knowledge that the Lord surely did, and He would, in His good time, make clear what was necessary. It was this and other words of encouragement that kept us hanging on through this emotionally difficult time.

Meanwhile, however, other events in our life were starting to take a most interesting turn. In May of 1997, our first spring in our Mentone house, we bought some flowers and bulbs to plant in our front beds, hoping to dress up the house a bit. One sunny late morning, I stepped outside to see how the young plants were doing and was walking across the yard when I spotted a blue car just pulling into our long driveway. On our rural road, such an event was a rare occurrence, and I was somewhat nervous. I thought seriously about heading back to the front door, but somehow my feet remained planted as firmly as my flowers.

A young blond woman emerged from the car clutching a stack of papers and approached me with bold enthusiasm. Her first words were neither "Hello," nor "How are you?" but, "Would you be interested in hosting an exchange student?" I was so taken aback that all I could manage to mutter was, "Well, ...uh, I really don't know." The woman didn't miss a beat, but continued to talk energetically about the prospect of our being host parents. It would have been difficult enough to deal with an intrusive door-to-door salesman, but here I was, face to face with a total stranger who was eagerly trying to convince me to spend the next year of my life living with someone else's teenager!

In truth, the experience of having an exchange student was not utterly new to me, since Allen had been, for several years, the Youth Exchange Coordinator for his Rotary Club back in Massachusetts, and we had hosted a lovely German girl for a week during the early 1980s. Nonetheless, I was decidedly uncomfortable with the pressure I felt being exerted by this woman, and I was silently wondering how to excuse myself when she suddenly invited herself into the house!

Soon, we were seated on the sofa, pouring over the pictures and applications of several students which had been spread out across the coffee table. It was in the midst of this bewildering activity that Allen walked in, only to be cheerily confronted with the same blunt question: "Hi, would you be interested in hosting a foreign exchange student?" The upshot of it all was that a few weeks later we were the proud host parents of Hanno, a sixteen-year old boy from Germany. We soon fell in love with him and had a great year, even taking him along with us on a trip to Israel with a group from our church. I might add that this blond woman, Kimberly by name, was to grow to be a dear friend.

Meanwhile, we had heard almost nothing from DHR regarding adoptable children. During these long months of waiting, we continued to periodically contemplate and pray about the possibility of an overseas adoption, but we held fast to the Lord's instructions that we were to take no initiative on our own to close any doors.

Amusingly enough, during this time Allen was given a most interesting vision. He wrote:

"I saw an image of two men in business suits looking at something through a large window. It seemed like a room in a hospital nursery, but it was very dimly lit. The men looked vaguely foreign, but not extraordinarily so, and they were white, I thought. The suits were wool and not very fashionable—rather staid. One of the suits was brown and, perhaps, one of the men had a mustache. They both were tallish and rather slender."

At the time, we had no sense whatsoever of the implications of the vision, despite the fact that it had come during prayer about the adoption. We dutifully stayed with DHR and waited, but with waning hope and interest. Two factors were at work. One was the ongoing lack of response from DHR, and the second was our exchange student experience which had affected us so profoundly. We began to genuinely wonder if we had really heard the Lord right to begin with. Perhaps the word about a child had really been about our exchange student all along.

Upon our return from our Israel trip, our hearts began to be heavy with the thought of Hanno's inevitable June departure, and so we decided on another exchange student for the following year: Revital, a vivacious and engaging girl from Holland. We began to communicate with her, and we looked forward enthusiastically to her year with us. All the while, our adoption efforts remained barren, and, frustrated and discouraged, we found ourselves increasingly losing the vision.

Finally, one morning in March of 1998, I sat down to have my usual morning quiet time and wistfully wrote these words: "Lord, I have come to realize that perhaps the word about the adoption did have to do with our ministry to exchange students. If that is true, it is a relief, for I have really not had much heart for the other lately. Perhaps I am to raise spiritual children. Lord, I would ask if that was indeed Your meaning and my purpose." I immediately and strongly got the following Scripture from II Corinthians 3:11: "And if what was fading away came with glory, how much greater is the glory of that which lasts!" Again, I failed to grasp the implications of the Scripture I had received. The words I had penned seemed to have a ring of finality, and I was oddly content or, perhaps, comfortably resigned.

However, it was a mere three weeks or so later that I had another amazing experience. I had again sat down to have my quiet time, but, after praying for a short while, I did something quite unusual for me. I arose instead, went to the family room, and turned on the TV, flipping to the Trinity Broadcasting Network just in time to catch the closing portion of a Bible study by Marilyn Hickey. Her thesis, illustrated with several examples from Scripture, was this: "Every dream that is from God must die, but He will resurrect it." This statement impacted me so greatly that I quickly arose again, returned to my desk, and wrote the thesis sentence in my journal. Ironically, I'm not sure just how clearly I made any connections.

Some time, shortly after this, finally sensing a release, Allen and I phoned DHR and asked them to take our names off of their waiting list. We were busy with church, with Hanno, and with the prospect of Revi's year ahead. In addition, we had finally made the decision to move my father to a nursing home near us in Alabama, and so we flew to Connecticut to undertake the enormous task of emptying out his house and putting it up for sale. We also decided to make a trip to Germany to visit Hanno and his family. Our lives were more than full, and we never gave the adoption another serious thought.

Nearly one year later, in March of 1999, Allen received an invitation, along with the other clergy in the diocese, to go to The Club in Birmingham to have dinner and hear an address by George Carey, the then Archbishop of Canterbury. The night's weather was dramatic and memorable with torrential rains and violent gusts of cold wind.

The ballroom at The Club was elegantly set for dinner for about six hundred people. However, since we were still fairly new in the diocese and knew only a small handful of clergy, we spent the hour before the meal floating about rather pathetically in a sea of unfamiliar faces. The room hummed with the sound of hundreds of voices engaged in polite conversation, but we somehow seemed a tiny, mostly silent island in its midst.

After two or three brief exchanges, we ended up alone in the center of the room, no doubt looking rather at loose ends. Suddenly, from the crowd emerged a couple, the wife of whom, from her black shirt and clerical collar, was obviously a priest. They approached us and struck up a conversation, and we soon discovered that we had once lived in Massachusetts in towns only thirty minutes apart. It was soon announced that dinner was ready to be served, and we were all asked to find tables and be seated. Sensing that we knew few people at the gathering, this couple, Ben and Kathryn, invited us to join them at a table for eight.

As we settled into our chairs, Ben, still making conversation, asked us if we had any children. "Well, not exactly," I replied, "we have exchange students!" His tongue-in-cheek response was, "We just went to Russia and bought two children." (Anyone who has done an overseas adoption can grasp the humor in that remark, though I hasten to add that of course the fees are for the services rendered, and not for the child!)

As the salad was served, Kathryn began filling us in on their story, focusing especially on her daughter Gulia and the difficult conditions in her orphanage. Then, with a certain intensity, she began to tell of Gulia's best friend, a girl named Oksana. Kathryn described her as a beautiful and sensitive girl of about twelve, with long blond hair. Oksana, she said, also wanted very badly to be adopted, and Kathryn had a heart to see that happen. To underscore Oksana's desire, Kathryn told of Gulia's going-away party. It seems that, as the two girls tearfully said their good-byes, Oksana lifted Gulia's chin, looked into her eyes, and said, "Don't cry, Gulia. I will see you in America." It was a second-hand statement made halfway around the world by a child we had never laid eyes on, but its blind conviction and against-all-odds determination and faith were to change our lives forever.

What happened next still astonishes me, as it no doubt astonished everyone else seated at our table, for I suddenly began to weep uncontrollably. One by one, I proceeded to produce several soggy napkins-worth of tears, while the others at the table, probably equally chagrined, focused politely on their salads, lifting their eyes only occasionally to give me a quick but kindly glance. After a good twenty minutes of this, I excused myself, got up, and fled to the ladies' room, past hundreds of clergy and the Archbishop of Canterbury, all the while still sobbing with yet another limp napkin pressed to my nose. I locked myself in a stall and continued to bawl. I was puzzled, confused, and agitated. "What in the world is wrong with me?" I asked myself. I even began to feel some anger, not a small amount of which was directed at God. I had, after all, put this whole adoption thing aside and was quite comfortable, thank you. What right did He have to blind-side me and rip my heart open? Or was it my heart that was deciding?

When I felt I had regained enough composure to be an acceptable dinner companion, I returned to the table, but, as I sat down, another flood of tears poured forth. Everyone else was on their dessert, while my salad still sat there, half-eaten. As I poked at my chicken, Allen gave me several consoling looks and comforting pats on the back. At last, with the evening drawing to a close, Kathryn and Ben knowingly offered, "Look, there's obviously something going on here. Perhaps we need to talk further. Here is our card. If you'd like, give us a call."

Allen and I drove home in a blinding rainstorm, our long silences punctuated by short episodes of thinking out loud to each other. That night and the next day, we felt compelled to again pray about the issue of adoption, centered this time on Oksana, and we immediately felt a release as well as an unmistakable urging to move forward. This was it, we sensed. We called Ben and Kathryn and drove to their home to talk and pray. On leaving, Kathryn gave us a few group photos taken at Gulia's going-away party. However, I was still anxious. How could we incorporate this adoption into our busy lives, and how would the addition of our own children affect our relationships with our exchange students? The Lord's response was clear: "This is not just about fulfilling your needs, though I will certainly do that as well. You are blessed to be a blessing, and I will provide what is necessary to fulfill My commitments." The idea that these were the Lord's commitments, and not ours, filled me with astonishment and wonder.

We began to include this new adoption concern into our daily prayer life together, and we continued to get confirmation that the pursuit of a Russian adoption, focused on Oksana, was indeed the path. Marilyn Hickey's theme rushed forcefully back to my mind, for the dream of adoption, which had died, was now suddenly being resurrected.

In retrospect, we would realize that the Lord had not really forgotten or put aside the matter at all. On reviewing our journals, we saw that we had continued to get words, Scriptures and visions pertaining to the adoption, though we hadn't been able to recognize them. I later chuckled to myself as I came upon these little tidbits: "rubles," "Ukraine," "Izvestia," "Moussorgsky" (the Russian composer), an image of the Kremlin. Most amazing, in January of 1999, Allen had received an exploratory employment letter from a church in another state. When we had prayed about the possibility of taking this position, the Lord had shown Allen an image of a large, gangly brown bear which was standing upright and moving its head back and forth sideways as if to say "no," in a classic gesture. The bear, we now remembered, was the symbol of Russia. If we had moved, we could not have been at the dinner, met Ben and Kathryn, or heard the story of Oksana. A week after meeting Ben and Kathryn, I asked the Lord if we were actually going to go to Russia, and when we would go. His adroit answer was, "*Bear* with me a while longer."

The Lord's other words to us during this time were comforting but, to our minds, frustratingly unspecific. As to our ongoing queries regarding the choice of the child, he replied, "Don't make it so complicated. However you proceed, you will end up with what I wish, if you are genuinely seeking My will." When I pleaded confusion, He said, "Of course you're confused. Part of dependence is not having absolute certainty. It is good news, for it means your heart is waiting." The wait, it seems, was only beginning. Things were starting to fall into place a bit, but the subsequent days of prayer and discernment proved to be far less fruitful than we, in our limited reasoning, would have wished.

After a few weeks, Allen began to experience a strong sense that he wanted not only one child, a girl, but a boy as well. I balked at the thought. After all, it was frightening enough to think of the responsibility of caring for one child, never mind two. The thought of a second child had previously never entered our minds. We soon came to the point where we couldn't even pray effectively about this together, as our divergent wills drowned out our ability to hear what the Lord might be saying. Frustrated, we called Kathryn and asked her to drive out from Huntsville and pray with us about the question of a second child.

In the meantime, we had excitedly brought the few pictures we had of the kids at the orphanage to our church to share, and an older woman quickly expressed some interest in Oksana. Since we were now, albeit somewhat unwillingly on my part, at least considering two children, we put the thoughts of Oksana aside. For one thing, someone else had shown some interest in her. For another, Kathryn believed, based on having seen no other siblings of Oksana's at the orphanage, that she was an only child. We now began searching the few pictures we had from the orphanage to find another girl and a suitable boy, perhaps a sibling pair, and we began to focus on a little girl named Katya.

In the midst of all of this, Kathryn did drive to our house one morning, and we sat on the sofa to pray about the idea of adopting two children. In a moment reminiscent of our search for an exchange student, the orphanage pictures were spread out on the coffee table in front of us. After we had been in deep prayer for some time, Kathryn looked up, glanced most deliberately at me, and spoke. "Well," she said thoughtfully, "I'm not sure you're going to like this, but I don't think it's two. I think it's three." We gasped.

She proceeded to describe a vision she had seen as she was looking at a group picture which included Katya. A strong beam of light had appeared, having three rays. The first was pointed down, seemingly toward Katya, while the other two pointed straight outwards in opposite directions, as though directed at two other children not in the picture and not together either. We were in shock. We entered back into prayer, and Allen pleaded, "Lord, we don't normally ask You for signs, but this is really serious! If You do intend for us to adopt three children, You will have to show us that very clearly sometime in the next few days."

The next morning, I got up and went to the kitchen to make myself some breakfast. While I usually have a bowl of cereal, I sometimes like to have a couple of fried eggs, and this particular morning seemed to be of one of those. I opened the refrigerator door and reached into the egg basket, taking an egg from the very front, but, as I reached out to take the one next to it, I felt a fleeting nudge to take the second egg from the very back of the basket instead, and so I did.

The frying pan was heating on the stove, and I cracked one of the eggs into it, but, when I glanced down at it, I was stunned for the egg was double-yolked! The second egg proved "normal," and so I now had two eggs in the pan, but three, happy, little, yellow yolks looking back at me! I can still remember the sound of the scream that jumped from my mouth. It had been literally decades since I had seen a double-yolked egg. Many people have since told me that they have never seen one.

Allen had gone to take out the trash, and I grabbed the hot pan and ran to find him. "Look," I exclaimed as I held it out to him, "do you think this is the sign?" The symbolic connection between yolks and progeny was not lost on us.

To our complete astonishment, this egg phenomenon happened several more times in the space of the next three weeks or so, and one day I asked the Lord if He did, in fact, have something to do with the eggs. "It's My little yolk," He replied. Somewhat testily, I said, "I'm not sure this is funny, Lord." "It may not be funny to you," He shot back, "but it's sure fun!"

The repeated occurrence of the double-yolked eggs was indeed an amusing statistical impossibility. One day our friend Kim, who knew of our egg adventure, inquired of the stock boy she found working near the egg case at Wal-Mart, where we had been buying our eggs. "Ma'am," he chuckled, "that's impossible. They candle these eggs, and the double-yolked ones get screened out. We never get them here."

During the following weeks, we began to commit to the Lord that, in obedience, we would indeed adopt three children, though we didn't know who they would be. We found it fascinating that, when we were at last solidly committed to adopting three children, the double-yolked eggs stopped and only reoccurred once more, though we continued to buy them from the same egg case at Wal-Mart!

A short time after Kathryn's vision, we followed up on Katya and discovered that she had a brother named Yuri. We even discovered that we had a picture of him. During this same time, the woman from church who had expressed some interest in Oksana backed away from the idea, and we began to reconsider her ourselves. Would our three children now be Oksana, Katya and Yuri? However, as the days went by and Allen continued to look at Yuri's picture, he became increasingly uneasy and negative. Something was wrong. Allen's uneasiness was soon fairly intense, and, while we didn't altogether abandon this sibling pair of Katya and Yuri as a possibility, we began to look at other sibling pairs to fill out our three children. Our attentions focused on two other pairs: Denis and Alona, a brother and sister, and Alyosha and Natasha, whom we later discovered were cousins.

One day, I complained to the Lord that I still did not understand the process we were in at all. "I'm not asking you to be detectives," He reasoned. "Detectives ultimately draw their own conclusions, often shaped by their presuppositions. I don't want you to draw any conclusions just yet. I am leading you down a pathway to a door which will be obvious. What seems on the surface is not always what is." Then, "You do not control the process, but I allow you to participate. It will work out well if you continue to seek Me. You want more certainty than is healthy. I am teaching you even as I bless you. Just persist in following My path."

So, despite our feeble understanding, we committed ourselves to following those instructions. During this time, we continued to receive interesting words from the Lord and to have confirming experiences relating to the adoption. One night, for example, as we were praying about the matter before going to bed, Allen had a vision. It consisted of a small, white, letter-sized envelope which was partly opened. He could see that it had either a scarlet interior or a scarlet wax seal which was broken. The Lord, I thought, seemed to be saying that some message from Him, some piece of information, had already been or was soon to be made known to us. A short while later, as Allen was turning out the light, he suddenly thought he got the word "flax."

The only connection I could make with the adoption was that Oksana's hair was decidedly that same, pale, straw-blond color. However, the depth of the word's significance would shortly become even more evident, for, soon afterwards, as we were again praying about the adoption, Allen thought he got this Scripture from Deuteronomy 16:1: "Observe the month of Abib and celebrate the Passover of the Lord your God, because in the month of Abib he brought you out of Egypt by night." When I turned in my Bible to the Hebrew calendar and read about the month of Abib, I nearly wept when I realized that it fell in March/April, the month of the heavy spring rains and, also, the time when the flax harvest began. It was also, of course, the month during which *Passover* fell, the time when the Israelites celebrated their miraculous deliverance from bondage. The date when we had met Ben and Kathryn and had first heard about flaxen-haired Oksana was March 13th—a dark and torrentially rainy spring *night* just two weeks before Passover. The whole thing was even more remarkable since, from almost the beginning of our awareness of the call to adopt, I had had a very strong sense, also confirmed by a friend, that something would somehow happen in the "springtime."

Perhaps not by coincidence, that spring produced another amazing experience, for the Lord's hand was in evidence again. Allen and I are great fans of contemporary Christian music, and we periodically add to our list of recordings. While browsing in our favorite Christian bookstore, I had listened to some portions of a tape by a new group called Burlap to Cashmere and had decided to buy it. One track was entitled Eileen's Song. I was gradually drawn to pay closer attention to the lyrics, and it struck me that the words, in some ways, related very poignantly to our adoption. I mentioned this to Allen, and we listened to the words together in the car one day. The refrain went as follows: "...you have one wing, I have another....seeking shelter like sister and brother....through the winter, through the summer....like one angel we'll fly far away. So my friend now this I say—I won't leave you hanging on. Hold on tight and don't fly away, until one angel we have become."[ix]

Some weeks later, we were in prayer again one night about the choice of our three children. We asked how we would know if the choices we'd been trying to make were the wrong ones, and we asked the Lord if He would be willing to grant us more clarity. Allen wrote that he was immediately shown a vision of the upper part of a polished wood staff. It had a gold head which was in the form of *one wing* going straight up, an obvious reference to the song! Along with the image came a Scripture, Mark 6:3-4, in which specific mention is made of Jesus' own brothers and sisters. In time, "Eileen's Song" came to be for us something of a theme song for the adoption, though we couldn't yet comprehend its full relevance, for despite this and other scattered gems of insight, we remained utterly confused as to the actual choice of our children.

Ironically, while still wrestling with this ongoing mental and emotional confusion, we were now being propelled into the actual hands-on process of doing the massively detailed paperwork which an overseas adoption entails. The first thing on the agenda was to file an application with the U.S. Immigration and Naturalization Service. Obediently, we applied to adopt three children, since one of INS's regulations stated that we could always adopt fewer children than had been declared for but never more. We also had to declare for the ages of the children we would adopt, and the same principle applied. We would not be allowed to adopt any child who was older than our upper declared age limit. We had been advised to list the acceptable ages of our children as eight to fourteen. However, I was home alone one day filling out this particular piece of paperwork, and, at the last minute, I suddenly felt moved to change the upper age limit from fourteen to fifteen. Like the choice of the second egg, it was a small, split-second decision but a momentous one. As required for this application, we were also fingerprinted in Birmingham, and the prints were sent off to the FBI.

Meanwhile, Kathryn, anxious to be helpful, had been strongly encouraging us to do an independent adoption, using the contacts in Russia that she and Ben had already made. The idea of avoiding the large agency fees had an obvious appeal for us, especially given our financial situation. We pursued this concept for nearly three months but, finally, began to get some clear warning signals urging us to steer clear of this course, and we conceded that we needed to try to find an agency that could work with us. Later, we would discover, to our amazement, that the Russian adoption laws had actually been in the process of changing radically during this time, and, unbeknownst to us, the route that we had been attempting would have been impossible. The law changes would prove to be providential from several standpoints, but, at the time, all we knew was the frustration we felt at what seemed like three months of lost time and effort.

Other than having finally realized that we needed the covering of an agency, I confess that we were so baffled at this point about how to proceed that our endeavors came to a virtual standstill.

Nonetheless, during these weeks, we persisted in praying about the choice of our children, and, though our prayer produced no clarity as to names, we were given a further window into the Lord's ways. Among His words to us were these:

"Your process is not complete yet, and I will have some interesting surprises along the way. Don't worry, it is under My control."

"Things are fuzzy because you're not moving forward."

"You have choices, you make choices, I choose—you will not understand this."

"Going the hard way is always safer."

Mindful of the Lord's exhortation to move forward, we decided we had to do something concrete, so Allen turned to the internet to find an agency that could work with our orphanage in Chelyabinsk. After much looking, we realized that only one or two agencies worked in Chelyabinsk at all—none at Oksana's orphanage. Finally, after some phone calls, we settled on Rainbow House International, based in Belen, New Mexico. Although the list of orphanages they worked with had not included Oksana's, they agreed to make this new contact, and suddenly we were off and running! We quickly found ourselves spending much time on the phone with Sonia Baxter, the agency's representative in Pittsburgh.

Now the paperwork began in earnest, as large envelopes-full of applications and forms began arriving from the agency. Voluminous as it all would have normally been, in our case everything had to be done three times over. I frequently commented that raising three kids had to be easier than slogging through these reams of paperwork! However, when I joked with Sonia about this, she assured me that I was laboring under a delusion! At any rate, the relentless stream of applications, forms, notarizations, apostilles, medical shots and screenings, and a dizzying host of other tasks were to plod oppressively on for over a year. The only way I coped, sometimes, was to remind myself of the nine months of pregnancy endured by other women. It was just that my "triplets" were triplicates!

It was already the middle of September, 1999, but we were still no closer to resolving the identity of our three children. We had eventually discerned that the pursuit of Yuri and Katya was to be put aside. After we had done so, the Lord confirmed: "You are not walking by sight; I do work through feelings as well, if they do not contradict my Word." However, we somehow seemed utterly unable to settle on any other known pair of kids. To make matters worse, there were, in fact, no real assurances with regard to even Oksana since, being past ten years of age, she would have to give her own consent to the adoption once she had met us. Again we turned to prayer, and this is what we thought we heard: "I am in charge, though it doesn't seem so to you. You are where I wish you now, though you would never have guessed the path. I am the Lord of what you would call mistakes, as well as of what you would call wisdom. Don't let your hearts be troubled. Remain open to my action, for as you move, so I can adjust circumstances. Be of good cheer, this is a fine adventure."

Despite this encouragement, I had bouts of nervousness and genuine fear. Again, the Lord spoke: "You would be foolish not to be scared on such an adventure as this. Even Paul was afraid on his adventure. Fear gives you the proper respect for the task, but it must not deter you. Doing the task in spite of the fear is faith. It is not a giddy certainty, but an assurance that all will turn out well despite the difficulties on the way."

One day in late September, nearly seven months after meeting Ben and Kathryn, I was again home alone when I got a startling phone call from Sonia Baxter. Still focused on Oksana, we had asked Sonia if she could get us any further information at all about her. We had Kathryn's two photos, but, beyond this, all we knew about this child to this point amounted to her name and approximate age. If Oksana were to be adoptable, it was required that her name be registered for a period of time in the data bank in the Chelyabinsk Region. The process could be likened to our laws regarding the probating of a will. In this case, a three-month public declaration of availability had to be made in order to insure that there were no relatives able and willing to adopt. In an understandable effort to safeguard them, the Russian government was intensively protective of these children and would give virtually no information to prospective adoptive parents until after the completed, official dossier—the formal, apostilled adoption paperwork—had arrived at the regional Department of Education.

In the course of making this basic check for us as to adoptability, Sonia reported that she had made a remarkable and unsettling discovery: Oksana had a brother! All Sonia could learn was that his name was Maxim, that he was about eight years old, and that he was living with an "auntie." It was completely unclear as to whether or not she would release him for adoption, but it didn't seem likely.

Now we were more befuddled than ever. Was Maxim part of the picture, or not? If he was, we now had two children potentially lined up, but we still needed a third. Needless to say, this meant that our months of looking at and praying over the two other possible girl/boy pairs were thrown into chaos. In addition, none of the other children we might have considered from our orphanage pictures was an only child, as far as we could determine from Kathryn and Gulia. Months passed as we continued to do paperwork while struggling to discern who our three children could now possibly be. The day that we received the startling news about Maxim, we got this word from the Lord:

"The path is no more or less certain than it has always been. What do you think My choosing means? I will work out the details. I know you want everything to be settled, but I don't work that way while I'm teaching. This is a special journey; don't fight it, enjoy it—for I will surely bless You. You must merely remain attentive, for I understand the deficiencies in your human hearing, and I take them into account. I will not fail you, for to fail you would be to fail Myself, and I am incapable of doing that. Stay on the path as far as you understand—that is all I ask—and take My blessing."

Despite this word of wisdom, I was so unsure of things at this point that I even went back to questioning whether we were supposed to be adopting Russian children at all. Allen thought he heard:

"I am seeking to fulfill your needs, but I have greater plans than you can imagine. Each small obedience leads to final victory. I have arranged the circumstances so that your choices led you this way. Know that you have freedom, but I have My purposes, and I make them coincide, though you surely cannot understand that. The things which seem so difficult now will seem obvious in retrospect. Stay on the path you understand to be the way, until I give you a clear sign. I will not let you go astray, for I am, after all, the Good Shepherd. I know you do not think I've answered your question, but I have. Rest and enjoy My peace and My plans."

Mid-October arrived, and one evening while in prayer the Lord gave Allen what seemed to me to be a confirming vision. As we asked about the issue of Oksana and her brother, Allen wrote that he had an image of a young lady from the neck down and the waist up. She was wearing a dark, rather closely tailored jacket with a V-neck, and she had a white scarf puffed up in the neck area. She was rather slender and had her arms crossed near her waist in a very confident posture. Though it was interesting that the Lord had not shown this girl's face, I remembered that Oksana's clothing in the two pictures we had of her was much like that in this vision. When I actually compared the vision to the photos, I was stunned to see that there was more than just similarity, for the vision had captured her appearance with amazing accuracy. What's more, the confident posture of the girl in the vision was a direct allusion to Oksana's bold statement to her friend Gulia that she would see her in America. Either the vision was a bold hint, or Allen's imagination was working overtime, enabled by his subconscious mental recollections of the photos. Fearing the latter, we were skeptical, but now the Lord had us over a barrel. When what we received was oblique, understanding eluded us, but, when the message was this direct, we distrusted ourselves. Was this the Lord speaking, or not? In my heart, I believed it was, but the experience made me realize that, despite our years of intense frustration with the veiled nature of the visions and words we received, I somehow felt safer with mystery.

The next few months found us largely preoccupied with assembling our dossier, and the Federal Express truck made increasingly frequent trips to our door to carry away the fruits of our labors. We soon knew the driver on a first-name basis, and he always cheerily asked us how our process was going. I looked forward to the day when I could actually introduce him to the children rather than to another stack of documents!

As the Lord had repeatedly urged, we continued to seek His will, alone and with others, about the adoption. We didn't get any definitive answers and, in fact, were specifically denied them, but we garnered much wisdom, and that strengthened us. One of my favorite conversations with the Lord was in regards to my ever-present worry about the identity of the kids. The Lord began with this encouragement:

"You are worrying unnecessarily— there will be clarity when the time comes. You do not know all the circumstances, but I, of course, do. I will not fail you. I never fail anyone who trusts in Me. As you walk the path, I will lead in the right direction. Worrying about your final destination will not help, for I am in charge of that. Trust and you will get your heart's desire."

My openly frustrated response was that I was not the least bit sure what my heart's desire even was. The Lord patiently answered:

"I'm not talking about your knowledge. You do not know the fullness of your desires, but I know your heart and what it needs. I will choose the right children to meet your needs and their needs. I recognize that you are confused, but, if you read My Scriptures, you will see that faith is following Me despite apprehension and uncertainty. There can be no other way than faith, because, otherwise, you would be tempted to think that your wisdom had led to the outcome you desire. It is the greatest temptation. I only show you a little bit of the path at any one time in order to protect you. I am shaping you to My call, but you will be blessed beyond imagining."

In April of the following year, we received another stunning phone call from Sonia, who had just discovered that Oksana also had a sister! By now I guess I should have been used to surprises! This time, Sonia did not even know the girl's age, name, or whereabouts, except that she was with neither Oksana nor her brother but was "somewhere else" in the institutional system. The one piece of information which Sonia had been able to acquire was that this third child had a diagnosis of "oligophrenia."

An unfamiliar term in American medicine, this word covered a wide range of mental and social developmental delays ranging from mild to severe, including mental retardation. It was categorically described as "slowness." Due to this diagnosis, Sonia informed us that Oksana's sister *could* be adopted but was not required to be. Russian adoption laws normally insisted that siblings be adopted together to retain the family unit, but exceptions were allowed if a child was living with a relative or had a disqualifying medical condition. Our initial reaction was to assume that, at our ages and with two other potential children to care for, we were not likely to consider adopting a third child with this kind of difficult condition. In the meantime, we were still not the least bit sure about the situation with Maxim or even fully about Oksana. Confusion continued to be the order of the day.

To add to our bewilderment, tucked into a longer word which we got one day with regard to some other issues was this: "You are My children, and I will be giving you some others of My children. I have entrusted much to your care...." We had pondered and prayed for months about who our three kids would be, and, now, with that issue no more resolved than ever, the Lord seemed to be saying that there were some other children of some sort out there somewhere. What in the world could that possibly mean? We had so much else to think about and deal with that this little prophetic parenthesis was nearly forgotten.

The spring of the year 2000 proved to be an extraordinarily difficult time for us. Allen was running into serious doctrinal and other conflicts at church which would lead to his resignation at the end of June. My father, who had remained in the local nursing home near us for two years, passed away on May 30th. Katharina, Hanno's sister and our third exchange student, went home at the beginning of June after spending the year with us, and we missed her greatly. With all of the physical and emotional stresses, I developed a miserable kidney infection and felt utterly wretched for weeks.

In the midst of all this, another call from Sonia informed us that the adoption process, which had seemed to drag on endlessly for so long, was suddenly moving into high gear. We had received our invitation from the Russian government, she said, to travel to Chelyabinsk for the purpose of identifying the children whom we would adopt, and we needed to make applications for visas immediately! I remember filling these forms out while seated on the sofa at the home of friends in Massachusetts, for we had flown up there to bury my father next to my mother in the family cemetery plot in Connecticut.

I also remember commenting to Allen on my observation that a death in a family seemed very often to be closely connected in time with a birth. This arrival of new life seemed to be the Lord's way of comforting, of giving new hope, of reaffirming life, and, yes, even at the practical level, of distracting from the pain and grief. However, in our case, we were even further awed by the Lord's timing, since my father's death now provided the resources for the large agency placement fees, by far the single biggest chunk of our adoption expenses. Up until this time, we had been proceeding on faith, having no idea how we would actually be able to pay these fees when the time came. On reviewing our journals, I later discovered that, over three years previously, while praying about how we could possibly finance an overseas adoption should we choose that route, the Lord had given Allen the number "eighty-four." We were naturally baffled and had never grasped the number's significance—my father's age at his death.

I mentioned earlier that the Russian adoption laws had been in the process of changing, and one effect of those changes was that we would now be required to make two trips, rather than one, to complete the adoption. The first trip was to be for the purpose of meeting, choosing and declaring for the children. On our return to Russia some weeks later, we would have our court date, get U.S. Embassy clearance and, finally, take the children home. We dreaded the inevitable exhaustion of this new two-step process, unaware that it was to be critical to the miracles which would soon unfold.

Meanwhile, with a definite timeline now before us, we grew ever more fretful. Yes, we would soon be going to Chelyabinsk to identify the three children whom we would adopt, but which three? In prayer about this, the Lord replied:

"Do not be anxious. You are on a path I have laid out, and I will do what is necessary. You don't have to worry about which child to choose, though your hearts will be pained at leaving any behind. The way will be clearer the closer you get. I will put my light on the faces of the three I have chosen. It will seem fleeting, but you will both see it. I cannot tell you more just yet. I know you have much uncertainty, but you should remember how much you have been blessed by uncertainty in the past."

"I will put My light on the faces...."—another mystery, another fleeting sign. What would the light look like? Could we miss it? And what if we didn't agree on what we thought we'd seen?

Our visas gave us a window of time in which to travel, and we were next told to make our airline reservations. Sonia suggested that we arrive in Moscow on a Friday, rest for a day, and then fly to Chelyabinsk on Sunday in order to be ready to interview children beginning on Monday. The system worked as followed, she explained: Apparently, there was one woman at the Department of Education in Chelyabinsk whose job it was to release the names of the children to be seen by the prospective parents and to arrange for those meetings at the orphanage. We would be allowed to see up to three children a day, and Sonia suggested that we allow ourselves four business days in Chelyabinsk, meaning that we would potentially see up to twelve children. While we dutifully accepted this system as something required of us, a part of us deplored and detested it, for it had a disturbing resemblance to picking over fruit in the supermarket. As difficult as it would be for us, we could only imagine what it would be like for the children involved for whom rejection was already their paramount life issue.

We soon had our flight scheduled for the seventeenth of August, with still no real idea of who our children would be! Graciously, during our prayer time one morning in July, the Lord promised us one final sign of His will. We didn't know when or how it would come.

Despite our intense busyness, I did periodically find time to muse on the process in which we found ourselves. Though we had lived it, we were sometimes in prayerful amazement at how we had gotten to the place where we were. Why Russia? Why this particular orphanage?

"I work through odd things. It is My favorite way to work, for, in these things that might otherwise seem like chance, you and others can see My unmistakable Hand. Consider all the odd twists that brought you to this particular place at this particular time. In a sense, nothing that I do is "normal" in that it is completely predictable by your limited viewpoint. Oh, I am completely dependable, certainly, but really not predictable. I reveal what I wish to reveal, but You can depend on My goodness."

Nine days before our departure, we saw that goodness manifested in the oddest of places: Wal-Mart! Having assessed our luggage space, we had decided that we really needed another small rolling duffel bag. Entering the store, Allen headed toward the back where the luggage was, while I made a brief detour to get a few groceries. When Allen rejoined me with his purchase, he remarked with amazement that, while selecting a bag, a poignantly familiar song had come wafting over the store intercom—the Burlap to Cashmere song that we had come to associate with the adoption! Since the album was overtly Christian in content, it struck us as rather unusual that it was being played in a secular merchandising setting!

Not long afterwards, Sonia informed us that two days before our flight to Moscow, she would make one final call to go over last-minute instructions regarding travel. She was to call at 9:30 A.M. On that Tuesday morning, we sat at home to await Sonia's call, but she was uncharacteristically late. When the phone did ring, she sounded flustered, and it became obvious that she was not only chagrined but disturbed. It seems that the woman from the Department of Education in Chelyabinsk who was to arrange for us to meet the children had suddenly and inexplicably decided to go on vacation for two weeks, was, in fact, already gone, and would not be there during our stay! We groaned in disbelief. However, Sonia hastened to add that the woman had done one thing for us before she took off. Since she knew that we had from the onset maintained an interest in Oksana, she had arranged for us to see the first day's set of three children, and they were to be Oksana, her brother, and her sister.

Instantly, the Lord's early words came rushing back to me: "Even though you think you've picked, I've picked." My mind began to race. Either this was the Lord and this was the way He had picked our three children, as He had said all along that He would do, or we were in the middle of a colossal mess. Sonia was apologetic. "I'm really uncomfortable with this," she said. "If I were you, as soon as we get off the phone, I would call your travel agent to see if you can reschedule your flight in order to arrive two or three weeks later." We did call the travel agent, but we also decided that we needed to sit down to pray immediately since our emotions were swinging back and forth like a church bell in a hurricane. One moment we were confused and panicked; the next we felt an odd calm. Was this the instantaneous resolution to a year and a half of prayer?

Allen had previously made plans to meet our doctor for lunch, and we were already running late, but we knew that we desperately needed to pray first. "Lord," we pleaded, "should we in fact change our flight and go later, or do we stick to our original plans?" Allen thought he heard the Lord say, "The airlines will decide for you." "Oh, swell," I moaned. "Now we've really reached the height of the absurd! After a year and a half in which we and everyone we know have been fervently praying about the choice of the children, now British Air is going to do the picking." When I wailed my complaint that over the next few hours we would have to make a decision that would affect the rest of our lives, the Lord replied, "Don't take it too seriously. I'm still in charge, you know." I could almost see Him wink.

"Well," I pondered out loud to Allen, "it's certainly not going to be a matter of our being able to go or not. After all, all you have to do to get a seat on some later flight is to wait long enough. It's probably going to come down to how much we are willing to pay in extra rescheduling fees." A moment earlier, I had felt that the absurd had been reached. Now things were even more ridiculous: the selection of our kids, which we had once assumed had at least something to do with us, was likely going to come down to the relative cost of a ticket change.

We continued to pray, and Allen got the further sense from the Lord that an amount of five hundred dollars was the acceptable upper limit on the cost to delay our flight, and that that would be the sign. With that, we left and went to meet our friend. Once at the restaurant, we poured out our tale of woe, but our friend, who had been praying for us for months, quickly, and somewhat exasperatedly, replied,

"What's the matter with you people? Isn't it obvious? These are your three kids. Just go and get them!" My spirit told me that he was right.

On our arrival back at the house, there was a message on the answering machine from the travel agent. Our return call to her informed us that we could indeed change our tickets in order to arrive two weeks later, but the cost would be steep—between five and six hundred dollars a person! Two days later, we were at the Atlanta Airport preparing for our flight to Moscow.

The flight, with stopovers in New York and London, was uneventful, even pleasant, but our arrival in Moscow was to prove tortuous. We de-boarded the plane at Sheremetyevo 2 and proceeded with the other passengers down a corridor which came to a wide, descending flight of stone steps. Below was the customs and immigration room, a dim and airless space already jammed with several hundred people from the past few incoming flights. Behind us, hundreds more were pouring in. A suddenly formidable expanse away, just beyond the four or so officials' stations at the other end of this room, was the baggage claim area. The more that people crowded in, the more stifling the room became. People were pressed against each other in the hot, stale air, and there was a constant jostling, shoving and straining forward, even though there was no place to go. Several times, I glanced back at the staircase behind me, as I fought off waves of panic. Being short, I almost continually found myself with my nose pressed against the back of some person in front of me, and there were moments when I was afraid I would suffocate. I wanted to struggle my way back through the crowd to the staircase and escape back up into the corridor, since that was the shorter distance, but Allen reminded me that it only went back out to the runway. There was no choice but to proceed forward through this hell.

On several occasions, I feared that there would be a crushing stampede, for, periodically, a large group off to our right somewhere would angrily stomp and shout in a burst of enraged voices, calling for the addition of more customs officials. Incredibly, there was only one working. Off to our left, about twenty feet away, we were aware that a woman had vomited and nearly fainted from the heat and closeness of the room. There was nothing for her to do but drop some newspapers over the mess and remain in her place. As we inched forward, others had to walk over or stand on the newspapers. There was no way to leave, sit down, get any water, or use the restroom.

We were to endure this agony for three horrible hours. As the room was somewhat funnel shaped, the closer we were able to get to the immigration control booths, the more intense the pushing and crowding became. After perhaps two hours of this torture, we became aware that another two customs officials had been finally added, but it scarcely seemed to make a difference in our rate of progress. We were exhausted, hot, thirsty and frightened—not to mention disgusted. When we were finally within about ten feet of the booths, the pressure and shoving increased to what seemed an intolerable level. At this point, the pushing was so intense that I was at times pressed so tightly against other people that my feet were off the ground. I got separated from Allen, and, though he was but a few feet away, I could not see or touch him. I was afraid that, as I came nearer to the customs booth to which I was headed, I would be crushed against the side of it.

Finally, I somehow stood in front of a uniformed woman who gruffly took my passport and visa. From reports filtering backwards through the crowd, I had become aware that what was causing much of the endless delay, in addition to the shortage of workers, was the fact that these bureaucrats were interrogating each traveler at great length. With the baggage claim area now visible just beyond me and freedom so close, I dreaded the prospect of this new assault, but I smiled and said a kindly word to this woman, expressing my genuine sympathy with her probable weariness. She smiled briefly in return, muttered a thank-you, and dispensed with the interrogation. I breathed my own thanks and slid past her into the baggage claim area.

Later, when I described this experience to friends at home, I suddenly had an acute awareness of having lived out a parable of childbirth. I reasoned that the Lord, knowing I had never experienced this part of womanhood, had given me a vivid, physical experience of the process from the perspective of both mother and child. The funnel-shaped room, after all, was not unlike a womb, and the tightness, pushing and agony were much like labor. At the end, when it was all the most intense, I was finally propelled through the narrow space between two booths and then, suddenly, released from the pressure, exited into the large baggage room. There we were met by Tanya, our Moscow social worker, and Volodia, our driver.

We rode, at length, through the busy streets of Moscow on that late Friday afternoon until we finally turned into the parking lot next to the apartment building where Galina, our hostess, lived. As we got out of the car and began to unload our bags, Tanya, with a waver of emotion in her voice, informed us that there was good news about Olesya, the third child, whose name we now heard for the first time. "The diagnosis isn't true," she exclaimed. "She is normal. And she is the top student at her school." I don't recall what I said in reply, but I remember that I wept a little, partly for joy and partly out of a mixture of amazement and relief. However, I was also so exhausted that I couldn't fully internalize the truth of her words, and so a shadow of doubt remained.

Meanwhile, the Lord's hand had also become evident in other ways, for, during the time just before we had left for Russia, we had received word through Sonia that we had been misinformed in another way as well. Maxim had, apparently, never been with an aunt, after all, but had been living for the last seven and a half years with a foster family! The news was, though we didn't fully realize it then, monumentally significant. What's more, we learned that, only a short time prior to our arrival in Russia, his foster mother, who had eventually been able to have a child of her own, had made the decision, while still unaware of our impending visit, to place Max in the orphanage system.

Tanya now led us up the several flights of stairs to Galina's flat. She saw to it that we got settled in and, then, announced that she would return after our supper to give us some further instructions about our travel on to Chelyabinsk—a two-and-a-half hour flight away in the south Ural Mountains, just over the Asian border. I pondered the realization that we would soon be eleven time zones from home!

Since it was now Friday night, and we had been told to anticipate going on to Chelyabinsk on Sunday morning, we were looking forward to Saturday as a day to rest and perhaps do a little sightseeing in Moscow. To our surprise, when Tanya returned, the first words she spoke were, "You must repack your bags tonight, since you are going to Chelyabinsk in the morning." So much for a chance to rest! I remember challenging her about this arrangement three or four times, until finally, a bit peeved with me, Tanya said, "Look, you are going to Chelyabinsk tomorrow. I have already bought your tickets." She then proceeded to pull them from her briefcase and slap them into my hand. Her next instructions were that we would be met at the bottom of the airplane steps by two women: Lena Gordetskeya, our translator, and Lena Chaikina, our Chelyabinsk social worker.

Off we flew the next morning. On de-boarding the plane in Chelyabinsk and glancing around, we began to realize that there was, in fact, no one to greet us, but we figured that the two Lenas were just a little late. We continued on into the small baggage claim room, thinking we might encounter them there, but, again, no one greeted us. We located our bags and moved on into the terminal building, an old, unappealing and un-welcoming structure. Spotting a long metal bench along the left-hand side of the wall, we dragged our bags over to it and plunked ourselves down to wait for the Lenas, who were now considerably tardy.

After some time, the airport cleared out, as ours had evidently been the last flight of the day, and we were left sitting in the large room whose sole other occupant was the woman at the little soda stand, who spoke no English, and did not look happy. Allen left me on the bench two or three times to make little forays out into the parking lot, back to baggage claim, and out the door and around the side of the building to two of the other airport offices. Still there were no Lenas. His absences became lengthier each time he ventured out, and I was left to sit on the bench with my head in my hands, contemplating my fate.

Gradually, my annoyance and weariness began to turn to anxiety and then fear, as the realization dawned on me that we might have to spend the night sleeping on the bench, assuming we would even be allowed to stay in the terminal building at all. Out in the parking lot, a number of rough looking cab drivers leaned against their cars. At one point, I ventured out to see if I could spot Allen, only to be accosted with yet another offer to take me to my destination. The first problem was that I didn't know my destination. Since we were being picked up, no one had bothered to tell us the name of the hotel where we would be staying. The second problem was that these cab drivers didn't look like anybody I wanted to get into a car with, especially alone. I did my best to indicate disinterest, but one of them persisted, following me from a distance as I hastily walked back into the terminal.

As I sat back down on the bench, Allen reappeared to tell me that he had decided that he would go and try to call Tanya back in Moscow in hopes of finding out what had happened to our Lenas. "Why Tanya?" I asked. "She's there, we're here." "Hers is the only phone number we have," he replied matter-of-factly. Allen headed back out the door, while I sat and waited for what seemed an interminable length of time. I was near tears. Having pretty much given up on the two Lenas, I cried out, "Lord, please send someone to get us." I had no idea who that could even possibly be, for literally no one in the world, outside of Tanya, who was now twelve hundred miles away, even knew we were there!

It was, by now, getting quite late in the afternoon, and the last flights had long since come and gone. I watched forlornly as the concession stand lady began to close shop for the day, and I grew more panicked with each passing moment. After awhile, even she had left. Allen had now been gone for what seemed like forever, and, as I glanced nervously at my surroundings, I noted to myself that I was not only halfway around the world from home but completely alone in the colorless terminal building of a strange airport in a city of 1.2 million people, whose name, a few weeks ago, I had never even heard. I felt frightened and abandoned. My rational mind clung to the thought that God had sent us here, and that it would all work out, but a part of me was crying, "Why, Lord, did you put us through all of this only for it to end this way?" It now occurs to me that the Israelites in the wilderness said more or less the same thing!

Suddenly, in the midst of my despair, Allen returned and with him was an attractive and nicely dressed woman with a warm smile. Allen explained to me that, when he had gone out to try to make the phone call, he had finally ended up in the airport customs office. The officer there at the desk was scarcely able to understand him, but standing nearby was this woman, named Luda, who had overheard the struggling conversation, spoke a bit of English, and offered to help. Allen introduced her to me, and she explained that her daughter Lera, who was outside in the car with her stepfather, spoke some

English, and so Allen and I were led out to meet her and relate our plight.

We were introduced to a beautiful young girl with black hair and dark eyes, who appeared to be about eighteen or nineteen years of age. (We would later discover that she was only fourteen, though she had a worldly maturity that reached beyond her years). Her English, learned through several years of lessons at school, was surprisingly good, though she told us that she had never actually conversed with a native English speaker. Lera's stepfather, Vadim, was equally gracious and supportive. We were invited to sit in the back seat of their car and chat for awhile, while Luda finished attending to her business in the customs office. It seems that the family had come to the airport this day to do some customs work connected with Luda's and Vadim's jobs, and they remarked that they had not been there for several months previously.

As we walked towards their car, we stopped for a moment and stood on the curb, and Luda and Lera asked Allen who it was that was supposed to have picked us up at the airport. Since Chelyabinsk was such a large city, Allen thought it absurd to even offer the information, but he gave them a slip of paper with the names of Lena Chaikina and Lena Gordetskeya scratched on it. To his amazement, Lera brightened and exclaimed, "I know Lena Gordetskya. She went to high school with my father, and she is also a DJ on the local radio station. In fact, I've been sitting here in the car listening to her on the radio!" Well, that explained why Lena was not at the airport, we reasoned with amusement. Luda offered to go and call Lena G. at the station and, later, laughingly commented that the first startled reaction to her call had been, "Those people weren't supposed to be here until tomorrow!" We were beginning to realize that we were in the midst of a divine appointment. In fact, Lena Gordetskeya later informed us that in working with about two hundred and forty other adoptive families, she had never failed to pick up anyone else at the airport, although she did admit to being late once due to traffic.

Naturally, Lena G. could not leave work to come and get us, and so Luda, Vadim, and Lera generously offered to drop us off at our hotel, where the two Lenas arranged to meet us upon our arrival. So, off we went, two bemused Americans in the back seat of a car with a Russian family whom we had only met an hour or two before!

At the hotel, we were warmly greeted by the two Lenas, who apologized profusely for the misunderstanding regarding our arrival day. As our bags were unloaded from the trunk of the car, Vadim, Luda and Lera asked us if they could return after our supper to give us an evening tour of their city. Surprised and delighted, we said yes.

The following night, they returned to bring us to their home for a wonderful, home-cooked Russian meal prepared by Vadim's mother. Like the vast majority of Russians, they lived in a large, high-rise, concrete apartment complex adorned with small balconies. It was the first Russian home we had been in, and we were thrilled to feel a sense of warmth and belonging. Before we left Chelyabinsk, they took us out to dinner, eagerly encouraging us to contact them on our return three weeks later to get our children.

Meanwhile, our thoughts churned, and our hearts pounded as we faced the prospect of going to Verkniy Ufaley, one hundred and twenty miles north of Chelyabinsk, early on Monday morning to meet the first two of the kids. We spent that Sunday evening in our hotel room reorganizing and re-packing the gifts that we had brought for the children and for the orphanage, and talking and praying about the two days just ahead of us when we would at long last see and talk with what would likely be our new family. I was nervous, especially about Olesya and Maxim, since they were such unknowns to us. We had never seen so much as a single picture of either of them. I was particularly anxious about Olesya, for, despite Tanya's good word, there was still some real question about her diagnosis. When I expressed to the Lord my fear of taking a child who might be "slow," Allen thought he heard:

"I only ask you to be obedient to what you understand. I never force My people to do what they do not wish. I will give you under-standing in the next few days, and you shall see My heart. I do not expect you to do things which are not suitable, but I do expect you to recognize My blessings even though you are fearful. I know your fear. These are hard things which I ask you to do, because they make you so uncomfortable. I am stretching your mind and your heart—that is never comfortable. However, I have good ends in mind. Stay the course. Do not get overly anxious. Remember Who is your real tour guide. You have been surprised, you will continue to be sur-prised! Have fun!"

That night, as we were getting ready for bed, Allen told me that he had also gotten the very strong sense that the key thing that we were to look for in each of the children was a sense of humor.

Due to the combination of jet lag and excitement, we slept fitfully, but the long awaited day finally dawned. The two Lenas called us from the hotel lobby to announce that they were coming upstairs to fetch us, and, soon, we were on our way to meet Oksana and Maxim. Our driver was a long, lanky and sweet-tempered fellow named Andy, and our ride took us about two and a half hours north of Chelyabinsk, through a flat, lake-studded and heavily birch-forested Russian countryside reminiscent in some ways of Minnesota. The fields along the road were planted with golden yellow sunflowers, and, though it was late August and the air was gently warm, there was already a brooding hint of fall in the air.

My first memory of the village itself was that of the huge mountain of black slag which dominated the town, the refuse of the nickel processing plant which was its main industry. We made our way through the muddy, dismal streets until we, at last, pulled up in front of the orphanage, an old stucco building of World War II vintage.

We were led into the small library, where we were introduced to the director, as well as to Oksana's other caregivers, including her pediatrician. Oksana, interestingly enough, was not there, for she, like many Russian children, was at summer camp, and so our driver was sent to go and bring her back. In the meantime, we had two hours to talk with the staff while we anxiously awaited the arrival of this child for whom we had so long dreamed and planned.

At long last, we caught the sound of quick footsteps outside the room, the door gently opened, and Oksana entered, a strikingly beautiful, blond-haired girl in an emerald green dress. She was fourteen years old. She sat opposite us at the long table and, surrounded by the staff and by the two Lenas, with Lena G. translating, we began to get to know this child. Before long, we saw that she not only laughed easily at our jokes but had a quick wit of her own. It was explained to her that we had come to see her because she was a friend of Gulia's, and, after some time of general chatting about her interests, we began to direct the conversation to the possibility of her being adopted and coming to live with us in America. Without hesitation, she said yes! We all hugged tearfully, and preparations were made to serve us lunch.

In the midst of these preparations, Maxim arrived with his foster mother and was seated next to Oksana. For some time, the two siblings gave each other shy but curious sideways glances, for they had not seen each other for seven and a half years. Oksana had been seven and Maxim three when they were separated, and it must have indeed been strange for Oksana to suddenly find herself sitting beside this brother who, when she had last seen him, was a toddler.

We began the same process of chit-chat with Maxim, asking him questions about things like school, sports and favorite foods. We discovered that he had a disarming smile and that same lively sense of humor. One comment that I specifically remember had to do with the bed we had gotten for his room which was, due to a lack of space, the upper part of a bunk bed. When I asked him if he would be afraid of falling out, he quipped, "I usually don't fly in my dreams." Nonetheless, I was nervous and unsure about this child. He had evidently had a home haircut, perhaps with a shaver, but it had been done in such a way that he had several bald patches on his scalp, and I was concerned that he had some sort of scalp disease. His clothes and shoes were very worn, and his hands and face were far from clean. He also had a badly chipped front tooth. I began to panic, since I knew that, within a half an hour or less, I would be required to decide whether or not this boy would be my son.

Allen and I left the room to talk, through Lena G., with his foster mother. She described him as a good boy who needed a strong hand, since he had begun some rebellious behaviors. True to our natures, Allen was certain about adopting him, but I struggled for what seemed like an eternity, pacing back and forth in the large play room opposite the library. In retrospect, I cannot understand why any of our concerns about him really mattered, and, given the circumstances, I surely don't know what else I might have expected, but outward appearance and a few comments about him were all I had, and the situation was complicated by the fact that we were under intense time pressure. In the end, that was probably for the best, since I finally agreed, more out of fatigue and resignation than firm conviction, and we went back to our seats at the small table where we asked Max if he would like to be adopted. He readily said yes as well and, then, flashed me an enormous grin which I shall never forget.

Lunch was served, and we shared our first meal with the first two of our three children. I remember that we had a tasty combination of baked chicken, which was Oksana's favorite, bread, sliced tomatoes and cucumbers, bowls of fresh black currants picked from bushes in the orphanage yard, and the ever-present Russian tea, with cookies.

It did not take long for our children's personalities to emerge, we discovered. Oksana spent the remainder of our time at the orphanage snuggled on the couch next to me, with one hand tightly holding mine and the other clutching a stuffed animal. Max, on the other hand, announced after lunch that he wanted to get back to town so as not to lose his prepaid one-hour slot at the computer game room. Having taken a brief break in his day to make the most momentous decision of his life, it was now time to get back to the really important stuff—play!

The formalities finally completed, we proceeded to the happy and practical task of measuring Oksana for some clothes and shoes, since she had few of her own. We had been told to bring a tape measure for just that purpose, and a slightly embarrassed Oksana dutifully stood still, turned, and lifted her arms, as we took the various measurements needed to get her the beginnings of her new wardrobe. Most of the children's' clothing, we had learned, was the property of the orphanage and went to the central laundry room to be washed. When the children dressed in the morning, they would go to the laundry room and pick their day's attire from the pile of clean clothing there. To get Oksana's shoe size, we had her draw around her stockinged feet while she stood on a sheet of white paper.

These necessities accomplished, and after some final words with the staff, we said farewell to Oksana and Max, informing them that we would return in three weeks or so to take them to America. After we had left, however, Lena C. suddenly remembered that we had forgotten to measure Max, and so we drove across town to his house. He had missed his game time after all, and we found him playing in the neighborhood with some friends. We did the same measuring routine with him, while he stood more or less patiently in the street, surrounded by a small crew of curious and equally scruffy young boys.

Once we were back in the car again, Lena G. told us that Oksana had slipped her a hand-written note to give to Olesya, whom she knew we would see the next day. Oksana's note told her sister of our visit and included the words, "These are good people. Do not be afraid of them." She did not mention the adoption. We also discovered through Oksana's comments to Lena C. that the two girls had recently begun to communicate by letter with each other and had been writing about three or four times a year.

The next morning, Andy drove Allen and I and the two Lenas to Olesya's orphanage in Chelyabinsk—Boarding School No. 9. She likewise was at camp, and Andy again had the job of going to get her, another two-hour round-trip. Again, we met with the director, the staff, and the pediatrician, as well as with the psychologist. To our bewilderment, they all spent the entire two hours vigorously trying to convince us that Olesya was mentally slow, and they gave much subjective "evidence." We were not convinced and became less so as the conversation went on. Allen continued to press for some objective data. They had none. At one point, we even asked if there had ever been an EEG taken, and they replied firmly that there had not.

After perhaps an hour and a half of this, we decided to ask to see some of Olesya's school work, and the staff acknowledged that she was, in fact, the top student at the school! We examined her math and Russian copy books, and, though the work she was being given to do was not on a level with her age, which was fifteen, she was performing extremely well.

When Oleysa was finally ushered into the room, we were again astounded. She was a beautiful girl with long brown hair and sapphire blue eyes, slightly shorter in stature than Oksana, though a year and a half older. She was seated near us, and we began the now-familiar process of getting to know her a bit. She was given Oksana's note and told that we were there because we had met her sister the day before and wanted to meet her as well.

After we had had a short time of conversation with Olesya, Lena C. rose from her seat, leaned over, and whispered in my ear, "There is nothing wrong with this child." Allen and I had already reached the same conclusion. We immediately saw that Olesya had the same ready smile, quick wit and easy laugh as her siblings and was sharp in her responses during the conversation. Allen leaned towards me, saying that he was ready to ask her to be adopted as well. Olesya was then told that her brother and sister had already agreed to be adopted by us, and she was asked if she desired the same. With no hesitation, she said yes, and, again, we all hugged. From the corner of my eye, I saw Lena C. slip out of her seat and walk across the director's room to the window, where she stood with her back to the group. When I approached her, I saw that, despite all her years of tough experience in social work, she was weeping. Equally amazingly, the orphanage director shook our hands and, putting pride aside, said with a tremor in his voice, "You have taught us all a great lesson in psychology." I would have rather said faith, for we had but clung to the words the Lord had given us.

Olesya, too, endured the tape measure and the pencil and paper, and we then settled down to the necessary duty of going through her medical and other records. In the course of doing that, we were off-handedly informed that about a year earlier she had had a fall and had been taken to the hospital to check out a bump to her head and to her leg. During that brief hospital stay, she had apparently had an EEG, and, in the physician's handwriting on the back side of the report where no one had apparently ever looked, was this scribbled note: "NO ORGANIC BRAIN DAMAGE." Her brain activity was perfectly normal. The staff was chagrined. The horrible reality was beginning to dawn on us that this child had been placed in this particular institution for "slow" children and then, forever afterwards, labeled with a diagnosis which had never been real to start with. It had only been a self-perpetuating nightmare, unconsciously sustained by the nature of bureaucracy and, as we later learned from Lena G., by the fact that the orphanage staff received a thirty per cent higher salary rate for working with children with oligophrenia.

Once the records had been dealt with, we were offered the opportunity to take Olesya out to lunch, and, as we rode in the car, the two Lenas chatted with her in the back seat. Lena G., casually but pointedly, asked her why she had ended up at her particular boarding school, and she gave this explanation. When the children had been taken from their home, there had been one bed available at another orphanage in Chelyabinsk, and one at Olesya's. Oksana had been arbitrarily assigned to Olesya's orphanage, but she had begun to cry for some reason, and Olesya, being the older sister, had offered, "Don't cry, Oksana. I'll go instead." Her act of kindness had resulted in a life of being marked as slow, despite all of the obvious evidence to the contrary. Once more, the two Lenas choked back tears. After lunch with Olesya and a bit of shopping with her, we said our good-byes and told her we would return for her in about three weeks.

Now we had a new and interesting task assigned to us, for we needed to declare for the children and decide upon the names by which they would be called. That night, as we collapsed into bed, our minds sorted through the possibilities. Sonia had impressed upon us that the only permanent thing that these children would take away from Russia would be their names, and so she strongly advised, especially at their ages, that they keep their Russian first names. We also chose to use their middle names, where possible, in order to retain some of their history and identity, since Russians' middle names are patronymic, reflecting the first names of their fathers. The children's birth father's name was Michael, so Oksana became Oksana Michelle, while Maxim became Maxim Michael Robert (Allen's middle name). That left Olesya. We had some concern that her first name would always present something of a challenge for her, as it was a bit too unfamiliar to Americans. However, since it was the Russian equivalent of our English name Alicia, we decided to change her name to Alicia Marie. When we informed them all of their new names, they were delighted, and I'm sure it gave them each a new sense of belonging.

We still had three days left in Chelyabinsk, and we were happy to be able to enjoy some further contact with Lera, Luda, and Vadim. With each visit, we were all aware of an increasingly strong bond developing between us, and our hearts became heavy at the thought of having to leave them, knowing they would be so far away. However, our recent experience with our three foreign exchange students had caused Allen and me to begin to wonder if the Lord might not be nudging us to invite Lera to come and stay with us also, and so, with some trepidation, we broached the subject first with her parents. They were understandably shocked and confused by the proposal, and, feeling somewhat embarrassed, we concluded that we had been too bold. After all, only a few short days before, we and this family had been total strangers half a world away. We backed off and resolved that we would not bring up the subject again unless the Lord made it very clear that we should do so.

Our last evening in the city found us having a lovely dinner with them in, of all places, a Western-style restaurant with country music. Though we said little more to them about our thoughts regarding Lera, the subject of her visit still tugged at our hearts and lingered in our minds. On returning to our hotel room after saying our last good-byes, Allen and I prayed, thanking the Lord for bringing this family into our lives. When I asked the Lord if there was going to be further contact, especially with Lera, Allen thought he heard, "Nothing could be more certain."

As I continued to pray, not only about our connections with Russia and with this family, but also about the miracle of our children, the Lord added:

"I am working in this land, and you are among My instruments. Do not think that your faith and the amazing reunion of these three children has gone unnoticed. This story will affect lives for Me. There is much evil in this land, but there is a core of openness which will provide fertile soil for the seeds of the Gospel. Continue walking along my path, and you shall see great things happen. I am the Good Shepherd."

We had arrived in Russia a mere nine days earlier, full of anticipation, but having no clear idea of what to expect or how the adoption would ultimately be resolved. Now we were flying home again, this time leaving behind not only our own three precious children, but also a family who had already become very dear to us. Our lives were forever changed, and we marveled at how we had seen the Lord's hand move! We stopped briefly in Germany to visit Hanno and his family, who were all eager to hear of our adventure and to see the pictures we had taken of the kids.

We were comforted by the fact that we would be reunited with our children again soon, and that we would also have further contact with our new friends, but we also had an extraordinarily busy three weeks ahead of us. As soon as we got home, we "hit the ground running." There was unpacking to be done, clothing and shoes to buy for our three kids, new Russian visas to be applied for, new plane tickets to be purchased, and re-packing to be done, not only for us but now for the kids as well. In addition, now that the children had been declared for, we had an intimidating new ream of paperwork to be done for the U.S. Consulate in Moscow. These papers would grant the children their U.S. visas, as well as give them final legal and medical clearance to leave Russia. We had been repeatedly and sternly warned against having the slightest error or missing piece of information in this paperwork, and I was extremely nervous.

This new paperwork included an application for something called a ten-day waiver. Under Russian law, ten days had to elapse after the passage of a court decree before it became legally binding. This meant that adoptive families were required to remain in Russia for ten days after their adoption was granted at the court hearing, unless they were granted the waiver. Expense aside, the wait would have been enormously difficult emotionally for both us and the children since, in our case, the children would have had to return to their caregivers while we spent the ten days alone in our hotel room. Sonia had informed us that there was a new official in charge of granting these waivers, and she cautioned that, in the several months since he had taken office, he had not allowed a single family to leave early. She suggested that, given these circumstances, it was probably not worthwhile to even do the paperwork which involved providing letters from schools, psychologists, and doctors outlining the emotional, physical, and psychological needs of the children to go home with us as soon as possible. As weary as we were, it was tempting to want to resign ourselves to the ten-day stay and avoid the extra paperwork. However, Allen strongly felt that, though we were already greatly overburdened and running out of time, we should complete these waiver documents and bring them with us. Our friend Kimberly joined in the effort by getting her church to pray that we would get the waiver.

We were deeply exhausted but had no time to rest, and we plunged into all of our tasks with an acute awareness of the deadline which was racing towards us. As I look back, I know beyond a doubt that it was only by the Lord's grace that we accomplished all that needed to be done.

During these three weeks, when we were separated by an ocean and two continents from our children, we prayed daily for their physical, emotional and spiritual protection, and we eagerly awaited our reunion with them. Though we barely knew them, the separation was already painful. Through Sonia, Lena C. communicated that she was stopping in regularly to check on Alicia in Chelyabinsk, and that Alicia, upon spotting her, would run to her side, asking "When are my mama and my papa coming?"

Despite our busyness during this interval between our two trips, prayer was still our first priority, and we often expressed to the Lord our fear of the great changes which we knew would soon be coming upon us. He responded:

"I will give you grace as you all undergo these great transitions. I am about a work that you cannot fully understand, but you are agents of My mercy to these children, and they are agents of My blessing to you. You shall rejoice, even in the midst of challenge, for I will stretch you, but I am also growing you for My further work."

Three weeks later, we were back in Chelyabinsk, and we immediately phoned Lera and her parents. They were overjoyed to hear from us and extremely anxious to meet our children. Despite our hesitancy in bringing up the subject of Lera's visit again, we still sensed that the Lord might be intending that she come to stay with us for awhile, and we continued to submit this to prayer. What did the Lord have in mind for this bright and beautiful girl?

One evening, as we prayed for her, Allen received a fascinating series of Scriptures, words and visions revealing the Lord's greater purposes. The first Scripture was John 6:39: "And this is the will of him who sent me, that I shall lose none of all that he has given me, but raise them up at the last day." Immediately following was a vision—an image—Allen wrote, of what seemed like the figure of Christ in white garments and with a halo of light around his head, standing with arms outstretched on the top floor balcony of a large apartment complex. Another Scripture followed: "...yet for us there is but one God, the Father, from whom all things came and for whom we live; and there is but one Lord, Jesus Christ, through whom all things came and through whom we live."(I Corinthians 8:6)

It seemed clear that the Lord planned to work in the lives of this family, but I asked if He would have us come to Chelyabinsk to continue the relationship, since Lera, at fourteen, seemed too young to be undertaking a lengthy trip to America. In addition, the bureaucratic hurdles to be overcome in accomplishing this visit seemed enormous. Allen thought he heard:

"She is still at a time when she can be molded and influenced, and she must hear My gospel. She can have great impact on many others. I will give a clear signal of what you are to do over the next few days. Of course, I will eventually have you return to Chelyabinsk, but it is far more effective in many ways for your 'mission' to come to you. You should not be anxious about these things, Jan. You have seen Me work through circumstances when you could not imagine how all the details could work. I'm good at that sort of thing. I know your concerns, but your best and easiest path is to follow My leading, and I will show you the way. There will be untold impact from all of the contacts I have given in the next years as seeds planted bear much fruit. You are not in charge of the harvest. I am the Lord of the Harvest. You are only to follow as clearly as you understand. Be watching for a sign of My guiding hand."

Later, when I again asked the Lord how Lera, at fourteen and a high school student, would possibly be allowed to leave the country alone to come to the States for an extended time, He answered:

"You didn't know how I was going to choose your children either. If I have chosen to do something, there are no obstacles. The process may sometimes go by a different route because of unbelief, and some will miss blessings in those circumstances. However, you should not constantly focus on obstacles. I am not deterred from My purposes, for, in time, I will accomplish all that I purpose."

All we could do was to trust, watching and waiting to see how this part of the drama would unfold.

In the meantime, our final and greatest adoption hurdle lay just in front of us. Respectfully referred to by us as "The Big Day," it was the long awaited court date: Thursday, September 28th, 2000—the moment for which we had been preparing since the beginning of the process. Only after the judge had granted the adoption would the children be allowed to come to us. We approached it all with an odd mixture of nervousness and confidence. The day before the hearing found us up at 6 A.M. and in prayer. The Lord graciously reminded us that He had been in charge of this process from the beginning, that we were well-prepared, and that we had good people assisting us.

Finally the hour arrived, and we drove to the courthouse and climbed the stairs to the hearing room. In typical courtroom fashion, an entire team had been assembled for the event, including the directors and key staff from the orphanages, the regional prosecutor, the judge and, of course, our two faithful Lenas.

All of us sat on two long benches outside the hearing room while we waited for the judge to appear. The children had been brought by their respective caregivers, and they now sat together, reunited as a family for the first time since 1993. As related earlier, Oksana and Max had briefly met on our first day at Oksana's orphanage, but Alicia had, as yet, seen neither Oksana nor Max. Oksana and Alicia, separated as little girls, now sat next to each other as teenagers. It was a moment we will never forget.

We had been told that the hearing could take several hours, but, in fact, it mercifully lasted but two. When all the depositions had been made and we, as well as the children, had been examined by the judge, he methodically reviewed all our paperwork. It was a strange feeling to see our dossier, which had required such a mammoth amount of work and which had been sent on ahead to Chelyabinsk months before, now resting on the judge's desk as he sifted through the documents. As he worked intently through this formidable stack of paper, I studied his face to see if I could catch a glimpse of a kindly smile, for, though he was a fairly young man, he was quiet and serious. At length, his review completed, he adjourned the court to render his decision, both regarding the adoption and the ten-day waiver.

On his return, the judge had us all stand while he announced that both the adoption and the waiver had been approved! The courtroom burst into a buzz of relieved excitement, combined with congratulatory hugs. In an instant, all the agonizing months of working and waiting were over, and we were parents! It was more than I could grasp.

As we stood in the courtroom and talked with the two Lenas after the hearing, we had three incredible realizations concerning the miracles that the Lord had arranged in the adoption. The first concerned

Max. As I mentioned earlier, his foster mother, unaware of our impending visit, had made the decision only about two weeks before our first trip to Russia to place him in an orphanage. It was now explained that none of the kids would likely have had a chance to be adopted if Max's foster mother had not done this, due to the policy of the system to try to keep family groups together when adopted. However, in an odd twist, it was also clear that his availability was the result of her own unwillingness to adopt him. Nonetheless, if she had not made this decision to let him go, the adoption of all three of the children would have been severely jeopardized, if not rendered impossible. The Lord's hand in the timing was abundantly obvious.

The other two miracles concerned Alicia. First was the issue of her age. At the time of the adoption, she was less than four months away from her sixteenth birthday. I recalled the day, so many months earlier, when I had been suddenly moved to change the declared upper age limit of the children for whom we were applying from fourteen to fifteen. At sixteen, according to U.S. Immigration and Naturalization law, she would have been unadoptable. For months on end, we had wrung our hands, complaining to the Lord about why the adoption was taking so long. Now we knew. The Lord had sent us to get these three children at exactly the right point in time: just after Max's foster mother's decision to release him but just before Alicia's sixteenth birthday!

Second, we now realized the blessing in the necessity of having had to make two trips to complete the adoption instead of only one. If we had been required to make a decision about Alicia based on her erroneous "diagnosis" and without the ability to see her first, we might have chosen not to attempt, at our ages, to deal with a supposedly mentally handicapped child.

With the court decision behind us, we were all now more than ready to be a family together, but the children were not immediately released to us. Instead, they were required to return to their respective homes for two days to say their good-byes and collect their few belongings, so we said farewell to them once again. It had been arranged that they would come to us at our hotel on Saturday, two days hence.

The next morning we awakened early, despite the exhaustion of our previous day, and we sought the Lord concerning our new life with our children. Allen thought he heard:

"I have not brought you through this adoption process to abandon you now. There will surely be some challenges because sin is in the world, but I have good plans for them and for you as well. You are not to worry about the problems, but you are to love these children and share My love with them. These are both exciting and hard times for them. As difficult as their life is, it is at least familiar, but they are venturing out into the unknown right now. They hope that you will love them, and they certainly have an inaccurate view of the country to which they are going. They will learn, they will grow, they will find Me through you. They are going to help others find Me as well. You must have faith that this great adventure is all about My purposes."

Though it was now only late September, the weather in Chelyabinsk had turned unseasonably cold and snowy, and, due to the centralized system of heat control, there was no heat in the orphanages, no hot water, and no way to bathe or wash clothes. Oksana already had a deep cough in her chest. Alicia also had the sniffles, and she had been wearing the same white shirt for so many days that the collar and cuffs were turning black. Lena C. took pity on her and made arrangements for us to go to her boarding school on Friday, one day early, to bring her to us so that she could take a hot bath. I shall never forget standing on the steps of her orphanage as she stood below, in the center of a circle of what had been her family for the past seven years, and watching as she hugged her friends, their faces soaked with tears. My heart ached, for I was aware, perhaps more than she, that she was unlikely to ever see most of them again. What courage, what unspoken hope, I thought, for this child to have made this decision.

Back at our hotel room, off went the dirty clothes, and, after a long, luxuriating soak in the big tub, Alicia happily slipped into her new jeans, sweater, and shoes. The old clothes were bagged up to be taken by Lena C. back to the orphanage. As I looked down at her old brown ankle-length boots, I noticed that the laces had been broken and retied so many times that they were nearly in shreds. The day she had worn the boots for the last time, the laces had broken irreparably. Alicia had brought with her the few belongings which she owned, bundled up in an old plastic bag. They were the remnants of her childhood: a doll, a few photos, a small porcelain mug, and some mementos from her friends.

On our first night with our first child, we had supper in the hotel's restaurant and then spent the evening together in our room doing a puzzle, as it was the only activity we could think of that could transcend language. I should mention here that the children spoke not a word of English, and we communicated by means of a comical mixture of gestures and the few Russian words we had learned.

The next day, Allen and the two Lenas made the long drive to Verkniy Ufaley to get Max and Oksana. I stayed in the hotel room with Alicia, as there wasn't enough room in the car for us all. We passed the time by studying the picture book, <u>The First Thousand Words in Russian,</u>ˣ together, as we taught each other the words for familiar objects and persons and animals: dog—sabaka, cat—koshka, babushka—grandmother, etc.

After several hours, Allen and the two Lenas returned with Max and Oksana, and suddenly, miraculously, we were all together in one place, as a family. The kids had their own room down the hall and around the corner, and they began the intriguing and difficult process of re-bonding with each other. Though they each had their own bed, for the first couple of nights little Max snuggled in next to Alicia for comfort. Our idyllic notions were quickly shattered, however, when we saw how brief that honeymoon was, for it was not long before they all began to fight and argue like normal siblings. The challenge for us was that we had absolutely no idea of what they were shouting at each other! Max was the most comical. Periodically, their door would open, and we would hear him come racing down the hall, bursting into our room with great energy. We later learned that the girls, being too shy themselves to ask for things they all wanted, had delegated the job to their kid brother—the classic "*You* go ask them." He would fire bullets of excited questions at us in Russian and, when we failed to understand, would slap the heel of his hand to his forehead in mock disgust, turn, and run back to his own room. It was an exhausting, amusing, turbulent, and remarkable time.

After the kids had come to us, Lera, Luda, and Vadim made several visits to our hotel room, and they instantly fell in love with our children. One Sunday afternoon, they packed us all into Vadim's brother's van and took us to the Moscow Circus, which was touring that week in Chelyabinsk. The bonds between our family and theirs were clearly growing, but we were still anxious about the issue of Lera's visit to us in America. We prayed hard about it, and the Lord continued to indicate that he would make the matter clear.

To our delight and astonishment, it was they themselves who brought up the topic one evening, this time in positive tones. We knew this to be the sign that the Lord had promised, and we rejoiced that this amazing event would become a reality. Lena C. informed us that we needed to begin doing our part of the paperwork—a letter of invitation—while we were still in Chelyabinsk. And so, having just barely received our own three children, we suddenly found ourselves making preparations to host a fourth!

At last, it was time to leave Chelyabinsk and return to Galina's apartment in Moscow for the final few days of paperwork, additional vaccinations, and then the clearance from the U.S. Embassy to leave the country with the children. The two Lenas drove with us all to the airport, and we tearfully hugged and thanked these women who, by now, seemed like old friends. We boarded the plane for our night flight, in a light but steady snowfall, and watched from our seats while the plane wings were de-iced.

Once at Galina's, the kids were put to bed in the living room, while we collapsed into our own bed next to the kitchen. We were physically tired, but emotionally exhausted as well, for, without the two Lenas, we were now abruptly on our own in communicating with our kids. Gestures and the few words we knew somehow got us through. We walked the streets of Moscow together holding hands, and Galina took us all on a lengthy walking tour of Red Square and the surrounding area.

From Galina's apartment, we called home twice to talk to our neighbor Dianne, who had been left in charge of feeding our dogs and cats. On our first call to her, she greeted us with some amusing news: "There is a chicken in your front yard." "A what?" I asked incredulously. "A chicken," she repeated. On our second phone call, the chicken was still there and was refusing to leave, despite Dianne's best efforts. We had her contact our friend Kimberly, who kept chickens and was wise in their ways, but Kimberly had no luck in capturing the bird either. It was crafty, that chicken. However, dealing with a chicken that was thousands of miles away was not high on our priority list, and we promptly forgot about it.

The day before our clearance from the U.S. Embassy, the children had a required medical examination by a Moscow physician who came to the apartment. He indicated to us that he felt Max would grow to be tall and slender, (at this writing, 6'1"!), as his leg and arm bones were quite long, and I later remembered the vision of the men looking through the foreign nursery window from so long before. However, most sobering to us were the doctor's comments about Alicia. After reading through her records, he paused thoughtfully and, with a quaver in his voice, declared, "I want you to know that this is a true miracle. This is nothing less than the rescue of a life." It seems that, based on her "diagnosis," Alicia could have been allowed to stay at her boarding school until the age of twenty-three, at which time she may have been transferred to a mental institution, presumably out of deference to her "defenseless" situation, there to live out the rest of her life! We could scarcely comprehend the irrationality and horror of it all. We later learned from Sonia that it was after watching a documentary some years previously on precisely this kind of situation that she had decided to redirect her career from social work to adoption.

We cleared the U.S. Embassy with no problems and, in fact, received from the examining officer an amazed commendation on getting the ten-day waiver. How had we done it, he wanted to know? He repeatedly emphasized that no other adoptive parents in the previous several months had been allowed to leave the country early. We could only attribute this blessing to prayer.

The next morning, we were on our way home. After a long flight which began well and ended in great aggravation and much exhaustion, we finally arrived home at midnight. Waiting to greet us at the airport was a small but hardy group of friends bearing balloons and a large "Welcome to America" sign. We were no sooner home than we all collapsed into our beds.

Early the next day, I was walking through the living room when I was abruptly stopped in my tracks by what I thought was the sound of a clucking hen. Then, out of the corner of my eye, I suddenly spied the chicken strutting about, large as life, and bold as could be, on the front porch! The humorous symbolism began to dawn on me, and I realized that her presence there was no accident. After all, hadn't the whole adventure begun with the eggs? Kimberly seconded my suspicions. She sensed that, just when the finality of the adoption was really beginning to hit me, and I was starting to doubt my own sanity, the Lord had sent a living reminder that it had all been His idea in the first place and that He was still in control.

A few days and several phone calls later, we finally discovered that the bird was an escapee from a neighbor's roost some distance down the road. The husband and one of their kids came to fetch her on their four-wheeler, and she rode back home in style, sitting on a child's lap, never guessing that she had been a messenger of God's astounding grace.

Post scripts:

During the time between our first and second trips to Russia, we learned that Ben and Kathryn were moving to Minnesota and would be gone by the time we got back home with our kids. However, in June of 2001, they returned to Alabama for a brief visit, and Oksana and her friend Gulia were reunited. One evening, Gulia stayed overnight in Oksana's room, and, as I went in to say goodnight to them, I found them sleeping peacefully side by side, as they had done for so many years in the orphanage. Oksana had indeed seen Gulia in America, and I stood silently in the doorway for some time, marveling at the miracle the Lord had done.

Likewise, Lera arrived at our home in May of 2001 and spent eleven weeks with us. She repeatedly expressed amazement at the ease with which she had been granted a visa, but we were not surprised. After all, by now we were getting used to miracles.

Epilogue

As I look back on what I have written in these pages, I find that several points deserve to be reemphasized.

First, this book obviously cannot begin to plumb the depths of the why's and how's of God's speaking to us, nor of our hearing. What I have offered is merely a taste, a nudge, a glimpse through a crack in the door.

Second, the book is didactic, while at the same time personal: an invitation by way of example.

Third, this business of hearing God never ceases to impress me as an awesome thing, for it encompasses both the eminently practical and the eternally transcendent. It is concerned with the point of contact between heaven and earth; it is about God's mind meeting man's need, for our sake as well as for His eternal purposes.

Fourth, hearing God encompasses a number of intriguing dichotomies. It is an often scary process, but in it lies the only real security. It can be an exhausting and demanding discipline, but it is also the source of the only true rest. It functions in and through community, yet it is, at heart, intensely personal. It is our daily bread, yet it is part of a Story with an ancient beginning and no end.

Most importantly, hearing God, as I have said, is not a nice little addition to life: it *is* life. It is an option only in the context of free will.

In closing, then, it is my fervent hope and prayer that some, at least, will choose to join in what is both the greatest of adventures and the ultimate romance—and not just for their own sake but for the sake of the Kingdom, now and to come. Adventure and romance, fulfillment and intimacy are, after all, entwined, for they each reach their glorious destiny in the wedding of the Lamb:

"Then I heard what sounded like a great multitude, like the roar of rushing waters and like loud peals of thunder, shouting: 'Hallelujah! For our Lord God Almighty reigns. Let us rejoice and be glad and give him glory! For the wedding of the Lamb has come, and his bride has made herself ready.'"(Revelation 19: 6,7)

Appendices: Selections From the Journals

In closing, it seems appropriate to devote some space to some representative selections from our journals. My hope is that these will provide examples of hearing, offer some general principles for those seeking, and edify the Body. As I struggled with what to choose from among hundreds of fascinating entries, here is what the Lord said. I first asked Him for a suggestion as to a reasonable number of items to include. Allen thought he heard, "I kind of like the number twelve." (Well, yes!). Simultaneously, I thought I had also gotten the same number, providing a confirmation. Then,

"Choose the one which strikes you the most at the moment for a particular thing and then go to the next one, trusting that you will be guided. You can only pick one at a time. You will invariably leave out some things which you might consider important, but you cannot do everything, and people would not read it if you could. Trust me that I will arrange it so that what I wish is communicated to those willing to listen. Relax and choose to the best of your ability without excessive worry. After all, I am pretty capable in fulfilling My part of the bargain."

So, here goes. I will try to select things which cover a range of topics.

Appendix A: Selected Topics

From 9-3-01

I had been doing some reading on the spiritual warfare between angels and demons, and I realized that I had no real sense of how that takes place. "If they are spiritual beings," I asked, "and do not have physical bodies and cannot die, then what does this warfare look like?" Allen thought he heard,

"As regards your question, there are many things on earth and in heaven which you could not understand, because you are bound by limited conceptions. It is enough that you know there is warfare, and it is fierce. The warfare is played out among humans in the physical sense, and the terrible violence in the world is the counterpart of a spiritual battle. There is surely suffering, not only at a human level, for the angels identify most closely with My physical creation, though they are not themselves physical. When hurt is done to any part of My creation, the angels feel it, as though they themselves were being injured or killed. The demons, of course, do not empathize in a positive sense, but they are also subject to the relationships with those to whom they have become tied in their evil. Satan uses his own particular tortures to force obedience from those who have made themselves subject to him. This warfare at the spiritual level is not a game, for there is great pain and great emotion involved by association. More than that, you will not be able to understand. You must realize that there are mysteries in My universe which are so large that you cannot comprehend them. How is it possible that I can be in the vastness of the universe, yet have contact with each part of My creation in an intimate, specific way? How can I have untold numbers of plans all worked out to the smallest detail?

How can I speak different things to all humanity all at once? How can I...? There are so many questions that are beyond your ability to grasp to which I know you would love to have answers. I love the inquisitive nature of much of mankind, for it is a big part of what I created. It is the reason for seeking, and it is also the cause of much of the pain in the world. I will, over a period of time, however, share more of the mysteries of My creation in ways that will enable you to grasp a bit more of My goodness and My person."

From 5-30-00

My father died in May of 2000, and, on the evening of his death, as we prayed, I asked the Lord if those in heaven have any sense of us and what we are doing. Allen thought he heard,

"That is not permitted, for it would interfere with the growing that is desired. They can have awareness by report, but the way is not open for them to watch earthly actions. It is far better this way, for the plight of the world is not their current concern—it is My concern. They are instead learning to praise and seeing My wisdom in portions of their own history—as well as also seeing their sin. This is painful, but it is part of the plan for all who come to Me. There is so much you do not know, and they really also have much to learn—though they know more than you. There is a continual process here for all that come to Me."

From 9-17-00

We were praying about the relationship of Satan to sickness, as well as about other factors connected to healing. Allen thought he heard,

"Satan cannot directly cause illness—he does not have that power. He can work in the mind to make the body more susceptible to sickness, and he can tempt to behaviors which cause sickness. All sickness is the result of sin, though not necessarily the sin of the person who is ill. I surely do heal, but all physical healing does not lead to spiritual healing. In fact, often physical healing may be a barrier to spiritual healing. I am desirous that all come to Me and have their spirits healed. I do heal, of course, as a demonstration of the power of the Gospel, and that is ultimately for the same purpose— that the spirits of many be healed. Surely, Satan should always be rebuked, for he desires to control the mind, which always leads to death. However, the physical illness may remain, for it is necessary for a greater healing to take place. There are many things about this you will not understand. I must even allow some things that I hate because I have chosen to give humanity free will. Some of My people suffer terribly, and it is no fault of their own. I have great rewards for those who suffer for My Gospel. I do always desire the best for My people, and I do bless all those who follow with joy and peace, even when there is suffering."

From 4-12-01

We had taken our kids on an educational family trip to New Echota, Georgia, to visit the site of the last capitol of the Cherokee nation. Later, we were lamenting the terrible abuse suffered by the Cherokees and pondering the greed and the injustice which caused men to act in such awful and unchristian ways, though many called themselves Christians. As we prayed, I noted that obviously this nation had been blessed regardless of these things. Allen thought he heard,

"The blessing could have been so much more. Like all disobedience, the seeds planted by these terrible acts, motivated by the worst of human emotions, have born some terrible fruit. Yes, there has been much blessing, for many have followed My instructions over the same time, yet there has been awful strife. The Civil War and many other conflicts, not to mention countless other acts of ignorance and hatred, are born from sin unrecognized and thus not dealt with. The most grievous abuses get framed as "just business"—when men see their personal material benefit, they often throw all other considerations aside. Of course, I value legitimate enterprise, and I made humanity so that the use of intelligence and industry is part of My plan. However, these things have often been corrupted by sin, and the result is the terrible record of human history. Unfortunately for humanity, the effects of these grievous sins reverberate over time. I forgive individuals who repent, but every action has consequences, the vast majority of which are never foreseen or imagined. Sadly, the treatment of tribes like the Cherokee is the fruit of earlier sin and the beginning of other waves of tragedy. Remember the Good News. I have made a way for all who believe. I am at work. I will bring history to My conclusion. I do not allow injustice and hatred to stand eternally, but I must allow it to stand as long as I allow people to choose to love or hate. Some choose only hate, and I continue to woo them, but they continue to rebel. I will allow the tides of history to continue for a short time, but your redemption is nigh. Do not be anxious. There is much struggle, but there is also much blessing for those who obey."

I later asked the Lord what He meant by the words, "Your redemption is nigh." Allen thought he heard,

"Indeed, the time is short by My standards, but there is yet time. Do what I've called you to do, for the harvest is great. Do not be afraid to confront the evil in the world, for I am with you and will defend you. You cannot know the exact timing of events, nor would it be good for you to know, for you would be driven by response to those events rather than obedience to what I am calling you to do at any given moment. You know what the Scripture says, and it is enough for now. Just know that My timing is perfect. I may seem slow, but I do everything at exactly the right time."

From 6-18-00

This came during a time of prayer with a friend regarding some issues of uncertainty in our lives:

"Do not be afraid of the uncertainty of life, for it is My agent of blessing. I have blessed those who have held firm in the midst of confusing and distressing times. It has never been easy for those who live by faith, because all have wanted the future to be more clear. That is exactly the point, for poverty of spirit is letting My Spirit be the guide even through the wilderness. All of history has been about the desire of humanity to accumulate certainty and not trust in Me. The irony is, of course, that there is no certainty without Me in the end, and I only give the good end through faith which trusts Me in uncertainty. You are not to fear, for I have good plans—even plans that will astonish you, but you must trust that I know what I'm doing. I do, you know. I know that it is hard to walk a path where you can only see the very next step, and you fear that there may be a cliff about to drop you for a hard fall. I am the Truth. I am the Way. I do not do these things lightly. My purposes are immense, and you could not comprehend them even if I showed you. Just know that you are learning. You will stumble along the way, but I will be there. There is nothing hidden from Me. You know that I am very real. I have shown you that. You know I am good. I love you, and I want you to participate with me in My eternal symphony of salvation. Have fun! Be joyful! Recognize that I made this immense universe. Think of Psalm 2. I laugh at the feeble powers who rebel, but I want all to have the chance to be saved—even those powers. I have called each of you for a purpose, and, in that purpose, you will find astonishing blessing, even though there will always be struggle. The enemy is also very real. He has been defeated, but he still has power to deceive. Walk by faith and trust in My Word."

From 12-9-00

We were praying with friends about how the Lord would have us act in these circumstances where we see battles in the spiritual, moral, political, economic, and every other realm. Allen thought he heard,

"There is indeed a terrible battle raging, and praise is the source of strength and joy for My warriors. I expect only obedience and unswerving commitment to Truth. I do not expect you to do all things right, for you do not hear clearly—even at your best—yet I am present, and My power is available. Call upon Me and My power, and you shall see incredible things. The level of deception is so high that only the demonstration of My power will be able to win some hearts. For some, even the vastness of My action will not be enough, and they will refuse to see. Yet, you are to stand, holding up the sword of Truth. You cannot wield it alone, for you require My strength. I freely give My strength. I have promised, and I will fulfill My promises. I can do no other. There is a choice that all must ultimately make—either Me or themselves. It is My pleasure to give those who choose Me also themselves, and it is My great sadness that those who choose themselves will find only emptiness and suffering. I desire all to come, and I will continue to call, even though I know that many will not answer. I gave My life for all of them, and I weep for those who turn their backs. You must continue to reach out with love and truth, for it is a desperate time, but I am here, and I love My people with a deep, intense, abiding love."

From 12-2-00

This entry provides a good example of the conundrums we so often receive from the Lord, and it again serves to illustrate that God's ways are not our ways. We had been asking the Lord how He was working or was going to work in our present circumstances:

"I will do what I do, but you are to do all the things that I have gifted you to do. You cannot do what I do, and I choose not to do what I have trusted My people to do. It is the only way to grow. Trust in me for all that is impossible for you, but remember that I work through My people's hands, feet, and minds. You will have confusion about this: some of the things you assume only I can do can be accomplished by My people; some of the things you think you can do easily require My power to be accomplished. Submit it all to me, and ask for wisdom. I have plans. I want My people to know the joy of using all the power and the gifts I have given, and I, likewise, want them to be aware of the power which lies at My fingertips when all of their own resources fail. These are hard times, yet they are also joyous times. You will be astonished by what I will do, and also by that which I have entrusted to you. I know you have moments of struggle right now, and that is truly inevitable, but you will see My plans emerging as a green shoot breaking through the surface of the ground with the promise of growth and abundant fruit. You must simply do your work, and I will do Mine. I will take care of the details, for I'm very good at that sort of thing. Stay in prayer and keep listening. You will see the power of My Holy Spirit move."

From 1-13-01

"I love My people, and I always desire the best. I choose not to force anyone to accept My will, for that would violate My very nature. Nevertheless, My plans will go forward, and I will bring all things to conclusion. I hear all prayers, and I answer all prayers, though the answers are not the ones that are desired, in some cases. I, of course, understand the full story of the answers I give, and you cannot. I always choose the best path, though the best path may sometimes have much pain. Since there is so much sin in the world, there must also be much pain. I am at work in a new way in this time, and I am shaking the world. I am also bringing My power to work in a more visible way. I seek hearts which will follow. I don't expect you to know the right answers, but I do expect you to obey. If you continue to seek My will, you will see amazing things. I am with you always, even unto the end of the age."

From 4-22-01

We had been dealing with some health issues, and had been to see a friend of ours who is a nutritionist. As we later prayed about our visit, this is what Allen thought he heard:

"As you learn more about your bodies, you learn more about the intricacies of My design in every cell. The brain alone is unimaginably more complex and capable than anyone can fathom. The more you learn about these things, the more you learn about My power, My creative ability, and My grace and mercy. I give My people the ability to see Me in the way I've made them, but they don't often use that knowledge. There is much to be learned, and it is a joyous journey, if the seeker understands that I am the Truth and the source of all truth. Therefore, keep seeking, and I will keep leading you into more truth about many different things. What I have created is inexhaustible in interest, for I have wrought intricacy beyond what you will ever understand in every little piece of Creation. However, it is the journey which concerns Me. Those who are seeking after truth are seeking after Me whether they know it or not, and I, of course, am seeking after them. All of the pieces of truth, in every corner of My universe, are clues which must lead to Me if they are honestly and determinedly followed. Since I AM the Creator, I have left My imprint on all of My creation. Then, also, there is My rescue mission. Because I knew that, even with the most vigorous search for truth, mankind could not find certain things about me, I came to earth and showed who I really AM. The human capacity for sin and deception is very great, so many cannot accept My revelation of Myself and My gift of sacrifice and hope. I only offer. I put the truth everywhere, so that the Truth may be found by those who genuinely seek. I wish everyone to be saved, but I will not violate My own rules. People must choose Me freely, and I have given and am giving every opportunity. I have acted in your lives, as I do in the lives of many, to increase the chance that some will hear. I love My creation, but all must choose Me freely, for it is the only way I work, and it is also a blessing of unimaginable proportions."

From 4-29-01

This came in response to prayer about how to cope with all of the challenges and resistance which we were facing as we tried to lead others in learning to hear and obey. Allen thought he heard the Lord say:

"Imagine how I felt in the Garden, with My splendid creation all around. Even though I knew it would happen, it was still sad to see how easily humanity fell—with barely a thought. I gave the right to choose, and that is the painful cost—that, too often, those whom I love so much choose the things which will lead to destruction. I do and have done everything possible to rescue all, but they still must choose Me, and the situation in the Garden is repeated one way or another many times a day. The world is filled thus with the consequences of not only Adam and Eve's act, but also of the countless rebellions since then. Certainly, many repent and return, and I rejoice at those who come, but I grieve for the lost, who do not know the joy and the blessing I would give, even in the midst of sin's consequences. You are called to be bearers of the Light—the Truth you have been given—in order that some would be rescued. It is no small task, and it is thankless in the world's eyes, at least much of the time, but the reward is great, both here and eternally."

From 2-14-01

We were praying about the difficulties of trying to work with issues of personalities and expectations in small group settings:

"Where I am received, I rip away the veils of self-delusion and hypocrisy, and I bring repentance and joy. It is the nature of humanity to hide, just like Adam and Eve. You all desire the worst parts of your lives to remain hidden, but I desire all to come to the light for your own sakes. Truth is a universal acid which eats away all that is not right in your lives and in your thoughts."

From 5-25-01

As we were in prayer one night, the Lord gave me the image of a ship setting sail as it left shore and prepared to go out into deeper water. When I shared the image with Allen, he replied with amazement that he had simultaneously been given a strong desire to play a wonderful song by Canadian songwriter Steve Bell, entitled, "I Feel the Winds of God Today." The Lord followed with this:

"I surely constantly call My people to venture out in trust and reliance upon Me. It is the only way that you or anyone can find out about My real power. If everything you do is safe and does not require My help, then you can never know Me. It is in the adventure that I am most evident, and it is surely where My power is most visible. The image is one that certainly expresses My call for My people, for it is in risking the loss of the world's safety-net—which is not really a safety net—that My followers are most alive and most excited about life. Fear is wise, if it is the fear of God, and I do not ever call My people to take foolish risks for no purpose; however, fear is one of Satan's great tools to prevent My work from being done. The 'winds of God' do blow the sailor who believes away from the comfortable shore into unimaginable adventure and a knowledge of fulfilling My purpose in life, and that is a great gift."

Appendix B: Selections on Hearing, Obedience and Following the Path

I thought it would be appropriate here to include some further selections specifically dealing with the topic of hearing.

1) From 7-20-00
"Of course you know that the cares of the world and the emotions of your lives act as static, though it is unavoidable static. I only admonish you to continue seeking Me, and all will be fine. Do not despair or get frustrated, for things that you think are bad may just be preparation for blessing. The times must work themselves out, but the plans I have are always good. You have a choice—many choices—each day to continue to walk the path of faith or choose the way of secular wisdom. There are surely things you can learn from the world, but only focus on Me, and faith in My work will guard your heart. I know that hearing is difficult because you cannot focus completely, yet, as you place your trust in Me, it will become easier. You should surely also know that the enemy is very active, and there will be harassment as well. Stay focused on Me, and the guidance you need will come."

2) From 1-7-01
We were praying about the frustration of being met with the fear and sometimes disdain which has often greeted the prophetic. Allen thought he heard the Lord say,

"What do you think has happened with all My prophets? Do not be dismayed by all of this, for the prophetic is a means of discerning who is willing to listen to Me. You, of course, must recognize the limitations of your own hearing, but, nevertheless, you are hearing from Me, even if it takes a while for you to understand. I will speak and do speak to anyone who is willing to listen. Obviously, My Church has often been ineffective precisely because believers did not and do not understand that I am only expecting obedience, and not creative plans for evangelism. Even though people are rebellious, I am still pretty good at getting their attention and providing opportunities for witness. Most of the time, My people are so focused on their own plans that they don't even see My much-better plan. Do not be frustrated with this issue of the prophetic. Instead, recognize that those who will hear that I do speak to individuals in very personal ways are the ones who will come together as the core of My new plans. Even though I will still love them, I cannot use anyone who will not listen to Me, for they will be constantly pursuing their own plans rather than Mine. I have much work to which I am calling My people, and I need those to participate who would be conformed to Me."

3) From 2-13-01

"I do not act precipitously, unlike many in My human creation. I am the Master of the details, and I bring all things together in marvelous ways for those who would follow. I do not wish that you be very concerned with your own plans, but, rather, you should continue to discern My plan. I know how ephemeral My guidance may sometimes seem, because humanity is not tuned too well to the spiritual, even at best. I do not promise ease, but I promise joy and peace and love, and these are far better than mere ease. I am not a hard master, but I am a Master. You truly do not have even the beginnings of comprehension of how vast and unsearchable I AM. The more you know and seek Me, the more you will know that you do not know, but there is beauty and grace and mercy in living with My vastness—the great dance of My Creation. I do wish I could show My people, and some have seen a very little, but it is far more than your minds can comprehend. I continue to give you the pieces which you can comprehend, for even a small part of the full picture is a brightness and a glory which would bring terror at a level you cannot imagine. I share these things with you in order that you might understand that I have everything under control on a scale you cannot understand, yet simply knowing that must give you peace. I know you even doubt the accuracy of the words you write down, and I will assure you that you always filter My words through your own consciousness, yet I say what I need to have you hear, and you grasp enough. You would not wish the weight of having direct communication from Me which must be transmitted to many, for, though it is a great honor, it is also a burden beyond imagining. Right now, I speak and I guide in direct words, but not words which you can accept as dictation from My mouth. It is enough for the moment. Know that I am on the move. The great Lion has plans. I move them forth."

4) From 3-1-01

"People need to hear My voice. Of course, I speak through the Scriptures, and there is much instruction about who I am and how to live. Yet I also desire that My people know My best will for them in particular situations. It is very important that each member of My Body is listening, for I will spare you much unnecessary trouble. Yes, there is some trouble which is necessary, for there is great evil in the world, but there is also trouble caused by simply following the wrong path. It is not a matter of salvation, for, if you claim me as Lord and obey My revealed Word, you will be saved. It is, however, for your own good that I provide specific guidance, for I desire each of My people to receive the blessings I have planned. This is, certainly, not just blessings for yourselves, but it is also the immense blessing of knowing you have brought the Gospel to one or many who would have had to wait. I wish My people to claim all of their blessings, but many walk the path of life intensely concerned about being faithful, yet never seeking to hear My voice. There are blessings lying all around them, but they never know when to bend down and pick them up, for they are not listening. I will work in each believer's life, of course, and I do, but, in order to fully benefit and receive all that I have, each must listen and hear My voice. I am always consistent and I am always good. Urge them to seek Me."

5) From 4-6-01

"I do have good plans, yet they are not without challenge. Indeed, I would be insulting you if the tasks I gave you were too easy. I, of course, always help when you are in need, but the challenges help you grow and change in ways that are necessary. There are problems which are not part of My plan, also, which are caused by sin—your own and that of others. However, I give you guidance and correction to deal with those problems as long as you continue to listen to Me and study My Word. I have little patience with those who would use My Word and My name to their own ends, but I have great patience with anyone who is genuinely seeking to follow. There is great margin for error which is called grace. I do not call you to ease but rather to adventure, and, when you are doing much, you will occasionally trip and fall. The truth is, nevertheless, that a life of ease would be far more dangerous. You would be tempted to think you didn't need Me and fall into the worst sort of sin. When you are stretched and challenged in doing My will, you are also most dependent on Me, and that is the safest place to be. It sometimes feels precarious because you will not know exactly where I will lead, and you get anxious, but you can trust My good plans. You must know that all times are challenging, for, outside of Me, security is a delusion. Those who built great houses without Me are building on sand, and all their plans will come to naught. My plans are the only ones which will ultimately succeed, and I bless obedience with a line which will not end and a future which is completely beyond your imagination. Keep on walking the path I light for you. I show you what is necessary, and I don't show you things which might cause you to fear because your understanding is too small. You can only, at your best, see the consequences of a few steps ahead, with so many permutations and possibilities. I can see all, and it is not too much for Me. Know that I will make the right choices and do what is best. Though there will be challenge, I have the best possible outcomes in mind. You cannot avoid sin, but you can obey to the best of your ability. That is all I ask. I love you."

6) From 4-30-01

"This principle of hearing Me is central to all of the other work that I desire to do. This should be obvious, for, if you are not listening or don't know how to listen to My direction, how could you possibly take the right path? It is very important that you recognize the centrality of My Scripture in all of this. Your hearing may be imperfect or faulty, so the Scripture is both the final authority and the check on any action which might come from wrong motives or desires. I recognize the weaknesses of humanity, for, after all, I dwelt in flesh Myself, so I insist that all action be considered and tested against Scripture. However, it is essential that My people not be too afraid to hear. I provide the Scripture as their check—their boundary, if you will—so that they can freely seek Me, knowing that I will not let them go anyplace that is spiritually dangerous, for they know the Scripture is their fence. This is a sensitive thing for many, because they wish to be obedient, and they have seen the abuse of people saying they are hearing Me, when they are really only furthering themselves. Be aware and know that this is important, but many of My people are afraid. They should be in awe, yet not afraid."

7) From 3-20-01

"I wish people to hear My voice, to respect My Scriptures, and to listen for My guidance in their lives. This is a critical time for many people, and they must see Me as I really am. I am not some remote figure enshrined in stained glass, but I AM. I am the very essence of life. I lead to completeness in every human life which will follow Me. I have surprises around every corner. I have blessings in abundance. There is certainly trouble in this life, but I provide the means to cope with the worst evil which sin can cause. I provide the means to learn and to grow, and I provide ways to escape Satan's grasp, if My people will but listen and stand firm. So much pain and suffering could have been avoided if My people had stood firm and not been misled by those in the Enemy's service. Nevertheless, these things have happened, and, out of evil, I bring good for those who love Me and obey Me. Of course, there will be opposition—there always is for the Enemy will seek to harass—but I will help you overcome. You must stand firm in your testimony. Relax and know that I am in charge. Remember the image I gave you years ago. You are in the airplane, and you should enjoy the ride. You really do not have the controls, even though you may think you do. Of course, you can choose to get out of the airplane, but you'll miss many blessings and a great ride."

8) From 3-17-01

"I do demand honesty from each of you, though I know it is very hard to be totally honest. The only way you can fully be honest is to constantly seek Me. If you are seeking your own will in the disguise of My will, you will ever be deceived. I know that life has many distractions, and you will be drawn apart by some of those things, yet you must be seeking Me through these winds of life. I know the way, and I know the hearts of all. I seek the best for each of My people, but the best is found through My hand. Do not be afraid to hear My still small voice. I wish you all to hear Me. You will know Me through Scripture—that is how you recognize the bracing, joyful edge of My voice. I do still speak to My people, because you all need to hear. I have adventure beyond measure for everyone who will follow, and I have the power to make My will happen. Rejoice and listen, for I am working."

9) From 4-14-01

"I know you question how accurately you hear or whether you properly interpret certain things, but you can be sure I will honor every attempt at obedience, and I will ensure that you hear well enough to follow the path. Surely you know, by now, that this is not a science. You can't figure out My plans by observing and noting down various facts and drawing conclusions. I like surprises, and I have built it into your natures that you like them, too. I know that you are also wary of change, so I bring My plans about piece by piece. I only show you as much as you can accept, for even though My plan is wonderful, you would be overwhelmed and frightened if I showed you all at one time. You will know what you need to know, and your obedience will take care of the steps along the path. You may be sure of challenges, but you must remember that you need to grow into the tasks I have for you. The things which you see as frustrating can also be seen as funny, and you need to have a sense of humor. I've not given you more than you can handle, but, rather, I'm helping you grow so that you can handle more and more responsibility. There is much work in the kingdom of God, and I am building My workers."

10) From 4-22-01

"Remember, I've told you I like surprises. That is why there are surprises and hidden joys around every corner for those who follow My path—yes, even for those who are in the direct path of the worst evil Satan can do. I provide what is necessary for those who call on Me and My power. I am the source of eternal life for all who claim Me as Lord, and I will not abandon any who call on My Name. Yet, many who claim My Name will not hear My voice in particular ways for their lives. They believe My Scriptures and often do hard things in My service, and I reward that effort always. However, I always have better plans than the best which men can dream up in My service. It is only by listening (and of course testing against Scripture, for deception and sin are human conditions), that any believer can find the best path which I have chosen, and know how to stand before the evil becomes too great to withstand without great loss. Pain is often the only way humanity can learn, but I always provide the option of hearing My voice and obeying. The hard lessons, surely, must have pain because no human is capable of learning those without pain. You are still learning and will always be learning, but you have learned a little about how to hear and follow. My people must hear and follow in this time."

11) From 3-24-01

"It is not your might or your power or your cleverness or your excellent organizational skills, or whatever else any individual might possess, but it is by My Spirit that My will is accomplished. Do not think Me slow. I work at precisely the right time with those who are willing to seek Me and listen. The whole process is really simple. I speak. You listen. You obey to the best of your ability. You see the results. You continue to listen, and I continue to work. Without the listening, even the best structure cannot provide what is necessary."

12) From 5-30-01

"I work in My time, and I always do things right. Those who follow My will enjoy the benefit of how I do things, and those who hurry ahead in their own light—well, they struggle and trip and usually take the wrong path which seems so tempting. The right path is not always the obvious one or the one which seems most inviting, but it is the one which leads to My chosen destination, and it is abundantly filled with adventure and blessing. Of course, I always know that your hearing is imperfect, but I always give abundant opportunity to find the right path. You will know the way, for I will confirm My path. I do not make obedience hard, but I do require that I be Lord. It is both the only and the best way for those who serve me. Step out into the light through the doorway—there are wonders untold."

i.) Streams Ministries International, <u>Institute for Spiritual Development, Level 201.</u>

ii.) <u>American College Dictionary</u>, 1963 ed., Random House, N.Y.

iii.) <u>Book of Common Prayer</u>, 1979 ed., The Church Hymnal Corporation, N.Y., pg. 355

iv.) Roberts, Frances J., <u>Come Away My Beloved</u>, 1973 ed., King's Farspan, Inc., Ojai, CA, pg. 78

v.) Henry, Matthew, <u>Commentary on the Whole Bible</u>, 1961, Zondervan, pg. 1710

vi.) <u>American College Dictionary</u>, 1963 ed., Random House, N.Y.

vii.) Levy, David M., <u>The Tabernacle: Shadows of the Messiah</u>, 1993, The Friends of Israel Gospel Ministry, Inc., Bellmawr, N.J.

viii.) Stube, Edwin, <u>According to the Pattern</u>, 1995, Companion press, Shippensburg, PA., pgs. 66-67.

ix.) Delopoulos, Steven, <u>Eileen's Song</u>, Burlap to Cashmere, 1997.

x.) Amery, Heather, and Kirilenko, Katrina, <u>The First Thousand Words in Russian</u>, 1989, Usborne Publishing, London, England.

CPSIA information can be obtained
at www.ICGtesting.com
Printed in the USA
FFHW02n1517150818
47780918-51469FF

9 781598 584103